Also by FranklinCovey

4 The Disciplines of Execution

SECOND EDITION: REVISED AND UPDATED

ACHIEVING YOUR WILDLY IMPORTANT GOALS

Chris McChesney, Sean Covey, *and* Jim Huling
with Beverly Walker *and* Scott Thele

Simon & Schuster

NEW YORK   LONDON   TORONTO
SYDNEY   NEW DELHI

Simon & Schuster
1230 Avenue of the Americas
New York, NY 10020

This Simon & Schuster hardcover edition April 2021

SIMON & SCHUSTER and colophon are registered trademarks
of Simon & Schuster, Inc.

For information about special discounts for bulk purchases,
please contact Simon & Schuster Special Sales at 1-866-506-1949
or business@simonandschuster.com.

The Simon & Schuster Speakers Bureau can bring authors to your
live event. For more information or to book an event, contact
the Simon & Schuster Speakers Bureau at 1-866-248-3049
or visit our website at www.simonspeakers.com.

Manufactured in the United States of America

5   7   9   10   8   6   4

Library of Congress Cataloging-in-Publication Data is available.

ISBN 978-1-9821-5697-8
ISBN 978-1-9821-5699-2 (ebook)

To Jim Stuart, our friend and colleague and the originator of this content, for your brilliance, insights, and your passion for great execution. May God bless you in your new endeavors.

1946 to 2006

Contents

Part 3: Applying 4DX as a Leader of a Frontline Team

Foreword

As Commissioner of the Department of Human Services for the State of Georgia, and Director of the Department of Children and Family Services for the State of Illinois, Beverly Walker has applied the 4 Disciplines of Execution (4DX) to driving results in government agencies and to seemingly insurmountable challenges from infant death to mental health to child literacy. Among other extraordinary results, her work with 4DX was responsible for reducing Repeat Cases of Child Abuse in the state of Georgia by 60 percent. Currently, she advises senior government officials across the United States on their most challenging problems.

When I was introduced to the 4 Disciplines of Execution, I was facing the greatest challenge of my career. As a new commissioner of Human Services, I had twenty thousand employees who were completely demoralized, we were under constant media scrutiny because of deaths and accidents involving children, and I was their sixth leader in five years. As a woman who has spent over half her adult life working in the hardest arenas of government, I first tried to avoid using 4DX. I said to Governor Perdue, "I got this . . . just let me do my job." And then after being dragged kicking and screaming into the 4DX world of execution, I became one of its staunchest supporters.

If you are facing the hardest work you've ever had, you need this book. The toughest part of doing that which seems impossible is finding the sweet spot—what your Wildly Important Goal is and what concrete and specific things you can do to achieve it. In government, there are no miracle cures; you must look deep into the heart of your crisis. You must be able to figure out what problem needs solving most, or nothing else matters. And you must solve that problem while maintaining vigilant oversight of the day-to-day transactions—or else they will become your new crisis.

But what about my "noble" vision? Here's what I learned: At the heart of every vision, every aspiration, is a crisis. You can't save children if you don't know why they are dying. You can't prevent homelessness if you don't understand why people are homeless. You can't reduce violence and crime if you don't know where it is happening and who is involved. You can't teach children to read if you don't understand which skill they are struggling to master.

This is what the terrain looked like to me when I came to Georgia: people were dying, and we did not know why. There was little appetite in our human services agency to talk about death. However, serious injury and death were preventing us from being successful in our mission to help people. It was a war we could neither escape nor win. Day after day, we worried about dropping the ball and being blamed.

That forced me as a leader to pull a Wildly Important Goal right out of the heart of our fear: "Reduce by 50 percent the number of incidents that can lead to death and serious injury of people in our care, custody, and oversight."

There! Now it had been said out loud, and we could openly acknowledge and own it. Just saying it, scary as that was, freed us up to talk about how we could achieve it—opened up space for us to work on it. We did not yet know what to do or how to do it, but we knew that preventing bad things from happening to vulnerable children and adults was why we showed up every day.

Many of the seemingly intractable and immovable issues and problems facing our government systems defy solution—not because people are not working hard but because there is no consensus about what it means to win. In government, we have many ways to know what is wrong—lag measures publicly track our every move—but we often spend so much time worrying over the public measures that we don't take the time to figure out why we are struggling to make progress, what prevents us from winning. That's where the sweet spot is—the work on the things that matter.

Our Primary WIG of reducing incidents of death and serious injury for those in our care was translated into dozens of team-level WIGs that would enable our success. These involved everything from increasing patient-health observation in mental hospitals to reducing one of the nation's largest backlogs of cases for possible child abuse. Team by team, we got clear on what it meant to win. And it was only at this basic level that we could start identifying and tracking the vital lead measures that would predict success.

We stopped waiting for reports filled with lag measures to determine whether we were winning or losing—data that always arrived far too late to do anything about. I played softball for many years, and one of the things I learned is that it's less painful to lose an entire game than it is to endure failure inning by inning. When you operate using only lag measures, it's like posting the score only at the end of the game; but by then, it's too late to change how you play your game. I learned that one of my most significant jobs as a leader was keeping score. In government, we are not used to playing in a winning game. But you cannot know what it will take to win if you do not know the score.

With the score visible, my senior team, the division management teams, and all the frontline teams held twenty-minute WIG Sessions every week focused on lead measures and weekly commitments. This forced leaders to see and hear from the front line regularly, and conversely, it provided the front line with unprecedented access to the eyes, ears, and voices of executive leaders.

Why did this process work? Because we took it to the ground. We took it to the people doing this very difficult work. We took it to workers involved in child welfare and mental healthcare. When we gave them what they needed, they thanked us and made it happen! Our leadership team certainly believed in what we were doing. But our frontline people really believed! The people who touch the people every day who might die or have serious injury desperately needed to believe in what we were doing. They needed to know they were making a difference. In the words of one gentleman at a 4DX report-out meeting, "You wait until I am about to retire to finally give us something that works?"

When things are challenging, we are used to working the supply side—tossing more money at a problem, finding the next superstar to come in and fix things, passing new laws and regulations intended to force-feed change. In applying 4DX, we didn't do those things. Instead, we attacked the demand side: those working on the most urgent problems. We engaged the energy of our organization by working the problem in tandem with those who knew it intimately—those who worked inside it day after day. Tapping into that collective knowledge and experience is what 4DX does. It helps leaders leverage their most powerful asset—their people.

—Beverly (BJ) Walker

Foreword to the First Edition

Clayton Christensen was the Kim B. Clark Professor of Business Administration at the Harvard Business School and author of The Innovator's Dilemma, *along with many other business books and publications.*

The 4 Disciplines of Execution offers more than theories for making strategic organizational change. The authors explain not only what effective execution involves but also how it is achieved. They share numerous examples of companies that have done just that, not once, but over and over again. This is a book that every leader should read!

—Clayton Christensen

Andy Grove, who helped found Intel and then led the enterprise for years as its CEO and chairman, has taught me some extraordinary things. One of them occurred in a meeting where he and several of his direct reports were plotting the launch of their Celeron microprocessor. I was there as a consultant. The theory of disruption had identified a threat to Intel. Two companies—AMD and Cyrix—had attacked the low end of the microprocessor market, selling much lower-cost chips to companies that were making entry-level computers. They had gained a significant market share and then had begun moving upmarket. Intel needed to respond.

During a break in the meeting, Grove asked me, "How do I do this?" I readily responded that he needed to set up a separate autonomous business unit that had a different overhead structure and its own sales force.

In his typically gruff voice, Grove said, "You are such a naive academic. I asked you *how* to do it, and you told me *what* I should do." He swore and said, "I know what I need to do. I just don't know how to do it."

I felt like I was standing in front of a deity with no place to hide. Grove was right. I was indeed a naive academic. I had just shown him that I didn't know the difference between *what* and *how*.

As I flew back to Boston, I wondered whether I should change the focus of my research as an academic, trying to develop a theory of how. I dismissed the idea, however, because I really couldn't conceive how I might develop a theory of *how*.

My research has continued to focus on the *what* of business—which we call strategy—and it has been quite productive. Most strategy researchers, consultants, and writers have given us static views of strategic issues—snapshots of technologies, companies, and markets. The snapshots represent the characteristics and practices of successful companies at a specific point in time, not those of struggling ones; or of executives who perform better than others at the time of the snapshot. Explicitly or implicitly, they then assert that if you want to perform as well as the best-performing ones, you should copy what the best companies and the best executives do.

My colleagues and I have eschewed the profession of still photography. Instead, we have been making "movies" of strategy. These are not, however, typical films that you might see at a theater, where you see fiction conceived by producers and screenwriters. The unusual movies that we're making at Harvard are "theories." They describe what *causes* things to happen and *why*. These theories comprise the "plots" in these movies. In contrast to the plots of films shown in a theater, which are filled with suspense and surprise, the plots of our movies are perfectly predictable. You can replace the actors in our movies—different people, companies, and industries—and watch the movie again. You can choose the actions of these characters in the movie. Because the plots of these movies are grounded in theories of causality, however, the results of these actions are perfectly predictable.

Boring, you think? Probably, to those who seek entertainment. But managers, who must know whether their strategy—the *what* of their work—is right or wrong, need as much certainty as possible. Because the theory is the plot, you can rewind the movie and watch the past repeatedly, if you want, to understand what causes what and why to a certain point. Another feature of movies of this sort is that you can look into the future too—before it actually occurs. You can change your plans, based upon different situations in which you might find yourself, and watch in the movie what will happen as a result.

Without boasting, I think it is fair to say that our research on strategy, innovation, and growth has helped managers who have taken the time to read and understand the theories, or movies, of strategy to achieve and sustain success more frequently than was historically the case.

What remains is the *how* of managing a company during times of change. This how has been studied minimally—at least until this book.

The reason that good research on how has taken so long to emerge is that it requires a different scale of research. Causal theories of strategy—the what—typically come from a deep study of one company, as was the case with my disk-drive study. The how of strategic change, in contrast, arises incessantly in every company. Developing a theory of how means that you can't study this phenomenon once in one company. You can't take snapshots of how. Rather, you need to study it in detail over and over again, over years, in many companies. The scale of this endeavor is why other academics and I have ignored the how of strategic change. We simply couldn't do it. It requires the perspective, insight, and the scale of a company like FranklinCovey to do it.

This is why I am so excited about the book. This isn't a book filled with anecdotes about companies that succeeded once. Rather, the book truly contains a theory of causality of how effective execution is achieved. The authors have given us not snapshots of execution but movies—movies that we can rewind and study over and over, movies into which you as a leader can insert your company and your people as actors. And you can watch your future before it emerges. This book is derived from a deep study of many companies over time as they deployed new ways of doing how—store by store, hotel by hotel, division by division.

I hope you will enjoy this book as much as I have.

—*Clayton Christensen*
(1952–2020)

Introduction

When we began writing the first edition of *The 4 Disciplines of Execution* in 2009, it was after eight years of implementing 4DX with more than a thousand different organizations. By the time it was published in 2012, we had increased the number of implementations to over fifteen hundred. Today this second edition is based on the experience of *four thousand implementations*.

As is often the case in a work that continues to grow and evolve, this second edition of *4DX* is the book we wish we could have published in 2012, had we known then what we know now. We are incredibly grateful to the readers worldwide (through all sixteen languages in which the book is now available) for your feedback. Working with you has enabled us to not only refine the disciplines but also greatly simplify our approach in applying them.

One of the most impactful things we learned about our readers early on was that they didn't just read the book—they *implemented the disciplines*. They were *doers*. This may not seem surprising, but it's unusual with business books, which traditionally are simply read rather than applied.

Our readers would rarely say, "I read *4DX*." More often, they would say, "We're doing 4DX!" Realizing that individuals and organizations were actively following the disciplines placed an even greater responsibility on us to be not only accurate but also clear. Which leads us to one of the driving forces behind the second edition.

Over the years, we've too often needed to say, "I can understand why you thought that is what we were saying, but it's not exactly what we meant." By 2017, we'd had enough of these conversations to know where and how we could significantly improve the text.

The second edition contains over *30 percent new content* intended to bring new ideas, a clearer direction, and the elimination of confusion primarily in these three areas:

1. *Leaders of leaders* apply 4DX differently than *leaders of frontline teams*: The principles are the same, but how they are applied is different. We addressed this in the first edition, but we were too subtle. The second edition is now organized around this important distinction, with an entire section of the book (including five new chapters) dedicated specifically to how leaders of leaders apply 4DX in an organization.

2. Knowing *where* to apply 4DX is as important as knowing *how* to apply it. While valuable insight on this point was offered in the first edition, we now have better examples, clearer illustrations, and new knowledge to help leaders know where (and how) 4DX works most powerfully and where it doesn't.

3. While *launching* 4DX can change your results, *sustaining* 4DX can change your organization. Today we have the added advantage of partnering with leaders who have sustained 4DX for years—indeed, some for *more than a decade*. Producing results is one level of accomplishment; sustaining and improving them over the long term is far greater. We believe the new practices and insights offered on sustainability alone would have warranted writing a second edition because of their value to leaders, not only for achieving their Wildly Important Goals but, ultimately, for creating a culture of execution.

STRATEGY VERSUS EXECUTION

There are two principal things a leader can influence when it comes to producing results: your strategy (or plan) and your ability to execute that strategy.

Stop for a moment and ask yourself this question: Which do

leaders struggle with more—creating a strategy or executing that strategy?

Every time we pose this question to leaders anywhere in the world, their answer is immediate: "Execution!"

Now, ask yourself a second question: If you have an MBA or have taken business classes, which did you study more—execution or strategy?

When we ask leaders this question, the response once again is immediate: "Strategy!" It's perhaps not surprising that the area with which leaders struggle most is also the one in which they have the least education.

After working with leaders and teams in every kind of industry and in schools and government agencies worldwide, we have learned that once you've decided what to do, your biggest challenge is getting people to execute it at the level of excellence you need.

Why is execution so difficult? After all, if the strategy is clear and you as the leader are driving it, won't the team naturally engage to achieve it? The answer is no, and it's likely your own experience has proven this more than once.

The book you are reading represents the most actionable and impactful insights from all we've learned. In it, you will discover a set of disciplines that have been embraced by tens of thousands of leaders, and hundreds of thousands of frontline workers, enabling them to produce extraordinary results.

In creating this second edition, we have remained passionately committed to sharing everything we've learned about creating breakthrough results through 4DX. We've gone beyond the principles to also describe in detail the thought process, the methods, and the tools we've used to implement 4DX worldwide, often in the form of specific practices, illustrated by real examples. This is what we refer to as the "4DX implementation process" throughout this book. While it might seem unusual to share this level of our intellectual property, developed at a great expense over more than a decade, we hope it's a clear indication of our sincere desire to see you, and your team, gain a thorough understanding of 4DX.

However, it's important to know that this does not enable you to use what you've learned in this book to create training programs, workshops, or multi-team implementation programs for 4DX. These types of programs (i.e., the "4DX implementation process") are offered exclusively through FranklinCovey and are led only by our experienced consultants.

If you have an interest in going beyond the principles to implementing 4DX across multiple teams, or even organization wide, we would be honored to help you through our consulting services using the 4DX implementation process.

PART 1

Learning 4DX

CHAPTER 1

The Real Problem
With Execution

MARRIOTT

One of the hotels near Marriott International's headquarters, the Spartanburg Marriott at Renaissance Park, wanted to improve performance measures, an effort magnified by being so close to the company's leadership. General Manager Brian Hilger, his team, and the hotel's owners worked together on the first part of the equation: a $20 million renovation that included remodeled rooms, an impressive lobby, and a new restaurant—improvements critical to higher guest scores. The hotel looked fantastic, but the guest scores still didn't reach the desired levels. They then addressed the second part of the equation: ensuring that every associate raise their performance on their highest priority: the experience of each guest.

After one year, Brian and his team proudly celebrated earning the highest guest-satisfaction scores in the thirty-year history of the hotel. As Brian said, "I used to dread the arrival of our new guest-satisfaction scores every Friday. Now I'm excited to get up on Friday mornings."

COMCAST

LeAnn Talbot was the new Senior Vice President for Comcast, responsible for the Greater Chicago Region. This was one of the largest operating regions in the company, but was in last place out of more than a dozen regions on the company's internal performance rankings.

In LeAnn's words, "Over the prior nine years, the region had remained last in virtually every metric Comcast used to measure performance, despite a succession of leaders. This wasn't a happy place, and talented people didn't want to risk the move to the Chicago region because they thought it could negatively impact their careers. And because of the importance of the region, we were also getting a significant level of attention—what we refer to as 'the love'—that added additional pressure. We needed a disciplined plan to execute with excellence, and we needed it now."

Within two years, the Greater Chicago Region had moved from last place to first on Comcast's internal performance rankings. LeAnn said, "Beyond these operating results, the effect on the team was dramatic. The region was recognized as a Top 100 Workplace by the *Chicago Tribune*. I really wouldn't have thought all of this progress could have happened so quickly when we first began our journey."

CNRL

Canadian Natural Resources had invested approximately $20 billion in their Horizon Oil production facility in northern Alberta, Canada, and it was not meeting production expectations. Despite the multibillion-dollar investment, the Bitumen Production unit at the Horizon Oil Sands operation could not rise above 72 percent utilization. Casey McWhan, Vice President of Bitumen Production, knew they needed to act fast, especially since each percentage point below 100 percent represented $15.7 million a year in lost revenue. He knew that the problem wasn't from a lack of effort: his crews were working around the clock to keep the equipment and complex refining facilities online. Colin Savastianik, Operation Lead, expressed a frustration shared by everyone when he described sitting in his office at the end of the day, head spinning, and wondering, "What did I do today?" He knew he was working hard, but at the end of the day, it seemed nothing was really accomplished.

Within one year, Casey and his team had the plant running at near 100 percent availability. Although the windfall from these results enabled CNRL to purchase a primary competitor, Casey said, "What I am *most proud of* is this team—seeing how the superintendents and managers have grown and developed a culture of accountability and ownership."

———————

These stories from Brian (Marriott), LeAnn (Comcast), and Casey (CNRL) may all sound very different, but they aren't. For each of these leaders, the challenge was essentially the same. So was the solution.

When you execute a strategy that requires a lasting change in the behavior of other people, you are facing one of the greatest leadership challenges you will ever meet. With the 4 Disciplines of Execution, you are not experimenting with an interesting theory; you are implementing a set of proven practices that meet that challenge successfully every time.

THE REAL CHALLENGE

Changing a culture meant changing the conversation. And to change the conversation, people would need new words, especially words about behaviors that would lead to winning results.

—Liz Wiseman

Whether you call it a strategy, a goal, or simply an effort at improvement, any initiative you as a leader drive in order to significantly move your team or organization forward will fall into one of two categories. The first mainly requires a stroke of the pen; the second is a breakthrough, requiring a change in behavior.

Stroke-of-the-pen initiatives are those you execute just by ordering or authorizing them to be done. If you have the money and the authority, you can make them happen. It might be a major capital investment, a change in the compensation system, a realignment of roles and responsibilities, an addition to staff, or a new advertising campaign. While executing these strategies may require planning, consensus, guts, brains, and money, you know that in the end, it is going to happen.

Breakthroughs that require a change in behavior are very different. You can't just order them to happen, because executing them requires getting people—often a lot of people—to be highly engaged in a new or different approach to creating results. And if you've ever tried to get other people to change, you know how tough it is. Changing yourself is hard enough.

For example, have you ever tried to persuade a sales team to become more consultative in their approach to customers, or induce an engineering team to collaborate with the marketing team on product design, or convince a call-center team to embrace a new software platform? You can't just send out an email declaring: "Starting tomorrow, we would like everyone to be more consultative!" In fact, you may be trying to change routines that have been entrenched for decades. Even when everyone recognizes that the old approach will never lead to a new level of performance, getting human beings to change is hard! Even initiatives that appear to be stroke-of-the-pen can often evolve into those that require significant permanent behavioral change.

Initiatives to move the organization forward take one of two forms...

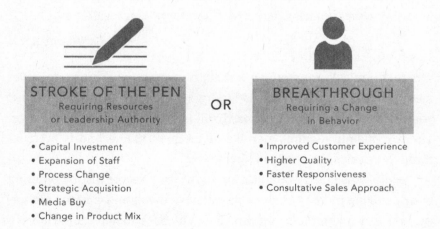

STROKE OF THE PEN
Requiring Resources
or Leadership Authority

OR

BREAKTHROUGH
Requiring a Change
in Behavior

- Capital Investment
- Expansion of Staff
- Process Change
- Strategic Acquisition
- Media Buy
- Change in Product Mix

- Improved Customer Experience
- Higher Quality
- Faster Responsiveness
- Consultative Sales Approach

Our colleague Jim Stuart summarized this challenge as follows: "To achieve a goal you have never achieved before, you must start doing things you have never done before." If it requires people to do something different, you are driving a *breakthrough strategy,* and it's not going to be easy.

Almost every leader has felt the pain and frustration of this challenge. Have you ever found yourself on the way to work muttering something like: "For the love of heaven, can't we do just this one thing?" If so, then you remember how it felt when the inability to get people to change was the one thing standing between you and the results you wanted. And you're not alone.

In a key study on organizational change, the global management consulting firm Bain & Company reports these findings: "About 65 percent of initiatives required significant behavioral change on the part of employees—something that managers often fail to consider or plan for in advance."[1]

Despite the significance of this problem, leaders seldom recognize it. You don't hear leaders saying, "I wish I were better at driving strategies that require people to do things differently." What you are more likely to hear is a leader saying, "I wish I didn't have Tom, Paul, and Sue to deal with!"

It's natural for a leader to assume the people are the problem. After all, they are the ones not doing what we need to have done. But you would be wrong. *The people are not the problem!*

W. Edwards Deming, father of the quality movement, taught that anytime the majority of the people behave a particular way the majority of the time, the people are not the problem. The problem is inherent in the system.[2] As a leader, you own responsibility for the system. Although any one particular person can be a big problem, if you find yourself regularly blaming the people, you should have another look at the situation.

When we began to study this challenge, we first wanted to understand the root causes of weak execution. We commissioned an international survey of working people and examined hundreds of businesses and government agencies. During the early stages of our research, we found problems everywhere we looked.

One prime suspect behind execution breakdown was clarity of the objective. People simply didn't understand the goal they were supposed to execute. In fact, in our initial surveys, we learned that only one employee in seven could name even one of their organization's most important goals. That's right—only 15 percent could name even one of the top three goals their leaders had identified. The other 85 percent named what they *thought* was the goal, but it often didn't remotely resemble what their leaders had said. The further from the top of the organization, the lower the clarity. And that was just the beginning of the problems we uncovered.

Lack of commitment to the goal was another problem. Even those people who knew the goal lacked commitment to achieving it. Only 51 percent could say that they were passionate about the team's goal, leaving almost half the team simply going through the motions.

Accountability was also an issue. A staggering 81 percent of the people surveyed said they were not held accountable for regular progress on the organization's goals. And the goals were not translated into specific actions—87 percent had no clear idea what they should be doing to achieve the goal. No wonder execution is so inconsistent!

In short, people weren't sure what the goal was, weren't committed to it, didn't know what to do about it specifically, and weren't being held accountable for it.

These were only the most obvious explanations as to why execution breaks down. On a more subtle level, there were problems with lack of trust, misaligned compensation systems, poor development processes, and poor decision making.

Our first instinct was to say, "Fix everything! Fix it all, and then you'll be able to execute your strategy." It was like advising them to boil the ocean.

As we did further research, we began to put our finger on a far more fundamental cause of execution breakdown. Certainly, the problems we just cited—the lack of clarity, commitment, collaboration, and accountability—exacerbate the difficulty of strategy execution. But in reality, they initially distracted us from seeing the deeper problem. You may have heard the old saying "Fish discover water last." That expression sums up our discovery very well. Like a fish discovering the water it's been swimming in the whole time, we finally realized that the fundamental problem with execution had always been right in front of us. We hadn't seen it because it was everywhere, hiding in plain sight.

THE WHIRLWIND

The real enemy of execution is your day job! We call it the *whirlwind*. It's the massive amount of energy that's necessary just to keep your operation going on a day-to-day basis; and ironically, it's also the thing that makes it so hard to execute anything new. The whirlwind robs you of the focus required to move your team forward.

Leaders seldom differentiate between the whirlwind and strategic goals, because both are necessary to the survival of the organization. However, they are clearly different; and more important, they compete relentlessly for time, resources, energy, and attention. We don't have to tell you which will usually win this fight.

The whirlwind is urgent, and it acts on you and everyone working for you every minute of every day. The goals you've set for moving forward are important, but when urgency and importance clash, urgency will win out every time. Once you become aware of this struggle, you will see it playing out everywhere, in any team that is trying to execute anything new.

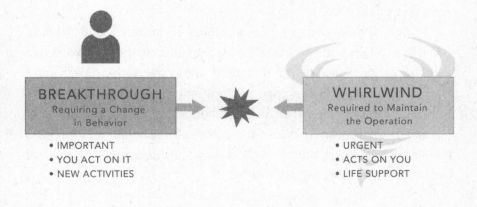

Think about your own experience. Can you remember an important initiative that launched well and then died? How did the end come? Was it with a loud crash and a tremendous explosion? Or did it go down quietly over time, suffocated by the whirlwind? We've asked countless numbers of leaders this question and we always get the same answer: "Slow suffocation!" It's like finding that faded T-shirt in the bottom of your drawer and saying, "Oh, yeah, Operation Summit. I wonder whatever happened to that?" It died, and you didn't even have a funeral.

Executing in spite of the whirlwind means overcoming not only its powerful distraction, but also the inertia of "the way it's always been done." We're not saying the whirlwind is bad. It isn't. It keeps your organization alive, and you can't ignore it. If you ignore the urgent, it can kill you today. It's also true, however, that if you ignore the important, it can kill you tomorrow. In other words, if you and your team operate solely from within the whirlwind, you won't progress—all your energy is spent just trying to stay upright in the wind. The challenge is executing your most important goals in the midst of the urgent!

Different leaders experience the whirlwind in different ways. A senior executive with one of the world's largest home-improvement retailers describes it this way: "We don't have dragons swooping down and knocking us off our priorities. What we have are gnats. Every day we have gnats getting in our eyes, and when we look back over the last six months, we haven't accomplished any of the things we said we were going to."

You've almost certainly found yourself facing the whirlwind when you were trying to explain a new goal or strategy to someone who works for you. Can you remember the conversation? Your mind is centered clearly on the goal, and you are explaining it in easy-to-understand terms. But while you're talking, the person you are talking to is backing slowly out of the room, all the while nodding and reassuring you, but trying to get back to what they would call the *real work*—another name for the whirlwind.

Is that employee fully engaged in achieving the goal? Not a chance. Are they trying to sabotage your goal or undercut your authority? No. They're just trying to survive in their whirlwind.

To illustrate, one of our colleagues shares this story: "I was chair of the community council for my local high school, and we as a council developed a serious goal of improving test scores. My job was to orient the teachers to the new goal, so I made an appointment with key teachers to explain what we were doing and get things started.

"At first I was baffled—they didn't seem to be listening to me. Slowly, I learned why. On one teacher's little desk was a stack that looked like a thousand papers. It was just one day's collection of essays she had to evaluate and grade. Plus, she had a parent conference to go to and the next day's lessons to plan. She looked kind of helpless while I jabbered on and on, but she wasn't really listening. There wasn't room in her brain for this, and I didn't blame her!"

Let's summarize what we've said so far. First, as you pursue results, you will eventually have to execute on a *breakthrough* strategy that requires a change in behavior. Stroke-of-the-pen initiatives will take you only so far. Second, when you undertake a breakthrough strategy, you will be battling the whirlwind—and it is a very worthy adversary, undefeated in many organizations.

We cannot stress enough that the 4 Disciplines of Execution are not designed for managing your whirlwind, and they are not designed to manage stroke-of-the-pen initiatives. The 4 Disciplines are the precise methods for accomplishing breakthrough results on your single most critical objective: your Wildly Important Goal.

Since execution is fundamentally a human challenge requiring new or different behaviors to produce improved results, you can best understand the impact of 4DX by first examining the most human reaction of all: resistance to change.

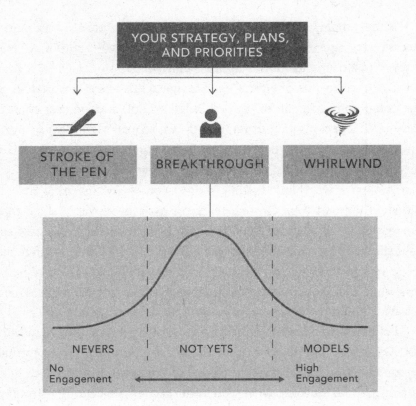

When it comes to adopting the new and different behaviors necessary for a breakthrough, you can expect people to fall into one of three categories. The first category is comprised of those people who engage quickly. These are your early adopters—the ones who energetically embrace and model the new behaviors that will create improved results. These are also the members of your team who are most open to new ideas, who have a willingness to try new approaches, and who are generally the most committed to *winning*. We refer to these individuals as Models.

There is another category (usually a much larger percentage of the team) who may appear to be in full support of the breakthrough, but in reality have embraced only a minimum of the changes required. They are doing just enough to appear supportive without ever really committing. We call these individuals Not Yets, because they have not yet fully engaged.

Finally, and unfortunately, a percentage of the team will never embrace the changes that breakthrough results require. We call this category the Nevers. Most often, the individuals in this category will never adopt, much less embrace, a significant change to the way they've become comfortable performing.

Models are found in both best-in-class organizations and those that are struggling. They create pockets of excellence, and are usually the source of outstanding results. Their high performance is valuable not only because it produces results, but also because it confirms that breakthrough results are possible on a larger scale. The greater your percentage of Models, the higher the performance of the team.

But pockets of excellence are also the bright side of a darker problem. Almost every organization also experiences significant variability in performance—highs and lows that are predominantly driven by the Not Yets and the Nevers. The greater your percentage of Not Yets and Nevers, the more inconsistent your results will be.

These two dynamics—pockets of excellence and variability of performance—exist in both the best- and worst-performing organizations. What actually separates the best and worst performers is the *shape* of their respective curves. The high performer's adoption curve is more "right and tight." So while leaders have to accept that they will always have an adoption curve, *they do not have to accept the shape of that curve.* Leaders who accept the shape of their adoption curve are, in a sense, giving up on improving *execution* and have limited themselves to improving results only through changing *strategy*. The purpose of the 4 Disciplines of Execution is to move the adoption curve right and tight, toward achieving a breakthrough.

THE 4 DISCIPLINES OF EXECUTION

Tim Harford, author of *The Undercover Economist*, said, "You show me a successful complex system, and I will show you a system that has evolved through trial and error."[3] In the case of 4DX, he is absolutely right. It benefited from well-researched ideas, but it *evolved* through trial and error.

In our initial research with Harris Interactive, we surveyed nearly thirteen thousand people internationally across seventeen different industry groups and completed internal assessments with five hundred different companies. Over the years, we've added to this foundation by surveying almost 300,000 leaders and team members. This research has been valuable as a foundation for the principles and in guiding our early conclusions, but the real insights did not come from research. They came from implementing 4DX with people like you in over fifteen hundred organizations for the first edition of this book, and over three thousand organizations for the release of this second edition. This effort is what enabled us to develop principles and methods we know will work, regardless of the industry or the geography in which they are implemented.

There is good news and bad news here. The good news is that there are rules—rules for executing a breakthrough in the face of the whirlwind. The bad news? The bad news is that there are rules—the kinds of rules that have immediate consequences if you violate them.

Although the disciplines may seem simple at first glance, they are not simplistic. They will profoundly change the way you approach your goals. Once you adopt them, you will never lead the same way again, whether you are a project coordinator, lead a small sales team, or run a Fortune 500 company. We believe they represent a major breakthrough in how to move teams and organizations forward.

Here's a quick overview of the 4 Disciplines.

Discipline 1: Focus on the Wildly Important

Basically, the more you try to do, the less you actually accomplish. This is a stark, inescapable principle we all live with. Somewhere along the way, most leaders forget this. Why? Because smart, ambitious leaders don't want to do less; they want to do more, even when they know better. Isn't it really difficult for you to say no to a good idea, much less a great one? Yet, there will always be more good ideas than you and your teams have the capacity to execute. That's why your first challenge is focusing on the wildly important.

Focus is a natural principle. The sun's scattered rays are too weak to start a fire, but once you focus them with a magnifying glass, they will bring paper to flame in seconds. The same is true of human beings—once their collective energy is focused on a challenge, there is little they can't accomplish.

Discipline 1: Focus on the Wildly Important requires you to go against your basic wiring as a leader and focus on *less* so your team can achieve *more*. When you implement Discipline 1, you start by selecting one goal where you would most like to achieve breakthrough results, instead of trying to significantly improve everything all at once. We call this a *Wildly Important Goal* (WIG) to make it clear to the team that this goal is critical and will be given special focus and attention.

If you are trying to simultaneously execute a number of new goals, each of which requires a high degree of engagement to achieve, you will inevitably be frustrated by your results. Even if each goal can be justified, the demands of the whirlwind leave you with limited capacity for anything new, especially a goal that requires a change in human behavior. Attempting to spread that limited capacity across multiple goals is the most common cause for failure in execution.

The word "focus" is most often used in one of two ways, and both are critical to Discipline 1. The first is when we talk about narrowing our focus, meaning to limit the number of things we are looking at to a single Wildly Important Goal. The second is when we talk about bringing that one thing *into focus,* the way you may adjust the lens of a camera until the subject is crisply clear. This is equally important. The Wildly Important Goal must be singular and completely in focus. This is achieved not only by selecting the specific area where you want to achieve breakthrough results (your WIG), but also bringing it into focus by defining a starting line (your current level of performance), a finish line (your desired improved performance), and a deadline for the WIG (the date by which this level must be achieved).

For example, instead of defining a WIG as "Improve subscription revenues," you would define it as "Increase revenue from new subscriptions from $3.5 million to $4.5 million by December 31." The process for defining a WIG should not be thought of as simply "this year's process for setting goals." The WIG represents a breakthrough result that can be achieved only by applying a special treatment. Without this level of focus, you likely won't get the results you want. Focus is the first step, but it's also only the beginning.

Discipline 2: Act on the Lead Measures

This is the discipline of leverage. It's based on the simple principle that all actions are not created equal. Some actions have more impact than others when you are working toward a goal. And it is those you want to identify and act on at the highest level if you want to achieve your breakthrough result.

Whatever strategy you're pursuing, your progress and your success will be based on two kinds of measures: lag and lead.

Lag measures are the tracking measurements of the Wildly Important Goal, or any other measurement you cannot significantly influence individually. These are usually the ones you spend most of your time agonizing over. Revenue, profit, market share, product quality, and customer satisfaction are all lag measures, meaning that when you receive them, the performance that drove them is already in the past. That's why you're agonizing—by the time you get a lag measure, you can't fix it. It's history.

Lead measures are quite different in that they are the measures of the most impactful actions (or behaviors) your team must do to reach the goal. In essence, the lead measures are the new behaviors that will drive success on the lag measures, whether those behaviors are as simple as offering a sample to every customer in the bakery or as complex as adhering to standards in jet-engine design.

A good lead measure has two basic characteristics. It's *predictive* of achieving the goal, and it can be *influenced* by the team members. To understand these two characteristics, consider the simple goal of losing weight. While the lag measure is pounds lost, two lead measures might be a specific limit on calories per day and a specific number of hours of exercise per week. These lead measures are predictive because by adhering to them, you can predict what the bathroom scale (the lag measure) will tell you next week. They are influenceable, because both of these new behaviors are within your control.

Be careful to not confuse what we are calling a "lead measure" with the often-used term "predictive indicator." For example, inches of rainfall might be predictive of crop growth, but it is not something that can be influenced by the team, and this is the critical difference. Both lead measures and predictive indicators predict an outcome, but only lead measures include being influenceable by the team. For this reason, lead measures are the more effective element for tracking actions critical to WIG achievement.

The number of times preventive maintenance is done could be a lead measure for a WIG (or lag measure) of reducing machine downtime. A reduction in the out-of-stock count could be a lead measure for the WIG of increasing same-store sales. The number of times call-center supervisors do one-on-one coaching could be a lead measure for a WIG of improved customer service. Acting on lead measures is one of the little-known secrets of execution.

Most leaders, even some of the most experienced, are so focused on lag measures that the discipline to focus on the lead measures feels counterintuitive.

Don't misunderstand. Lag measures are ultimately the most important things you are trying to accomplish. But lead measures, true to their name, are what will get you to the lag measures. Once you've identified your lead measures, they become the key leverage points for achieving your goal.

Discipline 3: Keep a Compelling Scoreboard

People play differently when they're keeping score. If you doubt this, watch any group of teenagers playing a game and see how the level of play changes the minute scorekeeping begins. However, the truth of this statement is more clearly revealed by a change in emphasis: People play differently when *they* are keeping score. It's not about the leader keeping score for them.

Discipline 3 is based on the principle of engagement. The highest level of performance always comes from people who are emotionally engaged, and the highest level of engagement comes from knowing the score—that is, if people know whether they are winning or losing.

It's that simple. Bowling through a curtain might be fun in the beginning; but if you can't see the pins fall, it will soon become boring, even if you really love bowling.

If you've narrowed your focus in Discipline 1 (your WIG with a lag measure) and determined the critical lead measures that will keep you on course toward that goal in Discipline 2, you have the elements of a winnable game; but as of yet, you have only a "good bet." It won't feel like a winnable game until there is a compelling scoreboard.

The kind of scoreboard that will drive the highest levels of engagement will always feel more like a players' scoreboard than the more complex coach's scoreboard leaders typically love to create. It must be simple—so simple that members of the team can determine instantly if they are winning or losing. Why does this matter? If the scoreboard isn't clear, the game you want people to play will be abandoned in the whirlwind of other activities. And if your team doesn't know if they are winning the game, they are probably on their way toward losing.

Discipline 4: Create a Cadence of Accountability

Discipline 4 is where execution really happens. The first three disciplines set up the game, but until you apply Discipline 4, your team isn't *in* the game. It is based on the principle of accountability: that is to say, unless we consistently hold one another accountable, the goal naturally disintegrates in the whirlwind.

The cadence of accountability is a rhythm of regular and frequent meetings of any team that owns a Wildly Important Goal. These meetings happen at least weekly and, ideally, last no more than twenty to thirty minutes. In that brief time, team members hold one another accountable for producing results, despite the whirlwind.

Why is the *cadence* of accountability so important?

Consider the experience of someone with whom we've worked. He and his teenage daughter made an agreement that she would be allowed to use the family car if she washed it every Saturday morning. He would meet with her each Saturday to make sure the car was clean.

They met on Saturday for several weeks, and everything went well, but then he had to go out of town for two Saturdays in a row. When he returned, he found that the car had not been cleaned. He asked his daughter why she hadn't taken care of her job.

"Oh," she replied. "Are we still doing that?"

It took only two weeks for the accountability system to break down. If this is the case in a one-on-one situation, think how much more it applies to a work team or a whole organization. The magic is in the cadence. Team members must be able to hold one another accountable regularly and rhythmically. Each week, one by one, team members answer a simple question: "What are the one or two most important things I can do in the next week (outside the whirlwind) that will have the biggest impact on the scoreboard?" Then members report on whether they met the previous week's commitments, how well they are moving the lead and lag measures on the scoreboard, and what their commitments for the coming week are, all in only a few minutes.

As a leader, how you launch 4DX with your team is not as important as how you run 4DX with your team. The team must feel that this is not only a winnable game, but also a high-stakes game. That starts with how you as the leader treat this session. When held with perfect consistency, this session communicates that it's a high-stakes game. This is vital, because so many other competing priorities will actually seem more urgent than your WIG on a day-to-day basis. However, the real secret to Discipline 4, in addition to the repeated cadence, is that team members create their own commitments. It's common to find teams where the members expect, even want, simply to be told what to do. However, because they make their own commitments, their ownership increases. Team members will always be more committed to their own ideas than they will be to directives from above. Even more important, making commitments to their team members, rather than solely to the boss, shifts the emphasis from professional to personal. The commitments go beyond their job performance to becoming promises to the team.

Because the team commits to a new set of objectives each week, this discipline creates a just-in-time weekly execution plan that adapts to challenges and opportunities that can never be foreseen in an annual strategic plan. In this way, the plan is adapting as fast as the business is changing. The result? The team can direct enormous energy to the Wildly Important Goal without getting blocked by the shifting whirlwind of change all around them.

When your team begins to see the lag measure of a big goal moving as a direct result of their efforts, they will know they are winning. And nothing drives the morale and engagement of a team more than winning.

People want to win. They want to contribute in a way that matters. However, too many organizations lack this kind of discipline—the conscious, consistent regimen needed to execute key goals with excellence. The financial impact of a failure to execute can be huge, but it is only one of the impacts. Another is the human cost to people who want to give their best and be part of a winning team. By contrast, nothing is more motivating than belonging to a team of people who know the goal and are determined to get there.

The 4 Disciplines work because they are based on principles, not practices. Practices are situational, subjective, and always evolving. Principles are timeless and self-evident, and they apply everywhere. They are natural laws, like gravity. Whether you understand them or even agree with them doesn't matter—they still apply.

Just as there are principles that govern human behavior, there are principles that govern how teams get things done, how they execute. We believe the principles of execution have always been focus, leverage, engagement, and accountability. Are there other principles at play when it comes to execution? Yes. But is there something special about these four and their sequencing? Absolutely. We didn't invent them, and we freely acknowledge that understanding them has never been the problem. The challenge for leaders has been finding a way to implement them, especially when the whirlwind is raging.

HOW THIS BOOK IS ORGANIZED

The 4 Disciplines of Execution is organized into three parts to provide you with a progressively deeper understanding of the disciplines and their application to any team or organization.

Part 1, "Learning 4DX," presents a thorough understanding of the 4 Disciplines. This part also explains why these apparently simple concepts are actually so difficult to practice and why they are the key to successfully meeting any leader's greatest challenge. Every leader and, if possible, every individual should read and understand this text.

Part 2, "Applying 4DX as a Leader of Leaders," is a detailed presentation of the process used by our consultants for addressing the higher-level challenges involved in implementing 4DX across multiple teams or an entire organization. It also includes specific practices for modeling and sustaining high performance over the long term. The content here is the result of our experience over two decades of teaching, and learning from, some of the finest senior leaders in the world. In addition, leaders of frontline teams will find this material valuable both to understand the focus and direction of *their leaders* and to prepare for success as a leader of leaders one day.

Part 3, "Applying 4DX as a Leader of a Frontline Team," is designed like a road map. It details the process we use when implementing the disciplines as a leader of a frontline team, with a separate chapter devoted to each discipline. This section is the most specific and detailed instruction for implementing 4DX, and is designed to show you the process we use with leaders of frontline teams as they progress through 4DX. Leaders of leaders may find that this material provides valuable context for the activities of their frontline teams but is not meant to be required reading at their level.

Most business books share a lot of helpful ideas and theories but are shallow on application. In this book, we are heavy on application and will tell you exactly how we implement these disciplines—the specifics, the tips, the watchouts, the must-haves. We'll share everything we know. We hope you'll find this approach refreshing.

BEFORE YOU BEGIN . . .

We've learned that there are three things to watch out for when you begin studying the 4 Disciplines more deeply.

4DX says easy, does hard. First, the disciplines will sound deceptively simple, but they take sustained work to implement. As one of our clients put it, "Says easy, does hard." Don't be misled by this simplicity. The 4 Disciplines are powerful in part because they are easy to understand. But successful implementation takes significant effort over an extended period. It requires sustained commitment. If the goal you're seeking isn't one you must achieve, you might not make the sustained commitment necessary. The payoff, however, is that you will not only achieve this goal but also build the organizational muscle and capability to achieve the next goal and the next.

4DX is counterintuitive. Second, each of the 4 Disciplines is paradigm-shifting and might even fly in the face of your intuition. While it might seem instinctive to have a lot of goals, the more you have, the fewer you will achieve with excellence. If you want to achieve a certain goal, don't focus on the goal itself but on the lead measures that drive the goal. As you implement each discipline, at least initially, you'll be doing things that at first glance might not seem to make sense and will run counter to your instincts. Let us emphasize, though, that the 4 Disciplines are the result of serious, intense experimentation and hypothesis testing over many years; everything you learn here has been thoroughly vetted. The good news is that once you gain experience with the 4 Disciplines, what seemed awkward in the beginning will become more comfortable and more effective.

4DX is an operating system. Third, the 4 Disciplines are a matched set, not a menu of choices. While every one of the disciplines has value, their real power is in how they work together in sequence. Each discipline sets the stage for the next discipline; leave one out, and you'll have a far less effective result. Think of the 4 Disciplines as the operating system of a computer. Once it's installed, you can use it to run almost any strategy you choose, but you need the whole system for it to work. As we move through the next chapters, the reasons for this will become clear.

CHAPTER 2

Discipline 1: Focus on the Wildly Important

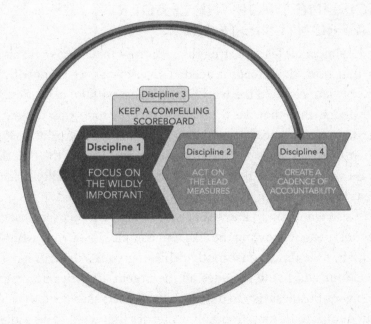

The first discipline is to *focus* your finest effort on the one thing that will make the biggest difference.

Execution starts with focus. Without it, the other three disciplines can't help you. But how you apply Discipline 1 will differ depending on whether you are a leader of a frontline team or a leader of leaders. This distinction is critical and will be used throughout the book to ensure we are always clear not only on *what* should be done but also on *who* should be doing it. This chapter will begin by discussing Discipline 1 from the perspective of a leader of a frontline team and then from the perspective of a leader of leaders.

> *It's difficult and resource-intensive to be great at everything—in fact, it's not necessary or even healthy. Instead, companies with highly effective operating models have decided to excel at only those few capabilities essential to realizing the strategy.*
>
> —Marcia Blenko, Eric Garton, and Ludovica Mottura[4]

DISCIPLINE 1 FOR THE LEADER OF A FRONTLINE TEAM

Why do almost all leaders struggle to narrow their focus? It's not because they don't think focus is needed. Every week we work with hundreds of leaders around the world, and almost without exception, they acknowledge that they need greater focus. Despite this desire, they continue to find themselves with too many competing priorities, pulling their teams in too many different directions. One of the first things we want you to know is that you are not alone. The inability of leaders to focus is a problem of epidemic proportions.

We also want you to know that narrowing your focus in Discipline 1 *does not* mean narrowing the size and complexity of your whirlwind (although, over time, consistently achieving your WIG will have that effect). Your whirlwind includes all the urgent activities necessary to sustain your business day to day, such as projects that need to be completed, quotas to be met, or baseline metrics that need to be achieved. As a result, these requirements will always be there, and they will (almost) always consume the majority of your team's time and energy.

Discipline 1 is different. It requires that you identify the *one objective* that will be separated out from your whirlwind and given intense focus, as well as the additional treatments of Disciplines 2, 3, and 4. This difference is signified by the name Wildly Important Goal. Your WIG is an outcome so significant that it cannot be accomplished without the finest efforts of your team and by performance that is above their day-to-day level. This is the one objective for which you apply 4DX.

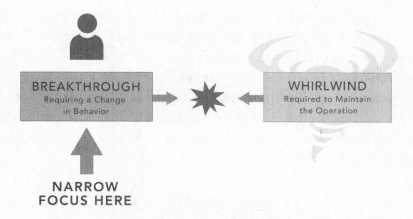

When you've defined your WIG, you will then view the work of your team in two distinct buckets. The first bucket contains everything the team needs to accomplish in the course of their day-to-day work (their whirlwind). This bucket is substantial and will likely require 80 percent of their time and energy. The second bucket is the Wildly Important Goal—the one specific outcome that represents the most meaningful breakthrough you'd like to achieve. Ideally, the WIG should be given the remaining 20 percent of the team's capacity.

Your WIG will be specific and clearly measurable, as in:

"Decrease speed of checkouts from 4:45 to 3:30 by end of year."

"Increase number of new subscriptions from 15 per month to 22 per month by July 31."

"Reduce machine shutdowns from 1.4 per day to 0.5 per day by March 1."

"Increase compliance to state budgetary guidelines from 58 to 63 percent by December 31."

Your WIG may be something new, something your team has not attempted before. But more often, it is something that has been part of your whirlwind that now needs to rise to a new level of importance and achievement.

Whether your WIG comes from within the whirlwind or outside of it, your real aim is not only to achieve it but also to make the new level of performance a sustained part of your team's operation. In essence, once a WIG is achieved, it returns to your whirlwind—it becomes part of your day-to-day operations, but at a new level. When this happens, your whirlwind changes. It isn't as chaotic, chronic problems are resolved, and new performance levels are sustained; in essence, it's a much higher-performing whirlwind. Ultimately, this is what enables your team to pursue the next WIG from a stronger foundation.

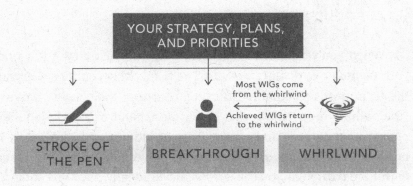

If you're like most leaders we work with, you will struggle to narrow your focus to just one WIG.

Here are simple guidelines that will help:

- **Think from the viewpoint of the team first.** No one individual on your team should focus on more than one WIG. For example, if you lead a marketing team that is comprised of an advertising team, a social media team, and a lead generation team, then each of those teams may have their own unique WIG. This might seem like three WIGs, but from the perspective of the team, no individual focuses on more than one.
- **Don't choose a WIG that encompasses your entire workload.** This might sound like you've narrowed your focus ("See, folks, we have only one WIG: 'Grow revenue'"), but you haven't. And everyone knows it. Separate your WIG from your normal results.

Instead of "Grow revenue," apply 4DX to a more specific portion of that overall outcome, such as "Grow revenue from midsize manufacturing companies in the southeastern region."

After coaching more than sixty thousand teams to apply 4DX, we have learned conclusively that if you want maximum results, you must narrow your focus to no more than one new significant goal beyond the whirlwind. We often refer to this as "whirlwind plus one." We understand that you might be someone who's great at multitasking and therefore believes that your team can accomplish lots of goals (requiring new and different behaviors) at the same time. But this isn't true. The science is very clear. The human brain can give its full focus to only one single object at any given moment. Most of us can't even give our best when we are driving a car while talking (hands free) on a cell phone, let alone juggle multiple important business goals all at once.

In our culture of multitasking, according to Professor Clifford Nass of Stanford University, "The neural circuits devoted to scanning, skimming, and multitasking are expanding and strengthening, while those used for reading and thinking deeply, with sustained concentration, are weakening or eroding."[5]

What's the consequence? "Habitual multitaskers may be sacrificing performance on the primary task. They are suckers for irrelevancy."

These same limitations apply to your team when you ask them to focus on multiple simultaneous goals, *at the same level of priority*. The more they focus on, the less they accomplish. This is why the idea of designating a single Wildly Important Goal is so effective.

Think of it this way. Right now more than a hundred airplanes might be approaching, taking off, or taxiing around, and all of them are very important, especially if you happen to be on one of them! But for the air traffic controller, only one airplane is *wildly important* right now—the one that's landing right at this moment.

The controller is aware of the other planes on the radar. They're keeping track of them, but right now all their talent and expertise is solely focused on one flight. If they don't get that flight on the ground safely and with total excellence, then nothing else they might achieve is going to matter much. They land *one airplane at a time.*

WIGs are like that. They are the goals you must achieve with total excellence beyond the circling priorities of your daily life. To succeed, you must be willing to make the hard choices that separate what is wildly important from the many other merely important goals on your radar. Then you must approach that WIG with focus and diligence until it is delivered as promised, with excellence.

Choosing a WIG doesn't mean you abandon your other important objectives. Your day-to-day responsibilities and metrics are always on your radar. The difference is that when you focus on your WIG, you give your finest diligence and effort in a precise way—because you're landing a specific plane *right now.*

Teams who try to focus to too many new goals at the same time usually wind up doing a mediocre job on all of them. You can ignore the principle of focus, but it won't ignore you. Or you can leverage this principle to achieve your top goals like landing planes one at a time, again and again.

THE LEADER'S CHALLENGE

So here's the big question: Why is there so much pressure toward expanding, rather than narrowing, the number of new goals? Even more simply, if you understand the need to focus, why is it so difficult to actually do it?

You might say that as a leader, you can always see more than a dozen existing things that need improvement and another dozen new opportunities you'd like to be chasing on any given day. On top of that, other people (and other people's agendas) are always adding to your goals, especially if they are from higher up in the organization.

However, more often than any of these external forces, there's one real culprit that creates most of the problem: you yourself. In the immortal words of Pogo from the comic strip, "We have met the enemy, and he is us."

Although the tendencies that drive you to add more and more new goals are well-intentioned, in a very real sense, you are often your own worst enemy. Being aware of these tendencies is a good place to start. Let's examine a few of them candidly.

One reason you may drive your team to take on too much is that as a leader, you tend to be ambitious and creative. You are exactly the kind of individual organizations like to promote. However, creative, ambitious people sometimes lose focus because they always want to do more, not less. If this describes you, you're almost hardwired to violate the first discipline of execution.

Another reason you might lead your team to go after too many goals is to hedge your bets. In other words, the more goals your team pursues, the more likely it is that at least some of them will be achieved. It also ensures that if you fail, no one can question the level of effort your team gave. Even though you know that more is not better, it *looks* better, especially to the person above you. Thus, you may resist the increased accountability for results that would come with fewer goals and instead rely on the sheer volume of effort to drive your success.

However, the greatest challenge you face in narrowing your goals is simply that it requires you to say no to a lot of good ideas. 4DX may even mean saying no to some *great* ideas, at least for now. Nothing is more counterintuitive for a leader than saying no to a good idea, and nothing is a bigger destroyer of focus than always saying yes.

What makes it even harder is that these good ideas aren't presented all at once, wrapped up in a nice little bundle so that the distraction they would create would be obvious. Instead, they filter in one at a time. Alone, each idea seems to make so much sense that it's almost impossible for you to say no. The more often you say yes, the more you fall into a trap of your own making.

We believe all leaders facing this challenge should have this quote prominently displayed in their office:

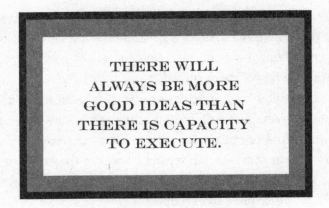

THERE WILL
ALWAYS BE MORE
GOOD IDEAS THAN
THERE IS CAPACITY
TO EXECUTE.

As a leader of a frontline team, you must be fanatical about ensuring that every individual focuses on no more than one WIG at a time, beyond their whirlwind. It's counterintuitive, but it must happen if you want real focus.

IDENTIFYING YOUR TEAM'S WILDLY IMPORTANT GOAL

A Wildly Important Goal is a goal that can make all the difference. Because it's your strategic tipping point, you're going to commit to apply a disproportionate amount of energy to it—the 20 percent that is not used up in the whirlwind. But how do you decide which of many possible goals should be your WIG?

As the leader of a frontline team, trying to define a Team WIG, you will be in one of two common situations:

1. **You have goal-setting autonomy.** This can occur when your team is actually the entire company, as with most small businesses. It can also occur when the leadership above you is not requiring new or significantly different results beyond your day-to-day. In this situation, you have the freedom to choose a Team WIG without high consideration for the goals of other teams.
2. **You do not have goal-setting autonomy.** This can occur when your team is part of a larger integrated strategy. In this situation,

your Team WIG may need to fit precisely within a larger plan for achieving a strategic result.

Sometimes the choice of a Team WIG is obvious, but at other times it can be confusing. For example, if you try to select your Team WIG by asking yourself what's most important, you may find your mind running in circles. Why? Because the urgent priorities in your whirlwind are always competing to be designated the *most important,* and a very good argument can usually be made for choosing any one of them.

When you *have* goal-setting autonomy, instead of asking, "What's most important for our team?" begin by asking, "If every other aspect of our team's performance remained at its current level, what is the one area where significant improvement would have the greatest impact?" This question changes the way you think and lets you clearly identify the focus that would make all the difference.

When you *don't have* goal-setting autonomy, it's more effective to ask, "What improved outcome would represent our team's greatest contribution to the overall strategy?" We recognize that if you are a leader of a frontline team with less autonomy, you may have many goals mandated from above. You may even be thinking, *My boss really needs to read* 4DX. We get it. Many leaders of frontline teams feel this way. Even though you may be responsible for a variety of goals, it's highly likely you will ultimately get to choose your Team WIG, because in the end, the leader of a team has the greatest influence on where the team applies deliberate focus.

We've never forgotten introducing 4DX to the plant managers of one of the largest consumer-products companies in the United States. After the session, one of the plant managers came up to us and said, "I have to tell you that I was just given the award for Plant Manager of the Year because of our results. But at the beginning of the year, I was assigned twelve 'performance priorities.' Even though I hadn't heard of 4DX, my own instincts told me I could not chase all twelve objectives. So we picked the one critical objective we thought would have the biggest impact, and we ended up with the best results in the company!"

Remember, 80 percent of your team's energy will still be directed at sustaining the whirlwind, so there's no need to worry that by focusing on a single WIG, your team will ignore everything else. It won't happen. What will happen, in the words of Discipline 1, is that you will increase your focus on the *wildly important*.

Another key aspect to recognize is that your Team WIG will either come from within the whirlwind or from outside of it. In simple terms, this means your Team WIG will represent either something *new* (an outcome you don't currently produce) or something *better* (an outcome that must be significantly improved).

Within the whirlwind, your Team WIG could be a result from an existing process so badly broken that it must be fixed, or a key element of your customer-service promise where delivery is failing. Poor project-completion time, out-of-control costs, or unsatisfactory customer service are all good examples. However, your Team WIG could also be an area in which your team is already performing well, but where a significant improvement could drive even greater impact. For example, increasing patient satisfaction in a hospital from the 85th percentile (good) to the 95th percentile (great) could help patients, increase revenue, and raise the entire organization to a new level.

Outside the whirlwind, your Team WIG will require achieving something it has never focused on before. This may take the form of a new opportunity to be seized, a new service to be delivered, or a response to a new competitive or economic threat. Whatever the focus, remember that this type of WIG will require an even greater change in behavior, since it will be completely new to your team. And changing human behavior is the greatest challenge of all.

DISCIPLINE 1 FOR LEADERS OF LEADERS

Let's start by looking at three common focus traps for leaders of leaders.

The first trap for leaders of leaders (as we've mentioned before) is the counterintuitive practice of saying no to good ideas. An illustration of just how important this one idea is was given by Tim Cook to company shareholders a few years before he became CEO of Apple.

"We are the most focused company that I know of or have read of or have any knowledge of. *We say no to good ideas every day* [emphasis added]. We say no to great ideas in order to keep the amount of things we focus on very small in number so that we can put enormous energy behind the ones we do choose. The table each of you is sitting at today, you could probably put every product on it that Apple makes, yet Apple's revenue last year was $40 billion."[6]

Apple's determination to say no to good ideas in order to focus has had devastating consequences for their competitors. We saw this first-hand when at the exact same time Apple was making history with their first iPhone, we happened to be working with a manufacturer who was their direct competitor. When we met with this company, the leader responsible for competing with the iPhone (how would you like that assignment?) was more than a little discouraged. "It's really not fair," he said, shaking his head. "Between our domestic and international operations, we make over forty different phones. They only make one." We couldn't have said it better ourselves.

> You have to decide what your highest priorities are and have the courage—pleasantly, smilingly, unapologetically—to say no to other things. And the way you do that is by having a bigger "yes" burning inside.
>
> —Stephen R. Covey

Saying no to good ideas, in order to say a focused yes to great ideas, is the key to extraordinary results.

The second trap for leaders of leaders is trying to turn everything in the whirlwind into a WIG. This is an approach that is appealing because it allows you to package your entire whirlwind into a single all-encompassing goal. While it appears that you've narrowed your focus, the reality is that you've simply given your whirlwind a new name.

Unless you can achieve your goal with a stroke of the pen, success is going to require the people in your organization to change their behavior, and they simply cannot change that many behaviors at once, no matter how badly you want them to. Trying to significantly improve every measure in the whirlwind will consume all of your time and leave you with very little to show for it.

The third trap for leaders of leaders is trying to create a WIG by identifying the *most important* objective. We mentioned this briefly as a challenge for the leader of a frontline team, but the challenge and the consequences are even greater for a leader of leaders, so we want to address it further here.

To illustrate the problem, imagine the leadership team in a manufacturing company having this conversation: "I'm telling you, quality is the most important thing, and it should be our WIG!" says one person. "Well, don't forget, it's our production that pays the bills around here," says another. "I'm sorry, but I disagree with both of you," says a third. "Safety has to be the most important. Have you ever had one of your people seriously hurt in an accident? If you had, you'd agree." The result is frustration and confusion, along with an inevitable (and paradoxical) loss of focus.

The problem in this conversation is that the leader here is asking the wrong question. They should not be asking, "What is most important?" but "Where do we most want to create a breakthrough?"

We know this may seem confusing, since we are talking about creating a *Wildly Important Goal,* so let's use an example. In the airline industry, no one would argue that airline safety is and always will be the most important objective. But airline safety would not be an effective WIG. Why? Because they are already so good at it. Their results are amazing, which leaves *little room for a true breakthrough*. However, if one day airline safety becomes a problem, the situation would change completely. It should immediately become a WIG.

Another problem with using the lens of *most important* is that it tends to direct your attention to an objective that is too high-level, and as a result, too broad. You lose your focus. A leader in a financially struggling company would resist choosing any WIG other than

EBITDA (or profit). But where is the narrowed focus in a goal that broad? EBITDA is actually a by-product of *all the activities* in the organization. It's like saying, "Get better at everything!" You've said nothing meaningful, and you certainly haven't narrowed your focus.

Instead, we would have you think about the *energy* a WIG at your level is actually directing toward an outcome. To do this, consider:

1. If each leader of a frontline team in your organization were to identify a Team WIG that represents a breakthrough for the team they lead . . .
2. Then if each team were to apply disciplined energy to their Team WIG every week (in addition to the effort they apply to their whirlwind) . . .
3. And if you thought of that cumulative energy, applied to all WIGs from all teams, as your "breakthrough currency" . . .

Then your role, as a leader of leaders, is to determine how you want to spend that currency. The more aligned and focused your investment is, the greater the return will be. And the more strategically effective that focus is, the greater the overall impact of 4DX. This is why the choice of the WIG at your level is so critical. Whatever you choose as the Primary WIG can be like a compass for the teams—each leader of a frontline team can align their Team WIG to the direction you set.

Below are the three most common approaches that you, as a leader of leaders, can take in defining WIGs at your level. Even though each of these graphics displays multiple WIGs within the same organization, they do not violate the primary guideline for focus: No individual focuses on more than one WIG at a time.

Approach A. Create a single Primary WIG.

When we use this approach, we have teams within the organization choose a Team WIG that aligns to the Primary WIG. It could look like either of the examples below. In the first example, the Team WIGs align directly to the Primary WIG; and in the second example, there are intermediate "sub-WIGs" (between the Primary WIG and the team, often referred to as "Battle WIGs") to which the Team WIGs are aligned.

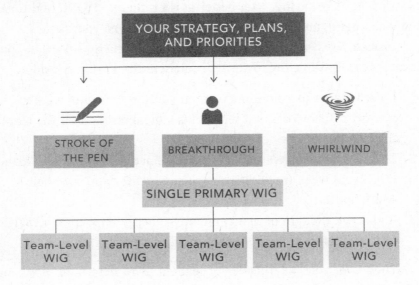

or . . .

There are two clear advantages to this approach. First, the energy of the organization is focused on a single Primary WIG, enabling you to produce the greatest possible result. Second, every member of the organization gets to contribute and participate in the same overall achievement. Whenever your frontline teams can have a meaningful impact on the Primary WIG, this approach is powerful. But if the frontline teams cannot find a way to directly or indirectly contribute to the Primary WIG, the forced alignment of their Team WIG can feel artificial and kills engagement.

Approach B. Create a small set of critical Primary WIGs.

When we use this approach, we know that even though these Primary WIGs are operationally unrelated, their combined accomplishment can lead to the achievement of the strategic objective. In this approach, the frontline teams within the organization align their Team WIG to the

one Primary WIG where *they can make the greatest contribution and impact*. Even though each team still has only one Team WIG, the organization can now divide its "breakthrough currency" between multiple objectives that are needed to fulfill the strategy.

Approach C. Leaders of frontline teams are given autonomy to choose their own Team WIG.

When we use this approach, the leader of leaders relies on the judgment of the leaders of frontline teams to decide what the WIG for their own team should be. This is particularly effective in organizations where the frontline teams have high operational autonomy and little or no interdependence with other teams for combined results. Small-box retail, grocery, and services operations are good examples. We have also seen this approach used in multiunit and franchised organizations.

––––––––––

Although we have seen other variations where elements of these approaches are creatively combined to address very unique business models and objectives, these three approaches represent the vast majority of 4DX implementations.

There are four primary rules for applying Discipline 1 as a leader of leaders.

Rule 1. No individual focuses on more than one WIG at a time. This rule acts like a governor on an engine. When you are deeply into the 4 Disciplines of Execution, there may be dozens or even hundreds of WIGs across the entire organization, but the key is not to overload any single leader, team, or individual. Remember, they are dealing with the incessant demands of the whirlwind. Keep this rule in mind as you consider the remaining three rules. If you violate this one, you will have lost your focus as an organization.

Rule 2. The battles you choose must win the war. Whether it's a military conflict or the war on hunger, cancer, or poverty, there's a relationship between battles and wars. The only reason you fight a battle is to win the war. The sole purpose of Team WIGs is to drive the achievement of the Primary WIG. It isn't enough that the Team WIGs just support or align with the Primary WIG. The achievement of the Team WIGs must *ensure* the success of the Primary WIG.

Once the Primary WIG is chosen, the next question is critical. Instead of asking, "What is the complete list of things we could do to win this war?"—a common mistake that results in a long to-do list—ask, "What is the smallest number of battles necessary to win this war?" The answer to that question determines which and how many Team WIGs will be needed to achieve the Primary WIG. As you begin to choose the battles to win the war, you have begun to both clarify and simplify your strategy.

Here's a meaningful example of the difference between Team WIGs that *support* achievement of the Primary WIG and those that *ensure* it. We worked with a provider of internet financial services who needed to increase revenues *within a specific market segment* from $160 million to $200 million by the fiscal year-end to fulfill the expectations of their investors. It's important to note that this was a narrowed focus on only a *portion* of their overall revenue. To achieve this result, the outside sales team committed to provide $8 million of new revenue and the major account division committed to the other $32 million.

It quickly became apparent that a major team—the technology division—had been left out of this plan. After all, what role could they play in a revenue WIG, since sales was not their direct responsibility? There were no easy answers, and this significant team soon felt left out of the WIG.

But after some careful research, they realized that they could have a great impact on the Primary WIG by improving their performance results for continuous uninterrupted service. After all, this was a major criterion that new customers would use to choose a provider. As it turned out, this Team WIG was the *most crucial* in achieving the Primary WIG of revenue growth, since it cleared the path for all other divisions. Without this contribution, the Primary WIG could never have been achieved.

Rule 3. Leaders of leaders can veto, but not dictate. The highest levels of execution are never reached when the strategy is devised solely by the top leaders of the organization and simply handed down to the leaders and teams below. Without the involvement of all, you cannot generate the high levels of commitment execution requires. While senior leaders will undoubtedly determine the Primary WIG, they must allow the leaders of frontline teams to have a significant role in defining the WIG *for their own team*. This not only leverages the knowledge of these frontline leaders, but also gives the team a greater sense of ownership and involvement. Frontline leaders will be more engaged in a goal they had a significant role in choosing. Senior leaders, as always, can then exercise their right to veto if the WIGs chosen will not achieve the Primary WIG.

Implementing Discipline 1 from a Primary WIG down to Team WIGs enables an organization to quickly turn a broad strategy into clearly defined targets at every level. It is not solely a top-down process, but neither is it exclusively bottom-up. It combines the best of both. The senior leader's choice of the Primary WIG (top-down) brings clarity, and the frontline leader's choice of a Team WIG (bottom-up) brings engagement. In the process, the entire organization mobilizes around the focus that matters most and takes ownership for driving the result.

A powerful example of this was illustrated by Dave Grissen, former Group President of the Americas for Marriott International, when he began the Marriott implementation that would eventually see 70,000 leaders certified in 4DX. In a candid presentation, he addressed a group of hotel managers by saying, "I'll let you in on a little secret. If you always want to have a job at Marriott, all you have to do is take care of the whirlwind. Run your day-to-day well and you'll always have a job. But if you want to get promoted, you have to drive results. Call your shot. Pick a WIG that improves our customer experience and then move the needle, whether it's arrival experience or event satisfaction or everything in working order." Not only did Dave Grissen say this, but "show me your result" became the first request to aspiring hotel managers in the interview processes.

Rule 4. All WIGs must have a finish line in the form of *From X to Y by When*. Every WIG at every level must contain a clearly measurable result, as well as the date by which that result must be achieved. For example, a revenue-focused WIG might be: "Increase percentage of annual revenue from new products from 15 to 21 percent by December 31." This *From X to Y by When* format recognizes where you are today, where you want to go, and when you plan to reach that goal. As deceptively simple as this formula may seem, many leaders often struggle to translate their strategic concepts into a single *From X to Y by When* finish line. But once they've done it, both they and the teams they lead have gained tremendous clarity.

Typically, however, goals lack this kind of clarity. We constantly see goals that no one can achieve because there's no finish line, meaning there is no way of telling whether you completed the goal or not and where you stand at any given point. Here are some examples:

From a major global retail company: "Improve inventory processing."

From a British publisher: "Develop and strengthen new and existing client relationships."

From an Australian tourist authority: "Influence effective tourism workforce development in Queensland."

From a European investment firm: "Successfully convert our portfolio to a life-cycle strategy."

From a multinational agribusiness company: "Identify, recruit, and retain the best employees."

These goals lack the measurement that can tell the team when they've won the game. "Improve inventory processing"? How much? "Strengthen new client relationships"? How do we measure "stronger"? "Successfully convert our portfolio to a life-cycle strategy"? How will we know if we've done that?

WIGs with clear finish lines look like this:

"Improve inventory processing by increasing per-year inventory turns from eight to ten by December 31."

"Raise our client-relationship score from 40 to 70 on the loyalty scale within two years."

"Move 40 percent of our customers from fixed categories to life-cycle categories of investments within five years."

"Launch the new CRM solution at an 85 percent quality beta rating by the end of our fiscal year."

If a goal is wildly important, surely you should be able to tell if you've achieved it or not. The formula *From X to Y by When* makes that possible.

In setting a finish line, we often hear the question "Over what period of time should the achievement of a WIG be spread?" Our answer is that it depends. Since teams and organizations often think and measure themselves in terms of a calendar or fiscal year, a one-year time frame makes a good starting point for a WIG. That said, remember that a WIG is not a strategy. A WIG is a tactical goal with a limited time frame. We've seen some WIGs that take two years and some that take six months. The length of a project-based WIG, such as "Complete the new website within budget by July 1," will usually correspond with the time frame of the project itself. Use your judgment. Just remember that a WIG should be within a time frame that balances the need to create a compelling vision with the need to create an achievable goal.

SHOOTING FOR THE MOON

In 1958, the fledgling National Aeronautics and Space Administration (NASA) had many important goals like this one: "The expansion of human knowledge of phenomena in the atmosphere and space." It sounded like many of the goals you hear in business today: "Become world-class . . ." or "Lead the industry . . ." Although the leaders at NASA had ways to measure various aspects of this goal, they lacked the clarity of a defined finish line. They also lacked the results that the Soviet Union was producing.

But in 1961, President John F. Kennedy shook NASA to its foundation when he made the pronouncement that the United States would "land a man on the moon and return him safely to the earth before this decade is out." Suddenly NASA had a formidable new challenge—the war it would fight for the next nine years—and it was stated in exactly the way WIGs should be stated: *X* is earthbound, *Y* is to the moon and back, and *when* is by December 31, 1969.

Just a glance at the table[7] on page 50 shows the difference between conventional organizational goals and a true WIG.

Consider the 1958 goals:

Are they clear and measurable?

How many are there?

Is there a finish line for any of them?

So, what kinds of results were these objectives driving for NASA? Russia went into space first with satellites and cosmonauts while the United States was still blowing up rockets on launchpads.

Contrast the 1958 goals with the 1961 goal: one clear, measurable WIG.

Now, with its reputation at stake on the world stage, NASA had to determine the few key battles that would win that war.

In the end, three critical battles were chosen: navigation, propulsion, and life support. Navigation posed the formidable challenge of moving a spacecraft through space at 18 miles per second to a precise location on the moon, which was also moving rapidly in its elliptical orbit around Earth. Propulsion was no less a challenge because a rocket heavy enough to carry a lunar module had never yet achieved a velocity sufficient to break free of Earth's gravitational pull. Life support was the most critical of all because it required developing a capsule and

NASA'S GOALS IN 1958	NASA'S GOALS AS OF 1961
1. The expansion of human knowledge of phenomena in the atmosphere and space;	*"I believe that this nation should commit itself to achieving the goal, before this decade is out, of landing a man on the moon and returning him safely to the earth." –John F. Kennedy*
2. The improvement of the usefulness, performance, speed, safety, and efficiency of aeronautical and space vehicles;	
3. The development and operation of vehicles capable of carrying instruments, equipment, supplies, and living organisms through space;	
4. The establishment of long-range studies of the potential benefits to be gained from, the opportunities for, and the problems involved in the utilization of aeronautical and space activities for peaceful and scientific purposes;	
5. The preservation of the role of the United States as a leader in aeronautical and space science and technology and in the application thereof to the conduct of peaceful activities within and outside the atmosphere;	
6. The making available to agencies directly concerned with national defense of discoveries that have military value or significance, and the furnishing by such agencies, to the civilian agency established to direct and control nonmilitary aeronautical and space activities, of information as to discoveries which have value or significance to that agency;	
7. Cooperation by the United States with other nations and groups of nations in work done pursuant to this Act and in the peaceful application of the results thereof;	
8. The most effective utilization of the scientific and engineering resources of the United States, with close cooperation among all interested agencies of the United States in order to avoid unnecessary duplication of effort, facilities and equipment.	

landing module that would keep astronauts alive, both for the journey to and from the moon and for the period while they explored the moon's surface.

President Kennedy's speech also included another key aspect of Discipline 1—saying no to good ideas—when he acknowledged that there were many other worthy objectives that the country would not pursue in order to achieve this goal. But as he asked, "Why, some say,

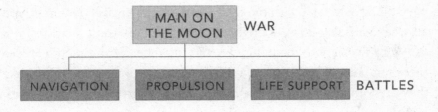

the moon? Why choose this as our goal? . . . That goal will serve to organize and measure the best of our energies and skills, because that challenge is one that we are willing to accept, one we are unwilling to postpone, and one which we intend to win."[8] In this way, he narrowed the focus of NASA to a finish line whose achievement became one of the most important ventures in human history.

What do you think happened to accountability within NASA when the challenge of putting a man on the moon was publicly announced? It went through the roof. This is particularly clear when you remember that the spacecraft they would use had only a tiny fraction of the computing power of the smartphone in your pocket. Even worse, the engineers and scientists still had no operational technology for winning the three necessary battles. Looking back, you might say human beings had no business being on the moon in 1969.

Now consider a different question: When accountability soared, what happened to morale and engagement? It, too, went through the roof. Most leaders find this surprising. We tend to think that when accountability is at its highest, the pressure makes morale go down. The reality is the opposite: Narrowing your focus increases both accountability and the engagement of your team.

When a team moves from having a dozen "we really hope" goals to one "no matter what" goal, the effect on morale is dramatic. It's as though a switch exists in every team member's head labeled "Game on!" If you can throw that switch, you have laid the foundation for extraordinary execution. When President Kennedy said to the moon and back by the end of the decade, he threw that switch.

Can you remember what it's like to be part of a team when the game-on switch is activated? It's a remarkable experience. Even though you still have to deal with the whirlwind and its myriad demands, you also have a finish line—something clear and important at which you can win. Even more meaningful, every member of the team can see that their contribution makes a difference. Everyone wants to feel like they are winning and that they are contributing to something meaningful. And when times are tough, they want it even more.

When we started on this journey years ago, we did not intend to focus on defining or even refining strategy. However, we quickly learned that the line separating strategy and execution is often blurry. Applying this discipline will sharpen your strategy more than you think it will. But what it will really do is make your strategy *executable*.

Think of it this way: Above your head is a thought bubble, and inside that bubble are the various aspects of your strategy, including opportunities you wish you were pursuing, new ideas and concepts, problems you know you need to fix, and a lot of versions of what to do and how to get it done. The contents of your bubble are complicated and chaotic. They are also completely different from the contents of the bubbles above every other leader.

This is why Discipline 1 requires you to translate your strategy from concepts to targets, from a vague strategic intent to the fewest number of specific finish lines at the front line of the organization. The four rules for implementing Discipline 1, outlined above, give an entire organization a framework for doing this successfully.

Finally, remember that the four rules of focus are unforgiving. At some point, you will want to cheat on them, even just a little. We understand. We often want to do the same inside our organization. However, what we've learned is that the rules governing focus are like the rules governing gravity: They aren't concerned with what you think or with the particulars of your specific situation. They simply yield predictable consequences.

When you think about it, the principle of focusing on the vital few goals is common sense; it's just not common practice. In one of Aesop's Fables, a young boy puts his hand into a jar full of hazelnuts. He grasps as many as he can possibly hold, but when he tries to pull out his hand, he finds the neck of the jar is too narrow. Unwilling to give up the nuts and yet unable to withdraw his hand, he bursts into tears and bitterly laments his disappointment.

Like the boy, you might find it hard to let go of a lot of good goals until you start serving a greater goal. As Steve Jobs often said, "I'm as proud of what we don't do as I am of what we do." Discipline 1 is about defining that greater goal, and it *is* a discipline.

CHAPTER 3

Discipline 2:
Act on the Lead Measures

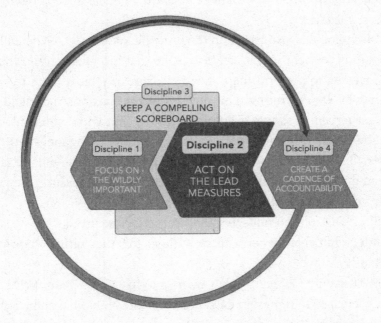

The second discipline is to apply disproportionate energy to the few actions (or behaviors) that will have the greatest impact on achieving the Wildly Important Goal. We call these actions "lead measures" because they are the measurable drivers that *actually lead* to WIG achievement.

Think of it this way: A lag measure shows you if you've achieved the goal. A lead measure tells you if you are *likely* to achieve the goal—meaning that the team is doing the things that are most critical to goal achievement. While a lag measure is hard for an individual (or a team) to directly affect, a lead measure is chosen to be both *predictive* of impacting the lag measure and within the team's control—what we refer to as *influenceable*.

It's important to note here that lead measures exist at the level of the frontline team and are designed to move the Team WIG (lag measure). Leaders of leaders may choose to use a particular metric, the Execution Performance Score (XPS), as a lead measure (a topic we'll address in Chapter 10), but otherwise do not have lead measures at their level. The descriptions of Disciplines 2, 3, and 4 presented here apply directly to leaders of frontline teams but represent a valuable understanding for leaders of leaders.

Discipline 2 is also based on the principle of leverage. When a lead measure is well chosen, it creates results that are greater than the effort invested to perform them. Lead measures enable a team to work smarter by concentrating their energy into the actions that yield the greatest return. A simple example would be that while you can't control how often your car breaks down on the road (a lag measure), you can certainly control how often your car receives routine maintenance (a lead measure). And the more you act on the lead measure, the more likely you are to avoid that roadside breakdown.

Since Discipline 1 and Discipline 2 interlock so precisely, it's easiest to understand them when you view them together rather than independently.

In Discipline 1, every team owns a WIG. These Team WIGs are usually created to represent each team's greatest possible contribution to the Primary WIG. The Team WIGs must be *aligned* (contributory) to the Primary WIG, and their combined results must *ensure* that the *X to Y* (lag measure) of the Primary WIG is achieved. It's important to note that once a WIG has an assigned *X to Y*, it is usually referred to as a lag measure.

In Discipline 2, each team then defines the measurable leveraged actions (lead measures) that will enable their Team WIG to be achieved. The illustration below shows the relationship between lag measures and lead measures in an overall plan to achieve the Primary WIG.

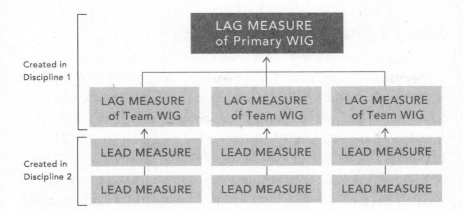

In a traditional planning model, you would begin by identifying your goal. Then you would create a detailed list of all the specific tasks and subtasks required to achieve the goal. But long-term plans are often too rigid. They lack the ability to adapt to the constantly changing needs and environment of the business. Not surprisingly, they often end up on your shelf collecting dust after only a few months.

With Discipline 2, you're going to do something quite different.

Discipline 2 requires you to define the daily or weekly lead measures, the achievement of which will lead to the goal. Then each week the team identifies the most important actions that will drive those lead measures. In this way, the team is creating a just-in-time plan every week that enables them to quickly adjust and adapt, while still remaining focused on the Team WIG.

CONVENTIONAL THINKING	4DX PRINCIPLE
Keep your eye on the **lag** measures: the quarterly results, the sales numbers, pounds lost. Stress out. Bite your nails while you wait.	Focus on moving the **lead** measures. These are the high-leverage actions you take to get the lag measures to move.

LAG VERSUS LEAD MEASURES

Now that you understand Disciplines 1 and 2, let's drill deeper into the distinction between lag and lead measures. Remember, a lag measure is the measurement of a result you are trying to achieve. We call them *lag measures* because by the time you get the result, the performance that drove it is in the past; the numbers are always lagging. In a Wildly Important Goal, the formula *From X to Y by When* defines your lag measure. Remember that your whirlwind is full of lag measures—quality, profitability, and customer satisfaction (to name just a few)—that will always be historical by the time you get them.

Lead measures are different; they foretell the result. Lead measures must always have two primary characteristics. First, a lead measure is *predictive,* meaning that if the lead measure changes, you can predict that the lag measure will also change. Second, a lead measure is *influenceable*; it can be directly influenced by the team. That is, the team can make a lead measure happen without a significant dependence on another team.

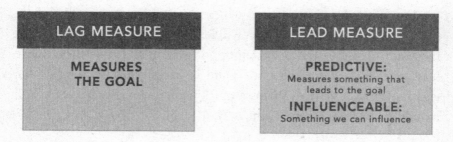

In Discipline 2, you create lead measures, the movement of which will become the driving force for achieving the Team WIG. In the months ahead, the team will invest consistent energy toward moving these lead measures. This investment will be the key to their success.

We believe that understanding lead measures will be one of the most important insights you take from this book.

Let's explore the two characteristics of a good lead measure further by first assuming you have a WIG to "Increase corn production from 200 tons to 300 tons by September 1." The *X to Y* of corn tonnage is your lag measure. You know that rainfall is an important factor in corn production, so rainfall can be predictive of the corn harvest. But is it a good lead measure? No, because you can't influence the weather to produce the right amount of rain. *Rainfall is predictive, but it isn't influenceable.* Rainfall fails the test because both characteristics are equally important.

Now take another illustration we referenced earlier: a WIG of achieving weight loss. Obviously, the lag measure will be your weight as reflected by the bathroom scale. If you format this WIG correctly, you might define it as "Decrease total body weight from 190 pounds to 175 pounds by May 30" (*From X to Y by When*). This is a good start, but what are the lead measures that will be predictive of achieving the goal and, equally important, that you can influence? You would likely choose both diet and exercise, and of course you'd be right.

These two measures fulfill the first characteristic of being predictive: if you decrease the calories you consume and increase the calories you burn, you'll lose weight. Just as important, however, these two lead measures are also directly influenceable by you. Achieve these two lead measures at the level specified, outside your daily whirlwind, and you will see your lag measure moving when you step on the bathroom scale.

LEAD MEASURES CAN BE COUNTERINTUITIVE

But there's one problem with lead measures. Where do leaders normally fixate—on lead measures or on lag measures? That's right. As a leader, you've likely spent your entire career focusing on lag measures, even though you can't directly affect them. And you're not alone. Think about your last meeting with the other leaders in your organization. What were you discussing, analyzing, planning, and agonizing about? Lag measures—including, usually, your inability to move them.

For example, it's easy for schoolteachers to measure the reading levels of students with a standardized test. Often they obsess over these lag measures. However, it's harder to come up with lead measures that *predict* how students will do on the test. The school might hire tutors or reserve more time for uninterrupted reading. In any case, the school is likely to do better if it tracks data on time spent reading or in tutoring (lead measures) rather than simply hoping and praying that the reading scores (lag measures) will rise of their own accord.

We see this syndrome every day in our work with teams around the world. The sales leader fixates on total sales, the service leader fixates on customer satisfaction, parents fixate on their children's grades, and dieters fixate on the scale. And in virtually every case, fixating solely on the lag measures fails to drive the desired results.

There are two reasons almost all leaders do this. First, lag measures are the measures of success; they are the results you have to achieve. Second, data on lag measures is almost always much easier to obtain than data on lead measures. It's easy to step on a scale and know exactly how much you weigh, but how easy is it to find out how many calories you've eaten today or how many you've burned? That data is often hard to get at, and it can take real discipline to *continue* getting at it.

Here's a warning: Right about now, you might be tempted to oversimplify what we're saying. If you're thinking something like *So all you're saying is that if you want to lose weight, you should diet and exercise? What's revolutionary about that?* then you've missed the point of Discipline 2.

There's a huge difference between merely *understanding* the importance of diet and exercise and *measuring* how many calories you've eaten and how many you've burned. Everyone knows you should diet and exercise, but the people who measure how many calories they've eaten and how many they've burned each day are the ones actually *losing* weight!

In the end, it's the *data* on lead measures that makes the difference, that enables you to close the gap between what you know the team should do and what they are actually doing. Without lead measures, you are left to try to manage to the lag measures, an approach that seldom produces significant results.

W. Edwards Deming, the management and quality expert, said it best when he told executives that managing a company by looking at financial data (lag measures) is the equivalent of "driving a car by looking in the rearview mirror."[9]

Lead measures also eliminate the element of surprise that a sole focus on lag measures can bring. Imagine this scenario: You and your team have been working hard on a goal to improve customer satisfaction. It's your most important measure and the one on which your bonus is based, and the new customer-satisfaction scores have just arrived in your inbox. As one of our clients expressed it, you are about to have one of two reactions: "Oh, cool!" or "Oh, no!" But either way, there is nothing you can do to change the results. They are in the past. That same client also pointed out, "If luck is playing a significant role in your career, then you're fixating on lag measures."

We couldn't agree more.

Imagine instead that you are tracking the two most predictive lead measures of customer satisfaction, and for the past three weeks, the team has performed well above the standard on those measures. Do you think your experience will change when the new customer-satisfaction results arrive? Absolutely. It will be like stepping on the scale knowing that you have met your diet and exercise measures every day. You already know that the lag measure will change.

DEFINING LEAD MEASURES

"Increase annual water production from 175 million liters to 185 million liters by December 31." This was the WIG for the water-bottling plant of a large beverage company when we began working to implement 4DX with the senior executive in charge of the supply chain. The plant had been struggling to meet its targeted water-production levels for several years, and the leaders were anxious to identify the lead measures that would drive water production to new levels.

We began by asking them to discuss what they thought a good lead measure for increasing annual water production would be.

"Monthly water production," they quickly answered.

"Sorry," we said, "that won't work."

They seemed confused. "Why not?" asked the plant manager. "If we hit our monthly water-production targets, then we'll hit our annual production, right?"

"You're absolutely right that monthly water production is predictive of annual water production," we replied, "but monthly production isn't any more *influenceable* by your teams than annual production. All you're doing is identifying a different lag measure that you can get more frequently than annual production. It is still a lag."

This dialogue is very common when teams first determine lead measures, and unfortunately, the leaders at the water plant still weren't quite getting it.

To help, we asked them what their lead measure would be for monthly water production.

"Daily water production!" they responded.

We knew that we weren't getting through.

The discussion grew more animated until the production manager finally demanded everyone's attention.

"I've got it," he said with real excitement. "I know what our lead measures should be!" He moved to the front of the room and began to explain. "We're constantly running shifts without full crews, and we have way too much machine downtime. Those are the two main things that keep us from producing more water."

Now we were getting somewhere.

Everyone in the room agreed with his diagnosis. They still didn't have usable lead measures—they needed to translate full crews and preventive maintenance into actual measures—but they had captured the idea. Quickly, they identified their first lead measure: Increase percentage of shifts with full crews from 80 to 95 percent. The second lead measure was even easier: Increase percentage of compliance to preventive-maintenance schedules from 72 to 100 percent.

Their strategic bet was that if the plant ensured full crews and a reduction in machine downtime, it would achieve a significant increase in water production. Over the next few months, the teams put a disproportionate amount of effort into those two lead measures, above their day-to-day whirlwind. Not only did their water production increase, it grew at a rate far greater than expected.

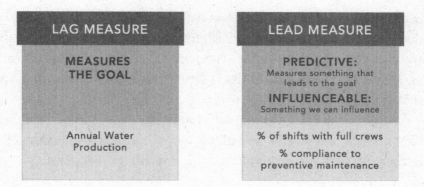

LAG MEASURE	LEAD MEASURE
MEASURES THE GOAL	**PREDICTIVE:** Measures something that leads to the goal **INFLUENCEABLE:** Something we can influence
Annual Water Production	% of shifts with full crews % compliance to preventive maintenance

This is a good illustration of the process for defining lead measures, but it also helps to make an important point. Our consultant on the project lauded the plant's results, but then asked an important question: "Why weren't you already doing those two things?"

His point was that their lead measures didn't come from Franklin Covey. The leaders at the plant already knew the importance of running shifts with full crews and compliance with standards of preventive maintenance, but despite knowing it, they weren't doing it. Why?

As with most teams, their problem was not that they didn't *know,* but that they didn't do—a matter of focus. Dozens of things needed improvement and focus, not just crew staffing and preventive maintenance; and by trying to improve everything, they remained trapped in their whirlwind. They spent every day spreading their energy across so many urgent priorities and trying to move all the dials at once that in the end, nothing moved.

Obviously, this problem is not unique to the leaders in this plant. If we followed you around for a few days, we would likely observe two predominant activities. One, you would spend most of your time battling your whirlwind; and two, a lot of your remaining time would be spent worrying over your lag measures. The problem with these two activities is that they consume enormous energy and produce little, if any, leverage beyond sustaining your whirlwind. And it's leverage that you need most.

The key principle behind lead measures is simply this: *leverage.* Think of it this way: Achieving your Wildly Important Goal is like trying to move a giant rock; but despite all the energy the team exerts, it doesn't move. It's not a question of effort; if it were, you and the team would already have moved it. The problem is that effort alone isn't enough. Lead measures act like a lever, making it possible to move that rock.

Now consider the two primary characteristics of a lever. First, unlike the rock, the lever is something we *can* move: It's influenceable. Second, when the lever moves, the rock moves: It's predictive.

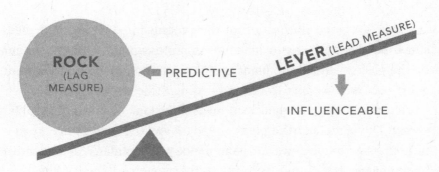

HOW DO YOU CHOOSE THE RIGHT LEVERS?

To achieve a goal you've never achieved before, you must do things you've never done before. When we work with clients, we encourage them to first look around. Who else has achieved this goal or something like it? What did they do differently? We then ask them to analyze carefully any barriers they foresee, and decide how to overcome them. We want them to use their imagination and often ask, "What haven't you thought of that might make a real difference?"

Our next step is to select the activities they believe will have the greatest impact on achieving the WIG: the 80/20 activities. Which 20 percent of what you do has as much or more leverage on the WIG than 80 percent of what you do? Finding the right lever among many possibilities is perhaps the toughest and most intriguing challenge for leaders trying to execute a WIG.

FINDING YOUR LEVERAGE

One of the most powerful examples of leverage we've experienced came a few years ago when we were engaged to use 4DX to drive an increase in revenue for the largest shoe retailer in the United States. The objective was familiar; the scale was not. Our engagement spanned 4,500 stores, crossing every demographic and geographic boundary imaginable, and engaging countless individuals in the greatest challenge of all: adopting a new approach to a business in which many had spent their entire careers.

We began by isolating a specific and measurable Primary WIG. Since "revenue" was too broad and represented virtually everything that happened in the stores, we narrowed our focus to a more precise outcome: Increase the percentage of customers who leave the store with new shoes (referred to as the conversion rate). On average, about 10 percent of adults entering the store were purchasing shoes, either for themselves or for the children with them. The leaders of the organization agreed that raising the conversion rate was the key to growth.

The next challenge was to determine which high-leverage behaviors would become lead measures capable of driving an increase this significantly. Initially, a list of ten lead measures was developed, and each store was allowed to pick two from that list. We knew that if the stores were allowed to choose their own, they would feel more ownership of the result. We also knew that if this many stores tried different approaches, the best lead measure would emerge. But when the most predictive of the lead measures became clear, it was one we would never have imagined.

If you think about your own experience buying shoes, you might expect the driver of increased conversion to be the friendliness of the staff, the availability of inventory in your size and style, or even the opportunity for a lower price. Certainly these are factors. But it turned out that the most predictive behavior for increased shoe sales was *measuring children's feet*. Let that fact sink in for a moment. Now imagine you're the adult responsible for the back-to-school shoe-buying adventure. You have multiple children with different shoe sizes, distinct preferences for style and color, and a very limited tolerance for shopping, all needing shoes today. At that moment, a salesperson approaches you and offers to measure the children's feet to ensure a quality fit before showing each child a selection that matches their preferences and your budget. What would your reaction be—especially in an industry where customer service is often sacrificed for lower prices and faster check-out times? Our client found that the simple act of measuring children's feet could become a *customer experience* that not only sold more shoes, but also created loyalty to the store for life.

Once the full impact of this lead measure was recognized, it became standard practice in each of the 4,500 stores. Every team constructed a scoreboard that identified each salesperson and the number of children's feet measured each day. At the end of the week, small prizes such as movie tickets and coffee-shop coupons were awarded to those who had the highest numbers. In essence, they made a game out of measuring feet to drive conversion—a game that was engaging and *winnable*.

When the final results were in, not only did they achieve the WIG, closing the X to Y gap across 4,500 stores, but they tripled the percentage increase they were hoping for.

Although each of the 4 Disciplines was necessary for this outcome, along with the talent, commitment, and hard work of a large group of people, it would not have been possible without the leverage of a predictive and influenceable lead measure.

The real insight of Discipline 2 is simply this: Regardless of the outcome you're seeking, a few actions or behaviors will create disproportionate results on your WIG. Working together with your team, you can find and then leverage these lead measures to produce extraordinary results.

In Part 3, we'll give you more specific insight on how to identify and deploy your lead measures, drawn from the lessons we've learned working closely with our clients.

Over the years, we've seen many leaders learn that an important key to execution is putting disproportionate energy against the leverage points by focusing on moving lead measures. If you have a big rock to move, you're going to need a lever that is highly predictive and controllable. The bigger the rock, the more leverage you will need.

TRACKING LEAD-MEASURE DATA

Younger Brothers Construction is a residential construction company in Arizona that had a big problem: a rising rate of accidents and injuries. Not only did each incident mean that a member of their crew was hurt, but it also meant a delay in the completion of a tightly scheduled construction project, increased insurance rates and, potentially, the loss of their safety rating. Reducing safety incidents had become the company's most important focus, so it wasn't difficult for them to arrive at their Wildly Important Goal: to reduce safety incidents from fifty-seven to twelve percent by December 31.

Once the WIG was established, we worked with them to determine the lead measures that were both predictive of fewer accidents and influenceable by the team.

The first idea they considered was to conduct more intensive safety training. This was highly influenceable, as they could simply make everyone go to more training. The leaders ultimately rejected that idea, however, since their people had already undergone a significant amount of training that had allowed them to achieve their current levels of safety. They decided that additional hours of training wouldn't be sufficiently predictive of achieving their new goal.

The leaders at Younger Brothers then looked more carefully at the primary causes of accidents plaguing the company and developed a different idea for their lead measure: compliance to safety standards. They decided to measure compliance via six safety standards: wearing hard hats, gloves, boots, and safety eyewear, as well as using scaffolds and roof braces to keep workers from sliding off the roof. They were certain that enforcing these six standards at high levels of compliance would be both predictive and influenceable in reducing accidents.

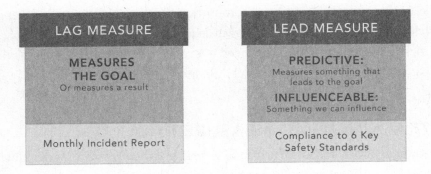

LAG MEASURE	LEAD MEASURE
MEASURES THE GOAL Or measures a result	**PREDICTIVE:** Measures something that leads to the goal **INFLUENCEABLE:** Something we can influence
Monthly Incident Report	Compliance to 6 Key Safety Standards

Within one year of focusing on the lead measure of compliance to safety standards, Younger Brothers Construction achieved the best safety record in the thirty-year history of the company. But it wasn't easy.

One of the most challenging aspects of their lead measure was simply getting the data. The lag-measure data of accidents and injuries came automatically from the company's system each week. The lead measure—compliance to safety standards—had to be physically observed.

This meant that construction supervisors had to move among the various crews to check whether workers were wearing their hard hats, gloves, boots, and safety glasses and if scaffolds and roof braces were firmly in place. Moreover, they had to do this despite a never-ending stream of distractions: subcontractor issues, late shipments, customer concerns, and weather delays. In the middle of that whirlwind, checking for safety compliance might not seem "wildly important" to a construction supervisor. However, because reducing safety incidents was the Wildly Important Goal, and because safety compliance was the primary leverage point for achieving it, they made it happen week after week.

The lesson in this story is that lead-measure data is almost always more difficult to acquire than lag-measure data, but you must pay the price to track your lead measures. We often see teams struggle with this, zeroing in on a high-leverage lead measure only to say, "Wow, getting that data is going to take real work! We're too busy to do that." If you're serious about your WIG, then you must create a way to track your lead measures. Without data, you can't drive performance on the lead measures; without lead measures, you don't have leverage.

And when the WIG is truly wildly important, you've got to have that leverage.

LEAD MEASURES AND ENGAGEMENT

Once a team is clear about its lead measures, their view of the goal changes.

Let's take a look at what happened when Beth Wood, a grocery-store manager, set out to achieve a very challenging goal of increasing year-over-year sales.

Beth called in Bob, her bakery manager, to get his support in improving their sagging year-over-year sales numbers.

Bob is a good-natured manager, and on a typical day, he would likely have said, "Sure, Beth, I'd be glad to help," even if he didn't have a clue what he could do to drive more sales. On this day, however, Bob had reached his limit and wasn't in the mood to just go along. "You want improved sales?" he said sarcastically. "Knock yourself out, Beth."

Startled by Bob's response, Beth responded: "Look, Bob, I can't do this alone. You're closer to the customers and your employees than I am."

Now Bob was really frustrated. "What exactly would you like me to do? It's not like I can hit people over the head and drag them into the store. I run the bakery. If you want a bagel, I'm your guy."

If you didn't know Beth and Bob well, you might think Bob has a chronically bad attitude or doesn't respect Beth, or worse, is just lazy. Actually, Bob likes Beth and really wants to help the store improve sales. But two things are holding him back: one, he doesn't know how; and two, he doesn't think he can. At this moment, what's really going through Bob's mind is, *We're a thirty-year-old store that just had a Walmart Supercenter move in down the street. We're also on the wrong side of the intersection and the traffic has to make a left to get in here, if they can even see our sign. And Beth wants me to improve store sales?*

Bob continues: "If I knew how to improve sales, don't you think I'd already be doing it? I'm not holding out on you!"

When you see Bob's perspective, you can better understand his response to this frustrating situation. Bob is representative of so many people. They can see the rock all too well. The problem is that they just don't see the lever.

Now let's replay this same scenario, but this time with Beth using a lead measure to drive her goal. She calls her managers together and poses this question: "Above sustaining our day-to-day operation, what is the one thing your team could do to improve year-over-year sales the most?" In effect, she is asking them what influenceable outcome or behavior is the most predictive of moving the lag measure of sales, but she's limiting it to a narrow focus.

They begin to discuss a lot of possibilities such as raising customer service, improving store conditions, or giving away more free samples. After a lot of back-and-forth, they finally agree that the single biggest thing they can do to improve sales in *their* store is to reduce the number of out-of-stock items.

This lead measure of reducing out-of-stocks is highly predictive of better store sales, a fact well known in the retail world. Equally important, out-of-stocks is a highly influenceable lead measure. Now Bob sees what he can do in the bakery to drive sales. Reducing out-of-stocks is something he and his team can influence. They can perform extra shelf reviews to check for items that are sold out, they can organize their back room so that fast-moving products are easier to restock, or they can change the frequency and volume of reordering. In other words, it's a game he and his team can win, and now *he's engaged*.

When a team defines its lead measures, they are making a strategic bet. In a sense, they are saying, "We're betting that by driving these lead measures, we are going to achieve our Wildly Important Goal." They believe that the lever is going to move the rock, and because of that belief, they engage.

Finally, we want to share that in more than two decades of doing this work, we have consistently seen that the lead measures with the most impact come from a collaboration between the leader and the

LAG MEASURE	LEAD MEASURE
MEASURES THE GOAL Or measures a result	**PREDICTIVE:** Measures something that leads to the goal **INFLUENCEABLE:** Something we can influence
Bakery Sales Report	Number of Out-of-Stocks

frontline team. This collaboration has taken different forms, but in all cases, the impact of the lead measures has been greater when the top-down influence of the leader provides guidance and direction, and the bottom-up influence of the team provides clarity on which actions actually produce the greatest results. And it is clarity on cause (lead measures) and effect (outcome on the WIG) that you are after. When done well, this collaboration creates a synergy that neither the leader nor the team could have created alone.

In some cases, the leader acts as a catalyst for the team's involvement by creating a sample of lead measures that might be most effective. But then the leader is careful to allow the team to go on to create their own ideas. In other cases, the team is allowed to create the opening set of ideas the leader can then review and respond to. In this approach, the leader can veto an idea they believe will not work, but they cannot dictate what the final lead measures should be.

Whatever approach is used, take heed of one of Stephen R. Covey's most powerful teachings: "No involvement, no commitment." If you want high engagement from your team, provide the opportunity for meaningful involvement. We will discuss this in detail in Part 3.

Disciplines 3 and 4 are designed to help the team put energy into moving the lead measures. However, the real impact and beauty of good lead measures in Discipline 2 is that they truly connect the team to WIG achievement. And ultimately, it's the front line of an organization that creates the bottom-line result you're after.

Coming up with the right lead measures is really about helping everyone see themselves as strategic business partners and engaging them in dialogue about what can be done better or differently in order to achieve the WIGs.

A good example of this comes from the advertising department of the *Savannah Morning News,* a venerable newspaper in the American South. When we met with them, they were trying to close a serious revenue gap. They had fallen into the trap of trying to focus on everything at once, including pushing new products, daily-inserts specials, and other add-ons in an attempt to incrementally move the revenue number. Their focus was spread across so many initiatives that they had taken their eye off their main product. So they began with Discipline 1, setting a Wildly Important Goal, to increase advertising revenue by refocusing on their core product.

Everything changed when they started practicing Discipline 2 and acting on the lead measures. Everybody on the team was involved in the dialogue. After thinking through ways to increase advertising dollars, they agreed together on three key actions (lead measures): increase their number of contacts with new customers, potential advertisers who had not done business with the newspaper; reactivate customers who hadn't advertised with the paper for six months or more; and upsell to their existing clients, finding ways to add value to the message—maybe adding color to an ad, giving it better placement, or increasing the size of an ad.

In practice, the plan broke down into simple lead measures. In the weekly WIG Sessions, people committed to hit a certain number of contacts with new customers, reactivate calls, and upsell offers. The next week they reported the results. Individual salespeople were both managing their own business more effectively and regularly communicating to one another best practices, refinements to approaches, and ways to overcome barriers.

The advertising director said, "I've been in this business for a lot of years, and I've spent my entire career basically agonizing over lag measures and putting out fires." For the first time, she could help her people achieve their goals in tangible ways. The newspaper closed their revenue gap and shot past their goals for the year. Acting consistently on the right lead measures made it all possible. Based on this success, Morris Communications, the parent company of the *Savannah Morning News,* went on to implement 4DX with their forty other newspapers.

We'll talk more about selecting the right lead measures in Part 3.

VISUAL EXAMPLES OF LAG AND LEAD MEASURES

One of the most important distinctions in 4DX is the difference between lag and lead measures. It's also been a frequent point of confusion, particularly when it is necessary to break Primary WIGs down into sub-WIGs (Key Battles). It's easy to think of sub-WIGs (and even Team WIGs) as lead measures, because everything below "leads" to the Primary WIG.

However, in 4DX, lead measures must also be directly influenceable by the team, and sub-WIGs (and Team WIGs) are too high-level to meet this requirement. Primary WIGs, sub-WIGs, and Team WIGs all represent lag measures. Lead measures exist at the level of the frontline team and are defined for the express purpose of driving the Team WIG (lag measure). They are chosen because they can be *directly* influenced and because they are predictive of Team WIG success.

We want you to avoid looking at your current set of metrics and wondering which of these metrics are lags and which are leads. Since the purpose of the lead measure is to drive the Team WIG, you can't create a lead measure until you have first defined the Team WIG. No Team WIG, no lead measures.

To ensure this is completely clear, the diagram below illustrates the difference between sub-WIGs (lag measures) and lead measures.

When people are new to 4DX, there is a tendency to confuse sub-WIGs (in gray) with lead measures (in white) because achieving sub-WIGs "leads" to achieving Primary WIGs, and achieving lead measures also "leads" to achieving Team WIGs.

However, there is a critical difference. Lead measures can be *directly* influenced by a team, while sub-WIGs cannot.

This is easier to understand by looking at a diagram that illustrates sub-WIGs in relationship to lead measures.

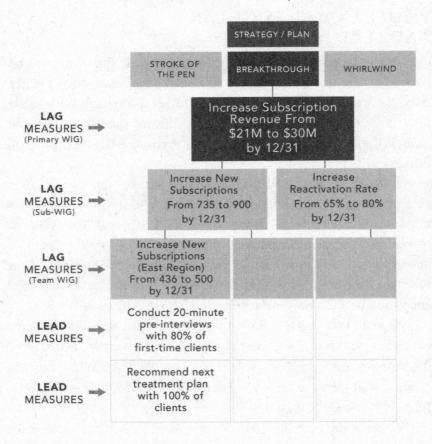

CHAPTER 4

Discipline 3: Keep a Compelling Scoreboard

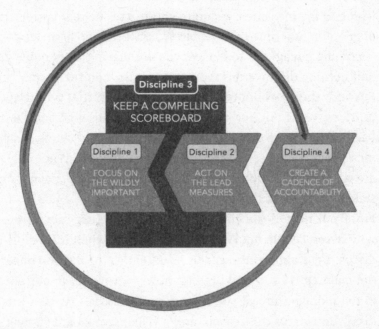

The third discipline is to make sure everyone knows the score at all times so that they can tell whether or not they are winning.

Discipline 3 is based on the principle of engagement.

Remember, people play differently when *they* are keeping score. The difference in performance between a team who understands their lead and lag measures simply *as a concept* and a team who actually knows their score is remarkable. If the lead and lag measures are not captured on a visual scoreboard and updated regularly, they will disappear into the distraction of the whirlwind. People disengage when they don't know the score. When they can see at a glance whether or not they are winning, they become profoundly engaged.

In Discipline 3, the execution bet (because it's yet unproven) is translated into a visible, compelling scoreboard. This scoreboard is designed to impact the team's performance in three specific ways:

1. **First, it provides a *visual* representation of the bet the team is making.** They can see that the plan centers on a bet that performing these lead measures will move this lag measure (WIG). It's one thing to talk about the correlation between lead and lag measures; it's quite another to see that correlation play out in real time on a visible scoreboard. The first step to becoming engaged is to believe you are playing a winnable game, and nothing displays this more powerfully than the scoreboard.

2. **Second, the scoreboard signals to the team that winning matters.** We're not just going to talk about this goal and then go back to managing the whirlwind. The scoreboard sends a clear message: "We are serious about this." It signals that not only are we playing a winnable game, but we are also playing a high-stakes game—one that really matters.

3. **Finally, it provides a counterbalance to the urgency of the whirlwind.** While the WIG may feel critical when it is being discussed, it almost never feels as urgent as the day job once the meeting is over. And urgency always overrides importance in the moment, unless you have discipline. WIGs are at a true disadvantage for this reason, and a visual scoreboard showing progress in real time helps level the playing field.

Several years ago, we were working with a group of leaders at Northrop Grumman to apply 4DX to the design and building of Coast Guard cutters. Our project began only a few months after Hurricane Katrina had significantly damaged their facility, and as we were introducing Discipline 3, they offered an example that perfectly illustrated the importance of having a compelling scoreboard.

On the previous Friday night, the local high school team had played an important game. As expected, the stands were full, and there was the usual excitement leading up to the kickoff. But as the game progressed, something was missing. No one was cheering. In fact, no one seemed to be paying attention to the game at all. The only sound from the stands was the dull hum of conversation. What was happening?

The scoreboard had blown down during the hurricane and had not yet been repaired. The fans couldn't see any numbers. One of the leaders described it this way: "No one could tell you what the score was, which down it was, or even how much time was left. There was a game going on, but it was like no one even knew."

This story caught our attention. Have you ever wanted to shout in frustration to your team: "Don't you get it? There's a game going on here, and it matters!" If you have, it's likely your team is missing the same critical element that affected the fans at the game: a clear and compelling scoreboard.

Great teams know at every moment whether or not they are winning. They *must* know; otherwise, they don't know what they have to do to win the game. A compelling scoreboard tells the team where they are and where they should be, information essential to team problem-solving and decision-making.

That's why a great team can't function without a scoreboard that *compels* action. Without it, the pent-up energy dissipates, the intensity lags, and the team goes back to business as usual.

We need to be very clear here. Visually displaying data is not new to you or your team. In fact, you may be thinking that you already have a scoreboard, or even lots of scoreboards, captured in complex spreadsheets inside your computer. And the data just keeps coming in. Most of this data is in the form of lag measures accompanied by historical trends, forward projections, and detailed financial analysis. This data is important, and it serves a purpose for you as the leader; but your spreadsheets are what we would call a coach's scoreboard.

What we're after in Discipline 3 is something quite different. In implementing Discipline 3, you and your team need a players' scoreboard, one that's designed solely to engage the players on your team to win.

If your scoreboard includes complicated data that only you—the leader—understand, it represents a leader's game. But for maximum engagement and performance, you need a players' scoreboard that makes winning feel like it's the team's game. Jim Stuart (one of the originators of 4DX) said it best: "The fundamental purpose of a players' scoreboard is to motivate the players to win."

We began this chapter with a critically important statement: People play differently when *they* are keeping score. This creates a very different feeling than when you keep score for them. When team members themselves are keeping score, they truly understand the connection between their performance and reaching their goal, and this changes the level at which they play.

When everyone on the team can see the score, the level of play rises, not only because they can see what's working and what adjustments are needed, but also because they now want to *win*.

You see here the contrast between a coach's scoreboard and a players' scoreboard.

TOTAL REVENUE							GROSS MARGIN							EBITDA						
2/12	Bud	Var	2/8	Var	2007	Var	2/12	Bud	Var	2/8	Var	2007	Var	2/12	Bud	Var	2/8	Var	2007	Var
0	0	0	0	0	0	0	0	0	0	143	(143)	0	0	0	0	0	143	(143)	0	0
(1)	53	(54)	182	(183)	1	(2)	(0)	35	(35)	0	(0)	1	(2)	(86)	(49)	(37)	(84)	(2)	(114)	28
0	0	0	0	0	0	0	0	0	0	0	0	0	0	(61)	(65)	4	(73)	12	(11)	(51)
1,008	1,080	(71)	1,150	(142)	1,146	(137)	699	754	(55)	812	(113)	892	(193)	384	384	1	439	(54)	530	(146)
		-6.6%		-12.3%		-12.0%	69.3%	69.9%	-7.3%	70.6%	-13.9%	77.9%	-21.6%	38.1%	35.5%	0.2%	38.1%	-12.4%	46.3%	-27.5%
699	843	(144)	700	(1)	963	(264)	486	594	(108)	498	(12)	730	(245)	242	297	(56)	218	24	392	(151)
		-17.1%		-0.2%		-27.4%	69.5%	70.4%	-18.2%	71.1%	-2.4%	75.8%	-33.5%	34.6%	35.3%	-18.8%	31.1%	10.8%	40.7%	-38.5%
592	682	(90)	524	68	613	(21)	422	483	(60)	361	62	459	(36)	260	276	(16)	187	73	270	(10)
		-13.1%		13.0%		-3.4%	71.3%	70.8%	-12.5%	68.9%	17.1%	74.8%	-7.9%	43.9%	40.5%	-5.7%	35.8%	38.9%	44.0%	-3.5%
879	937	(58)	840	39	828	51	607	695	(88)	582	25	539	68	354	370	(16)	292	62	235	119

A coach's scoreboard is complex and data rich, but it requires careful study to figure out if the team is winning.

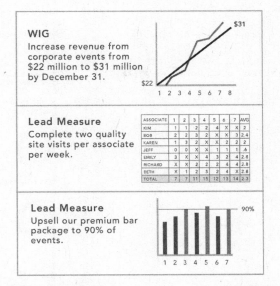

In this players' scoreboard, the goal (represented by the black line) is to increase revenue. The gray line is actual performance. At any moment, team members can see if they are winning.

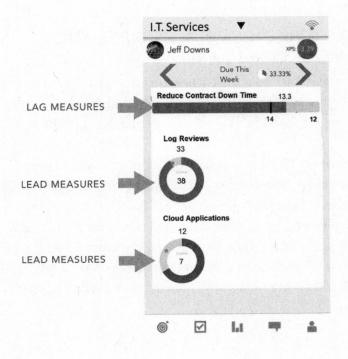

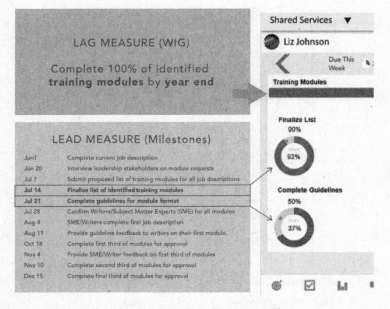

*The players' scoreboard is essential to
motivating the players to win.*

CHARACTERISTICS OF A COMPELLING PLAYERS' SCOREBOARD

We always ask four questions when determining if a scoreboard is likely to be compelling to the players, whether it's a physical scoreboard or one displayed from a technology platform like the 4DX app:

1. **Is it simple?** Think about the scoreboard in a sporting event. Usually, only a few distinct pieces of data are displayed. Now think about how many pieces of data the coach is tracking on the sideline: player performance, fouls and misconduct, goalkeeper positioning, shots on goal, and even saves. The list goes on forever. Coaches need this data to manage the game, but the scoreboard on the field shows only the data needed to play the game.

2. **Can I see it easily?** It has to be visible to the team. The scoreboard at a football game is huge and the numbers are gigantic so everyone can tell at a glance who's winning. If your scoreboard sits on your computer or hangs on the back of your office door, it's "out of sight, out of mind" for the team. Remember that you are always competing with the whirlwind, and it's a tough adversary. If you don't have a scoreboard visible, the WIG and lead measures could be forgotten in a matter of weeks, if not days, in the constant urgency of your day-to-day responsibilities.

    Visibility also drives accountability. The results become personally important to the team when the scoreboard is displayed where it can be seen by everyone. We've observed this again and again. We've seen a union shift at a giant juice-bottling plant in Michigan choose to skip their lunch break in order to increase the number of full truckloads they delivered. Why? So they can move past other shifts on the scoreboard. In another instance, we observed the night shift come to work at midnight and saw that the first thing they looked at was the scoreboard to see how their team was doing in comparison to the day shift. If your team is geographically dispersed, the scoreboard should be visible on your desktop computer or mobile phone.

3. **Does it show lead *and* lag measures?** It should show both the lead and lag measures. This really helps a scoreboard come to life. The lead measure is what the team can affect. The lag measure is the result they want. The team needs to see both, or they will quickly lose interest. When they can see both the lead and lag, they can watch the bet play out. They can see what they are doing (the lead) and what they are getting (the lag). Once the team sees that the lag measure is moving because of the efforts they have made on the leads, it has a dramatic effect on engagement because they know they are directly impacting the results.

4. **Can I tell at a glance if I'm winning?** The scoreboard has to tell you immediately if you are winning or losing. If the team can't quickly determine if they are winning or losing by looking at the scoreboard, then it's not a game, it's just data. Check your next report, graph, scorecard, or scoreboard before you dismiss this as obvious. Glance at the spreadsheets that show the weekly financial data. Can you *instantly* tell if you are winning or losing? Could other people tell? We call it the *five-second rule*. If you can't tell within five seconds whether you're winning or losing, you haven't passed this test.

This simple illustration comes from one of our clients, an events-management company responsible for booking trade shows for outdoor retailers. The WIG was to book a certain number of exhibitors by a certain date

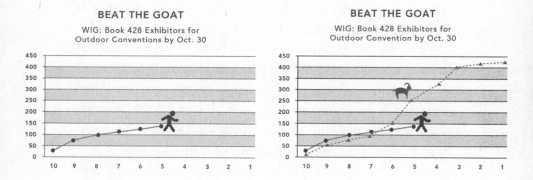

In the scoreboard on the left, you can see the status of the team's progress to date, but you have no idea if they are winning or losing. Winning or losing requires you to know two things: where you are now and where you *should* be now.

The difference in the scoreboard on the right is the addition of where the team should be, illustrated by the goat. Because so many of their customers were mountain climbers, they used a mountain goat to represent the performance needed each week to achieve their goal. Now you can easily see that they are losing, and several other important aspects of the team's performance are also immediately apparent. You know how long they have been losing (two weeks). You know that achieving the goal is getting harder, not easier. You know that the performance of the team is starting to level off instead of climbing. And you know that the team is closer to the end of the race than the beginning.

As basic as this may seem, when we ask leaders in our programs to report this sort of data on the spot, they will often say, "I think I can get most of that, but I'll need a few minutes to pull it together." Keep in mind that these are capable leaders. Their problem is not the absence of data; their problem is too much of it and little sense of which data is most important.

Imagine if not only you but every member of your team understood the team's performance this clearly. Would it change the way they engaged in the game? We can assure you that it would.

Like the first and second disciplines, Discipline 3 is not intuitive for most leaders. You don't naturally create a players' scoreboard. Your instinct will be to create a coach's scoreboard: a complex scoreboard with lots of data, analysis, and projections designed for the coach, not the players. And you're not alone. We seldom find even a single scoreboard in most organizations that meets the four criteria listed here.

In the end, it isn't actually the scoreboard that's compelling. Although teams enjoy creating their own scoreboards, what ultimately drives engagement is the game the scoreboard represents. You'll never hear a sports fan saying, "Did you see that game last night? What an amazing scoreboard!" The scoreboard was absolutely necessary, but it was the game that interested them.

One of the most demoralizing aspects of life in the whirlwind is that you don't feel you can win. If your team is operating exclusively in the whirlwind, they're giving everything they have just to sustain their day-to-day operation and survive. They're not playing *to win*; they're playing *not to lose*. And the result is a big difference in performance.

But with 4DX, not only do you create a game for your team, but you create a *winnable* game. And the secret to that game being winnable is the relationship between the lead and lag measures that plays out on the scoreboard every day.

In essence, you and your team make a bet that you can move the lead measures and that those lead measures will move the lag measure. When this starts to happen, even people who have shown little interest become engaged as the entire team starts to see that they are winning, often for the first time. Keep in mind that their engagement is not because the *organization* is winning or even that *you* as their leader are winning. It's because *they* are winning.

Some years ago, we were invited to help a low-performing plant run by a global manufacturing company to come up to the quality standards of the rest of the company. The plant was old, struggling with outdated technology, and in a remote location. For us, it required all-day flights and a long drive to the end of a forest road in Canada to reach the plant.

In twenty-five years, this plant had never hit its targeted production number. Additionally, they had massive quality issues in their products, particularly those made by the night shifts, which employed the least experienced workers. The quality score was in the low seventies, while the rest of the company was in the high eighties.

It wasn't until the scoreboards went up that things changed radically. They had been playing in the dark, and the new scoreboards "turned on the lights." Data is like light—an agent of growth. When winners are given data that shows they are losing, they figure out a way to win. With the lights on, they can see what they need to do to improve.

A shift would come in at midnight and get energized to go beyond whatever the previous shift had done. This was a hockey-playing culture: For entertainment in this remote locale, there were two hockey rinks and not much else. The workers knew they'd be playing hockey and drinking with the guys from the other shift on the weekends, and they wanted to be the shift with bragging rights about higher scores.

As 4DX leveraged the natural urge to compete, the quality score soared from 74 to 94, from worst in the fleet to best and far above the industry standard. And within a year, this plant that had never hit its production number exceeded it by 4,000 metric tons, adding at least $5 million to the bottom line.

The players' scoreboard is a powerful device for changing human behavior anywhere.

THE 4 DISCIPLINES AND TEAM ENGAGEMENT

We'd like to be able to say that we understood the connection between the implementation of 4DX and team engagement all along, but we didn't. We learned it through experience. As we began to implement 4DX with teams around the world, we saw significant increases in morale and engagement, even though the WIGs the teams were working with didn't mention morale and engagement. That outcome might not come as a surprise to you, based on how we've described 4DX so far, but at the time, it did to us.

FranklinCovey had built a worldwide reputation for helping increase the personal effectiveness of individuals and teams, and with it, their morale and engagement. 4DX was designed to occupy the other end of the continuum of FranklinCovey offerings, with an exclusive focus on business results. However, in our early implementations, the increase in engagement we observed as teams began to feel they were winning was not subtle. It was obvious. In fact, we would have to have been blind to miss it.

Our implementations usually involved several days of intensive work with leaders and teams, and these teams included their fair share of naysayers and resisters. To our surprise, we would return two months later and find that these initial resisters, along with everyone else on the team, were excited to show us what they were accomplishing.

Many believe that engagement drives results, and so do we. However, we know now, and have witnessed consistently over the years, that even small results can drive engagement. This is particularly true when the team can see the direct impact their actions have on the results. In our experience, nothing affects morale and engagement more powerfully than when people feel they are winning. In many cases, winning is a more powerful driver of engagement than money, benefits packages, working conditions, whether you have a best friend at work, or even whether you like your boss, all of which are typical measures of engagement. People will work for money and they will quit over money, but many teams are filled with people who are both well paid and miserable in their jobs.

In 1968, author Frederick Herzberg published an article in the *Harvard Business Review* aptly titled "One More Time: How Do You Motivate Employees?" In it, he emphasizes the powerful connection between results and engagement: "People are most satisfied with their jobs (and therefore most motivated) when those jobs give them the opportunity to experience achievement."

Forty-three years later in another *Harvard Business Review* article, "The Power of Small Wins," authors Teresa Amabile and Steven J. Kramer emphasize the importance of achievement to team members: "The power of progress is fundamental to human nature, but few managers understand it or know how to leverage progress to boost motivation."[10]

We have learned that scoreboards can be a powerful way to engage employees. A motivating players' scoreboard not only drives results but uses the visible power of progress to instill the mindset of *winning*.

If you still have doubts about the impact of winning on team engagement, think of a time in your own career when you were the most excited and engaged in what you were doing—a time when you couldn't wait to get out of bed in the morning, when you were consumed with what you were doing professionally. Now ask yourself this question: "At that time, did I feel like I was winning?" If you are like most people, your answer will be yes.

4DX enables you to set up a winnable game. Discipline 1 narrows your focus to a Wildly Important Goal and establishes a clear finish line. Discipline 2 creates lead measures that give your team leverage to achieve the goal. This is what makes it a game: The team is making a bet on their lead measures. But without Discipline 3, without a compelling players' scoreboard, not only would the game be lost in the whirlwind, but no one would care.

A winning team doesn't need artificial morale boosting. All the psyching up and rah-rah exercises companies do to raise morale— solving a puzzle, staging scavenger hunts, or holding a talent show— aren't nearly as effective in engaging people as the satisfaction that comes from executing with excellence a goal that matters.

Disciplines 1, 2, and 3 are powerful drivers of execution, yet they are only the beginning of the story. The first three disciplines set up the game, but your team may still not be *in* the game, as you are about to learn.

When we wrote the first edition of *The 4 Disciplines of Execution,* almost ten years ago, our focus was predominantly on physical scoreboards. Although physical scoreboards are still an essential tool used by many teams, today the most visible and easily accessible location for a scoreboard is on your tablet or phone. The 4DX app provides the ability to display and update a scoreboard for your team that is constantly available, simple to use, and compelling to display. As a result, we will use the 4DX app as a primary source for illustrations throughout this book.

CHAPTER 5

Discipline 4: Create a Cadence of Accountability

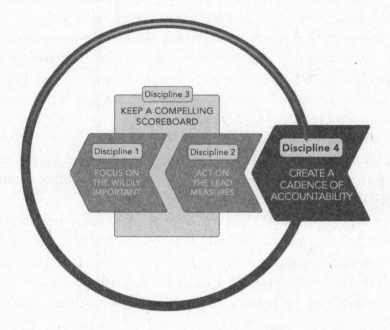

Leadership is about making others better as a result of your presence and making sure that impact lasts in your absence.

—Sheryl Sandberg

The fourth discipline is based on the principle of accountability. In this discipline, you create a *cadence* of accountability—a regular and recurring cycle of accounting for past performance, as well as committing to move the score forward.

Discipline 4 is where execution actually happens. As we've said, Disciplines 1, 2, and 3 set up the game; but until you apply Discipline 4, your team isn't *in* the game.

Many leaders define *execution* simply as the ability to set a goal and achieve it. After years of teaching these principles, we can tell you that this definition is insufficient. But as discussed above, what's difficult—and rare—is the ability to achieve a critical goal while living *in the midst of a raging whirlwind.* And it is even more difficult when achieving the goal requires changing the behaviors of a lot of people.

Great teams operate with a high level of accountability. Without it, team members go off in all directions with each doing what they think is most important. Under this approach, the whirlwind soon takes over.

Disciplines 1, 2, and 3 bring focus, leverage, and engagement, which are powerful and necessary elements for your success. But with Discipline 4, you and your team ensure that the goal is achieved, no matter what is happening around you.

In many organizations, accountability means the annual performance review, hardly an engaging experience whether you are giving or receiving it. It can also mean being called on the carpet for something you failed to accomplish.

On the other hand, in a 4DX organization, *accountability* means being truly committed, not only to the achievement of the WIG but also to your teammates. Each week, every member of the team makes personal commitments *to the entire team* that will move the score forward. Following the meeting, they then follow through in a disciplined way.

Dr. Ted James, Vice Chair at Beth Israel Deaconess Medical Center and Associate Professor of Leadership Development at the Harvard Medical School, offers this advice: "As a leader, you are ultimately responsible for your team's results. Unfortunately, when leaders fail to address performance and behavioral issues, this undermines the entire team, leading to lower quality and weak organizational culture. It sets a dangerous precedent as people start to learn that there are no real consequences for poor behavior or performance. Without accountability, engagement wanes and resentment can build in members of the team who are negatively impacted. Leaders lose their credibility, and top performers leave."

THE WIG SESSION

In Discipline 4, your team meets at least weekly in what we call a WIG Session. This meeting, which lasts no longer than twenty to thirty minutes, has a set agenda and goes quickly, establishing your weekly rhythm of accountability for driving progress toward the WIG.

Discipline 4 creates the critical difference between successful and failed execution. As one of our clients said, "How you run your WIG Session is how you execute."

The focus of the WIG Session is simple: to hold one another accountable for taking the actions that will move the lead measures, resulting in the achievement of the WIG despite the whirlwind. Easy to say, but hard to do. To ensure that this focus is achieved every week, three rules of WIG Sessions must absolutely be followed.

First, the WIG Session should be held on the same day and at the same time every week (sometimes even more often—daily, for instance—but *never* less often than weekly). This consistency is critical. Without it, your team will never establish a sustained rhythm of performance. Missing even a single week causes you to lose valuable momentum, and this loss of momentum impacts your results. This means that the WIG Session is sacred—it takes place every week, even if the leader can't attend and has to delegate the role of leading it.

It is truly amazing what you can accomplish by the simple discipline of meeting around a goal on a weekly basis over an extended period of time. There is nothing quite like it. Frankly, we're amazed that this discipline isn't practiced more frequently. We have asked a vast number of employees in various industries around the globe to respond to the statement: "I meet at least monthly with my manager to discuss my progress on goals." To our surprise, only 34 percent can respond positively to this statement, even when the review is only once each month, let alone weekly—the best practice of high-performing teams. It's no wonder that high accountability is absent in so many organizations.

What is so impactful about holding a WIG Session each week? you may ask. We have found that for most teams, the week embodies a perfect slice of "life." It is a short enough period of time to keep people focused and remain highly relevant, but long enough to allow for commitments made in these meetings to get done. In many operating environments, weeks represent a natural rhythm of organizational life. We think in weeks. We talk in weeks. Weeks have beginnings and ends. They are a staple of the human condition and make for a perfect cadence of accountability.

Second, the whirlwind is never allowed into a WIG Session. No matter how urgent an issue may seem, discussion in the WIG Session is limited solely to actions and results that move the scoreboard. If you need to discuss other things, hold a staff meeting *after* the WIG Session, but keep the WIG Session separate. This high level of focus makes the WIG Session not only fast but extremely effective at producing the results you want. It also reaffirms the importance of the WIG to every team member. It sends a clear message that, as it relates to achieving the WIG, no success in the whirlwind can compensate for a failure to keep the commitments made in last week's WIG Session. Many of our clients do exactly this: They hold a WIG Session for twenty to thirty minutes and then hold a staff meeting right after, during which they can discuss whirlwind issues.

Third, keeping your WIG Sessions to twenty to thirty minutes is a standard to strive for. When you first start holding WIG Sessions, they may take more time. But over time as you increasingly focus your attention on moving the scoreboard and nothing more, your sessions will become increasingly effective and efficient. We also recognize that, depending upon the particular function or nature of your team, they may take a bit more time. But even then, any team in any function can learn to conduct fast, efficient sessions centered on the Wildly Important Goal in place of protracted meetings covering everything under the sun. Often, to keep your WIG Sessions fast and focused, you may need to schedule other meetings to resolve issues that grow out of the WIG Session. For example, you might say, "Bill, you bring up an important problem that has to be resolved this week. Why don't we set up another meeting this Thursday to see if we can solve it?" and then continue your WIG Session.

WIG Sessions might vary in content, but the agenda is always the same. Here's the three-part agenda for a WIG Session, along with the language you should be hearing in the session:

1. **Account. Report on last week's commitments.**

   "I committed to make a personal call to three customers who gave us lower scores. I did, and here's what I learned . . ."

   "I committed to book at least three prospects for a site visit and ended up getting four!"

   "I met with our VP but wasn't able to get the approval we wanted. Here's why . . ."

2. **Review the scoreboard. Learn from successes and failures.**

   "Our lag measure is green, but we've got a challenge with one of our lead measures that just fell to yellow. Here's what happened . . ."

   "We're trending upward on our lead measures, but our lag measure isn't moving yet. We've agreed as a team to double our efforts this week to get the score moving."

   "Although we're tracking toward achieving our WIG, we implemented a great suggestion from a customer this week that improved our lead-measure score even further!"

3. **Plan. Clear the path and make new commitments.**

   "I can clear your path on that problem. I know someone who . . ."

   "I'll make sure the inventory issue impacting our lead measure is resolved by next week, no matter what I have to do."

"I'll meet with Julius on our numbers and come back
next week with at least three ideas for helping us improve."

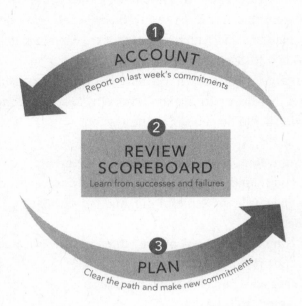

STAYING FOCUSED IN SPITE OF THE WHIRLWIND

In a WIG Session, you and every member of your team are accountable
for moving the metrics on the scoreboard. You accomplish this by committing each week (in the WIG Session) to one or two specific actions
that will directly affect your lead measures, then reporting your results
to one another in the next week's WIG Session.

To prepare for the meeting, every team member thinks about the
same question: "What are the one or two most important things I can
do this week to impact the lead measures?"

We need to be very careful here. The team members are not asking
themselves, "What is the most important thing I can do this week?"
That question is so broad that it will almost always take their focus
back to something in their whirlwind. Instead, they are asking a much
more specific question: "What can I do this week to impact the lead
measures?"

As discussed above, this focus on impacting the lead measures each week is critical because the lead measures are the team's leverage for achieving the WIG. The commitments represent the things that must happen, beyond the day-to-day, to move the lead measures. This is why so much emphasis is placed in Discipline 2 on ensuring that the lead measures are influenceable: so that the team can actually move them through their performance each week. Keeping weekly commitments drives the lead measures, and the lead measures drive achievement of the WIG.

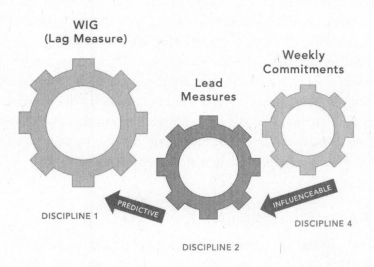

By keeping their weekly commitments, team members influence the lead measure, which in turn is predictive of success on the lag measure of the WIG.

Let's take the example of Sabria, a nurse manager whose lead measure is to reduce the time it takes to administer pain medication to patients. Sabria can see from her scoreboard that two of her teams, the seventh-floor day shift and the eighth-floor intensive care, are lagging behind the others. She knows that the seventh-floor team has a new supervisor who is still learning the procedures for pain management. She also knows that the eighth-floor team is understaffed. So Sabria's commitments to move the lead measures for this week might be to review the pain-management procedures with the seventh-floor team and to fill the open position on the eighth-floor team.

Now let's take the example of Tomás, a member of a sales team whose lead measure is to send out two new proposals each week, Tomás knows that his list of prospects is running low, so for this week, his commitment might be to acquire names and contact information for ten additional prospects, ensuring he has enough to successfully move two of them to the proposal stage.

In these two examples, both leaders and team members make weekly commitments. The nature of the commitments might change every week because the business, along with the performance of the team, is always changing; only the process is constant.

Realize that these weekly commitments are often not urgent or necessarily even new. They often are things the team should be doing naturally, but the reality is that these are the actions the whirlwind devours first. Without the steady cadence of accountability of Discipline 4, there will always be actions the team members know they should perform but never actually do with real consistency.

CREATING A CADENCE

MICARE, which produces the coal that fuels many of Mexico's power plants, is one of the largest private enterprises in Mexico. 4DX permeates everything at MICARE.

Monday-morning WIG Sessions take place in every department of this vast company. The meetings are connected by webinar to remote locations so that everyone will be on the same page at the same time. Every manager's results are visible on the screen for all to see.

Each group (production, delivery, human resources, finance, operations, and so forth) has scoreboards posted around the company and kept constantly updated. Everyone in the company—engineers, miners, maintenance workers—can recite their Team WIGs to you. When touring MICARE, we were reminded of this observation by Jack Welch, the legendary leader of GE:

Goals cannot sound noble but vague. Targets cannot be so blurry they can't be hit. Your direction has to be so vivid that if you randomly woke one of your employees in the middle of the night and asked, "Where are we going?" you could still get an answer in a half-asleep stupor.[11]

That is the level of strategic clarity and commitment evident throughout MICARE.

What has the 4DX operating system meant to the achievement of MICARE's WIGs?

Over a seven-year period:

- Lost-time accidents dropped from nearly seven hundred per year to fewer than sixty.
- Water consumed in processing coal—a major environmental concern—dropped by two-thirds.
- Annual rehabilitation of mined-out properties rose from six hectares to more than two hundred.
- Suspended particulates in the air around the mines dropped from 346 units per cubic meter to 84.
- Metric tons of coal produced per worker grew from 6,000 to 10,000 per year.

In summary, and according to MICARE's CEO, 4DX has produced dramatic hard business results for MICARE and enabled major improvements to safety and the environment as well. MICARE credits concentrated attention to the cadence of accountability as the major factor in MICARE's success. The regular WIG Session, as simple in concept as it is, keeps bringing the whole organization's focus back to what matters most.

Remember that the WIG Session should move at a fast pace. If each person simply addresses the three cadence items described earlier, it doesn't require a lot of talking. As one of our largest clients is fond of saying, "The more they talk, the less they did."

The WIG Session also gives the team the chance to process what they've learned about what does and doesn't work. If the lead measures aren't moving the lag, the team brings creative thinking to the table, suggesting new lead measures to try. If people are running into obstacles in keeping their commitments, team members can commit to clear the path for one another. What might be tough for a frontline worker to achieve might take just a stroke of the pen from the team leader. In fact, as the leader, you should often ask each team member: "What can I do this week to clear the path for you?"

It's also important to note that, if you are a leader of leaders, you will likely be in two WIG Sessions every week: one led by your boss, and one you lead with your team.

For now, let's apply Discipline 4 to the example of Younger Brothers Construction that we discussed earlier. Remember that the WIG for Younger Brothers was to reduce safety incidents from fifty-seven to twelve by December 31, and their lead measure was compliance to the six safety standards they believed would eliminate the vast majority of accidents.

Imagine you are a project manager at Younger Brothers responsible for a number of crews. In the WIG Session with your boss, you would do three things:

1. *Report on last week's commitments*: "Last week I committed to order new braces for the scaffolding so that conditions for my crews were up to code [one of the six safety standards], and I completed that."

2. *Review the scoreboard*: "My lag measure for safety incidents is currently averaging five per month, slightly above where we should be for this quarter. My lead measure for compliance to safety standards is green at 91 percent, but Crews 9, 11, and 13 are hurting the score because they aren't consistently wearing their safety glasses."

3. *Make commitments for the coming week*: "This week I will meet with the supervisors of Crews 9, 11, and 13, review their safety

records, and ensure that they have enough safety glasses for everyone."

Each commitment must meet two standards. First, the commitment must represent a specific deliverable. For example, a commitment to "focus on" or "work on" Crews 9, 11, and 13 is too vague. Because this type of commitment doesn't make you accountable for a specific result, it usually gets lost in the whirlwind. Second, the commitment must influence the lead measure. If the commitment doesn't directly target the lead measure, it won't advance the team toward achieving the WIG.

As you begin to understand the WIG Session, you'll also see more clearly the importance of the two characteristics of lead measures we discussed in Discipline 2. If the lead measures are influenceable, they can be moved by the weekly commitments. If they are predictive, then moving them will lead to the achievement of the WIG.

The WIG Session is like an ongoing experiment. Team members bring their best thinking as to how to influence the scoreboard. They commit to try new ideas, test hypotheses, and bring back the results.

For example, at the Minnesota Cystic Fibrosis Center at the University of Minnesota Medical Center, Fairview, staff doctors hold a weekly meeting to review lung function among their vulnerable patients, most of them infants and small children. Cystic fibrosis gradually reduces the victim's ability to breathe, so the WIG for this world-class treatment center is 100 percent lung function for their patients. They are not satisfied with 80 percent of normal, or even 90 percent, as a lag measure.

In these weekly meetings, the doctors review what they've observed that week about improving lung function, and they make commitments to follow up. For example, because body weight might be a lead measure in lung health, doctors carefully monitor it and give some infants supplemental feedings. They conduct experiments with mist tents and massage vests and other ways to clear lungs. Then they report back to the team on the outcomes.

Each week they learn more and share their learning.

Few people hold themselves as rigorously accountable for a WIG as the Fairview team does, and the results show the value of their cadence of accountability: They haven't lost a patient to cystic fibrosis in many years.[12]

Principal Kim Blackburn of Seven Hills Elementary in Texas has been passionately applying the 4 Disciplines of Execution in her quest to reach lofty goals. In doing so, she has spent countless hours attempting to crack the code around systems and routines that ensure a strong school implementation of 4DX. Kim will be the first to tell you that without a strong cadence of accountability for both students and adults, you will not see the results you desire. This isn't just her opinion; Kim has data to prove the power of Discipline 4.

Over time at Seven Hills, a strong cadence of accountability with refined systems has been established. Kim shared, "Not only are WIG Sessions changing the game in the classroom, but they are changing the game on our campus too! Last year, we knew we needed to create a model for our grade-level teams to meet weekly, and their sessions center around the Team WIG aligned to the campus WIG.

"Weekly commitments are things that the team should be doing naturally, but the reality is that these are the actions the whirlwind devours first. Without the steady rhythm of the WIG Session, there will always be things team members know they should do, but never do with real consistency.

"The focus of the WIG Session is simple. To hold one another accountable for taking action to move lead measures, resulting in achievement of the WIG despite the whirlwind. Having this structure in place prevents the urgent, or the whirlwind, from entering into the conversation. The structure we created helps us keep the main thing the main thing! What happens in the Team WIG Sessions is that each team member realizes the importance of their commitment to the success of the TEAM! And ultimately, the school. It becomes *personal*. They begin asking themselves, 'What can I do this week to move the lead measures?' WIG Sessions produce reliable results over and over again, but most important, what a good WIG Session does is produce a high-performing team."

ENSURING COMMITMENTS COME FROM PARTICIPANTS

While the leader of the WIG Session is responsible for ensuring the quality of commitments, the commitments *must* come from the participants. We cannot emphasize this strongly enough. If you simply tell your team what to do, they will learn little. But when they can consistently tell *you* what's needed to achieve the WIG, they will have learned a lot about execution, and so will you.

Having team members generate their commitments may seem counterintuitive, especially when you can see so clearly what should be done and when your team may even expect or want you to tell them what to do. However, you ultimately want each member of your team to take personal ownership of the commitments they make. As a leader, you may still coach people who are struggling to make high-impact commitments, but you want to ensure that in the end, they feel the ideas are theirs, not yours.

THE BLACK AND THE GRAY

Finally, the WIG Session saves your Wildly Important Goal from being engulfed by the whirlwind. Below is the calendar for a typical week. The black blocks represent your WIG Session commitments and the gray blocks represent your whirlwind. This simple visual on the next page shows what the balance of time and energy invested in execution looks like.

When we introduce Discipline 4, some leaders mistakenly picture a week that's mostly black, meaning the commitments are the predominant focus for the week. This seldom represents reality. The vast majority of your energy will still be spent managing your day-to-day priorities, as it should be. But the critical value of the 4 Disciplines is

Weekly Commitments

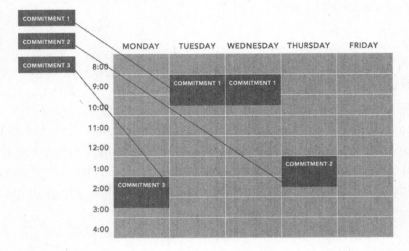

The gray blocks represent your day-to-day whirlwind; the black blocks represent your weekly commitments to move the WIG scoreboard. If you actively schedule them into your week, the whirlwind is less likely to draw your focus away from the WIG.

ensuring that the black—your investment over and above your day-to-day—stays consistently focused on your WIG.

What would happen if you pulled one of those black blocks out of your week? Would it remain empty?

Think about the last time you were relieved to learn that a meeting had been canceled, freeing an hour in your schedule. How long was it before three other meetings and five urgent requests were all competing for that one open spot? In terms of the diagram, how long would it be before the whirlwind devoured that open time, turning it gray?

When we ask this question in our sessions, every leader knows the answer: "Immediately!" The gray doesn't want the black in your week. In other words, the whirlwind will consume every moment of time and every ounce of energy it can. Parkinson's Law states: "Work expands so as to fill the time available for its completion," and nowhere is this principle of expansion and consumption of time and energy more true than with your whirlwind. Execution on your WIG is all about driving the black into the gray, no matter what it takes.

Now think of the diagram as representing the combined energy of a week from your entire team, not just from you. In this new context, the black represents the energy of every member of your team as they keep their commitments every week. This is the kind of focused energy that produces results. If you keep the cadence of accountability, week after week, your team unleashes this focused energy against the lead measures that have a direct effect on the WIG.

This weekly discipline also has a real effect on morale. Think about the last time you had an all-gray week, a week of long hours consumed by the endless crises of the whirlwind. The worst part was the sickening feeling in the pit of your stomach that despite the tremendous effort you gave all week, you didn't really accomplish anything.

If all-gray weeks become a regular experience, you feel the life draining out of you as a leader. Even worse, you will see the same feeling reflected in the engagement and the performance of your team.

WIG Sessions are the antidote to all-gray weeks. When the discipline of holding WIG Sessions is sustained—when you and your team force the black into the gray every week—not only will you make consistent progress toward your goals, but you'll also begin to feel that you, rather than the whirlwind, are in charge.

WIG SESSIONS AND ENGAGEMENT

Mark McChesney, the older brother of one of our coauthors, wanted only one thing growing up: to design cars. Mark worked very hard to achieve his dream and was eventually hired as a designer for one of the Big Three automakers in the United States. Almost all of the designers on Mark's team had the same dream—a dream they are now living by spending every day doing the one thing they wanted to do more than anything in the world: designing cars.

You would think that their level of engagement would be off the charts. However, here is the fascinating part of this story. This design department has the lowest engagement scores of any team within that giant organization. That's right, people who are doing the one thing they always wanted to do have the lowest scores. How can people who have made a career doing what they love report low engagement?

In his book *The Three Signs of a Miserable Job,* Patrick Lencioni describes brilliantly three reasons individuals disengage from work.

1. **Anonymity:** They feel their leaders don't know or care what they are doing.
2. **Irrelevance:** They don't understand how their job makes a difference.
3. **Immeasurement:** They cannot measure or assess for themselves the contribution they are making.[13]

All three of Lencioni's signs are present in the automotive-design department. First, the designer's original work is changed so much by the time it actually becomes a product that the originator is often forgotten (anonymity). Second, the product is released years after designers work on it, so they may not see their contribution in the final product (irrelevance). And third, evaluations of performance are extremely subjective (immeasurement).

Lencioni's three signs not only explain what's happening in the design department, as well as in many other jobs, but also describe life in the whirlwind perfectly—what we have called an "all-gray week." The good news is that Discipline 4, if done right, is the cure for all three.

On a team that keeps the cadence of WIG Sessions, the individual members are not anonymous. On the contrary, they are in the spotlight at least once a week. They are also not irrelevant, because they can see exactly how their commitments are moving the lead measures that drive a Wildly Important Goal. And they are definitely not suffering from immeasurement: They have a clear and public scoreboard that is updated weekly to reflect their performance.

The full impact of the WIG Session won't be felt right away. It often takes three to four weeks before a team establishes an effective rhythm in which they learn to stay focused on the WIG and avoid talking about the whirlwind. But soon the meeting feels more productive; and after a few more weeks, something important happens. The lead measures actually move the lag measure and the team starts to feel that they are *winning*.

A DIFFERENT KIND OF ACCOUNTABILITY

The 4DX app is an essential tool supporting the leading of WIG Sessions, having captured millions of commitments from teams all over the world, and more important, *whether those commitments were kept*. Worldwide, more than 75 percent of those commitments ever made have been kept, despite each team battling their whirlwinds. This actual data shows that WIG Sessions create real accountability and drive follow-through.

However, it's the particular *kind* of accountability created in a WIG Session that we want you to understand deeply.

Often the word *accountability* has a strong negative connotation. If your boss says, "Come see me in an hour; we need to have an accountability session," you can be fairly certain it's not a good thing.

However, the accountability created in a WIG Session is very different. It's not organizational, it's *personal*. Instead of accountability to a broad outcome you can't influence, it's accountability to a weekly commitment that you yourself made and is within your power to keep. And one by one, you report your results not only to your leader, but also to one another. The question you ultimately answer in a WIG Session is: "Did we do what we committed *to one another* we would do?"

When the answer is yes, when members of a team see their peers consistently following through on the commitments they make, they grow in respect for one another. They learn that the people they work with can be trusted to follow through. When this happens, performance improves dramatically.

Take the experience of Nomaco, a leading company in engineered polymer foam extrusions. In short, they make things out of colored foam—from high-tech insulation to swimming-pool toys.

As one of three Nomaco manufacturing locations, Tarboro in North

Carolina was considered a *good* plant. They were beating budget on all fronts—costs, profitability, and safety—but they did not yet feel that they were a *great* plant, because although they were improving, they were not producing breakthrough performance.

The plant's organizational structure was traditional, and despite an open and friendly environment, people still depended on the plant manager to supervise, monitor, and make the decisions. Essentially, it was up to the manager to ensure everyone in the plant was doing what they were supposed to be doing. This was an almost impossible responsibility for one person, and one that limited that person's ability to rise to the next level of performance.

4DX brought the breakthrough they were looking for. In the eighteen months after adopting 4DX, the plant in Tarboro:

- Cut more than $1 million in costs off the production line.
- Came in more than 30 percent below budget for the fiscal year.
- Experienced no lost-time accidents and only one recordable accident.
- Beat projected budget for the following fiscal year in the first quarter.

Of 4DX, the plant manager concluded, "It is simply a strong tool to ensure success in any type of initiative an organization chooses to bring on board. . . . 4DX will get you the results you are desiring to achieve."

The key to this shift was in the WIG Sessions and the accountability they helped to drive.

At Tarboro, every team held WIG Sessions weekly. Employees reported on how they were moving the needle, changing the score, and achieving the WIG. Each week, they came up with new ideas to keep the scoreboard green. The WIG Sessions kept them focused on achieving the Wildly Important Goals, but more than that, the sessions enabled them to think together, make decisions together, help one another, and celebrate their wins.

As a result, the Tarboro plant created a culture of highly engaged employees who held themselves, *and one another,* accountable for results.

Julian Young, president of Nomaco during the 4DX implementation, summarized the impact of WIG Sessions in this way: "The WIG Sessions have a lot more energy than your traditional, old-fashioned manufacturing meetings. They have improved productivity substantially at each of our locations and have made accountability incredibly simple."

ENSURING YOUR TEAM IS IN THE GAME

Over the years, we've observed countless WIG Sessions like those at the Tarboro plant, and this experience has made one thing clear: The accountability to their peers created in the WIG Session is an even greater motivator of performance than the accountability to their boss. In the end, people will work hard to avoid disappointing their boss, but they will do almost anything to avoid disappointing their teammates.

However, to reach this level, you still need to understand one additional point. We've said that the first three disciplines set up the game, but until you apply Discipline 4, your team isn't *in* the game. But now we want to say it even more clearly: The level of importance you place on the WIG Session will directly determine the results your team produces. Based on your consistency, your focus, and your modeling of making commitments and following through, you will establish the WIG Session as either a high-stakes game or a low-stakes game in the minds of your team members.

Think of this point applied to a game played in the preseason versus the playoffs. In preseason, you'd like to win—but lose in the playoffs, your team goes home. Which type of game drives the highest level of play? Candidly, if the game doesn't really matter, why should your team care? This is why real accountability inspires the team to engage at the highest level of play, and that level is established most directly in the WIG Session.

CREATING AN INNOVATIVE CULTURE

Some people don't like the fact that WIG Sessions are so structured. Actually, when done right, WIG Sessions are also highly creative. Structure and creativity together produce engagement, as eminent psychiatrist Dr. Edward Hallowell has discovered. "The most motivating situations," he says, are those that are "highly structured *and* full of novelty and stimulation."[14]

The cadence of accountability can *release* the creativity of the team.

When you think of a team that has a culture of discipline and execution, you don't expect to hear that they are also creative and innovative. However, we've regularly seen these characteristics in teams that apply 4DX well.

Because the WIG Session encourages experimentation with fresh ideas, it engages everyone in problem solving and promotes shared learning. It's a forum for innovative insights on how to move the lead measures, and because so much is at stake, it brings out the best thinking from every team member.

Towne Park is a great example. The largest provider of valet parking services for high-end hotels and hospitals, Towne Park has always been extremely well-run. When Gaylord Entertainment (one of Towne Park's largest customers) had great success as an early adopter of 4DX, the leaders at Towne Park became interested as well.

Towne Park was already measuring virtually every aspect of its business: Did attendants open the door for you and your guests when you arrived? Did they use the proper hotel greeting? Did they offer you a bottle of water? Their execs could tell you, as they were literally measuring everything they thought mattered to their *customers*.

Still, they decided to apply 4DX to the Wildly Important Goal of the company—increasing customer satisfaction—to see if they could improve it even more. While developing lead measures in Discipline 2, they realized that one thing they weren't measuring might be their point of highest leverage in pleasing the customer: how long it takes customers to get their car back when they are ready to leave.

So they chose "reduced retrieval time" as the most predictive lead measure for further improving customer satisfaction. The faster a car was delivered to the customer, the happier the customer was. Although Towne Park had always known retrieval time was an important aspect of the business, they had never measured it because it isn't an easy measure to get, even for a company that believes in measurement. They knew that collecting retrieval-time data would require them to clock when the customer called for the car and also when the valet arrived with the car. The elapsed time between the two points, the *retrieval time,* would then need to be consistently captured for all teams in all locations.

You can imagine how difficult it would be to gather this data in the whirlwind of incoming and outgoing cars; so difficult, that some leaders argued that it couldn't be done. However, because they were committed to their WIG of unparalleled customer satisfaction, and because they believed retrieval time was the most predictive and influenceable measure for achieving it, they committed to tracking it. As is true of all great teams, once the decision was made, they found a way.

Initially, they wondered if retrieval time was influenceable because of the external factors that impact it, such as the location of the parking area and the distance to the car. Despite these worries, they reduced retrieval time dramatically.

How? The teams figured it out because they were highly engaged in the game. Once the lead measure went up on the scoreboard, the valets began finding new ways to win. For example, they started advising arriving guests to call before checking out so their car would be waiting for them. Whenever the guest called in advance, the valet knew the retrieval time would be zero.

The valets also began to ask what day the guest planned on checking out. If it was later in the week, they would park the car in the back of the lot. As the day of departure drew closer, they would move the car forward so the retrieval time would be reduced.

These and a host of other innovations not only reduced the lead measure of retrieval time, but immediately raised the lag measure of customer satisfaction. Towne Park was winning, but without the team's engagement in the game, these ideas might never have surfaced, let alone been implemented.

However, a Towne Park team in Miami, Florida, faced an obstacle that seemed insurmountable: A four-foot-high concrete wall ran down the middle of the parking garage, forcing the valets to park multiple cars back to back. This in turn often required the valets to move more than one car when retrieving the vehicle they needed.

After several months of trying to compensate for the wall, a *literal* breakthrough came during their WIG Session. James McNeil, one of the assistant account managers, committed to his team that the wall was coming out. He obtained clearance from the hotel's engineer, who confirmed that the wall was not load-bearing. Then McNeil borrowed a concrete saw and recruited several other team members to help. Starting early the following Saturday morning, they cut and hauled out several tons of concrete; by the end of the day, the wall was gone.

If you're a leader, you should be fascinated by this story. If a Towne Park executive had ordered the team to do something as far outside their normal responsibilities as removing a concrete wall, what do you think the team's reaction would have been? At best, resistance, and at worst, mutiny, even from a good team. In the words of one of the Towne Park executives when discussing this story, "If this had been our idea, they wouldn't have done it at gunpoint."

But because the lead measure had become a high-stakes game—one the players didn't want to lose—the effect was the opposite. Taking out the wall was their idea; and their desire to win was so strong, you couldn't have kept them from doing it. Necessity really is the mother of invention. Once they made retrieval time a high-stakes game, the creativity and invention followed.

What's critical to understand is that this level of engagement seldom if ever comes from a command-and-control approach—that is, one that relies exclusively on the formal authority of the leader. Authority alone at best yields only compliance from a team.

By contrast, 4DX produces results not from the exercise of authority, but from the fundamental desire of each individual team member to feel significant, to do work that matters and, ultimately, to win. That kind of engagement yields true commitment, the kind of commitment that led a Towne Park team to tear down a wall. And it's only that kind of commitment that produces extraordinary results.

In Part 3, we'll give you deep insights on how to achieve commitment through the cadence of accountability.

THE POWER OF 4DX

Now that we've examined each of the 4 Disciplines of Execution, we hope you sense their power to transform your business results and your culture. When we introduce leaders to 4DX, they often believe they are already doing most of what we teach. After all, goals, measures, scoreboards, and meetings are familiar topics. But once 4DX is implemented, these same leaders report in their teams a dramatic Paradigm Shift that produces breakthrough results, often for the first time.

If you contrast 4DX with the familiar practices of annual planning, you can see how different this paradigm is from the typical mindset about goals.

The annual goal-setting process usually begins with the creation of a master plan for the year, focused on a large number of objectives. Then each objective is broken down into the many projects, milestones, tasks, and subtasks that must be accomplished over the coming months for the plan to succeed. The deeper the planning process goes, the more complex the plan becomes.

Despite this growing complexity, the leaders may feel symptoms of what we call the "planning high." It's that hopeful feeling they get as they say, "This could really work!"

Finally, they create a set of colorful PowerPoint slides to explain the plan and then deliver a convincing formal presentation. Sound familiar? If so, there's only one step left after the plan is presented: watching it slowly fall into oblivion as the changing needs of the business, none of which were accounted for, make the plan less and less relevant.

Now, in contrast, think back to the experience of Younger Brothers Construction and their WIG to reduce accidents. No matter how detailed or strategically brilliant their annual plan might have been, it could never have foreseen that in Week 32, a leader would need to meet with Crews 9, 11, and 13 to focus on safety glasses. In other words, the very information needed to drive the highest level of results that week would not be in the plan, and it never is.

However, in Discipline 4, the team plans weekly against their lead measures, thus creating a just-in-time plan based on commitments they could not have imagined at the beginning of the month, let alone the beginning of the year. The constant weekly energy applied against the lead measures creates a unique form of accountability that connects the team directly to the goal, again and again.

If Younger Brothers had attacked their WIG without the lead measure of safety compliance, they still would have made weekly commitments, but against a less specific target. Can you imagine each team member making a commitment to reduce accidents this week? It would seem so broad as to be overwhelming to them, like trying to boil the ocean.

Even worse, imagine the perspective of the leaders. Can you hear them saying in frustration, "These are adults who've been working construction for years. If they don't care about their safety, what am I supposed to do about it?"

Once people give up on a goal that looks unachievable—no matter how strategic it might be—there is only one place to go: back to the whirlwind. After all, it's what they know and it feels safe. When this happens, your team is now officially playing *not to lose* instead of playing to win. There's a big difference.

Think of 4DX like the operating system on your laptop. You need a powerful operating system to execute whatever programs you choose to install. If the operating system isn't equal to the task, it doesn't matter how beautifully designed the program, it won't work consistently.

Likewise, without an operating system for executing your goals, no matter how beautifully designed your strategy, it won't work consistently. Even if you achieve results, you won't be able to sustain them, or surpass them, year after year. 4DX ensures the precise and consistent execution of any goal you install in your team and creates a foundation for greater success in the future.

4DX works so powerfully because it's based on timeless principles. Furthermore, it's proven to work with virtually any organization in any environment. We didn't invent the principles of 4DX; we simply uncovered and codified them. Others have used the same principles to effectively change human behavior in the service of a goal.

THE 4DX OPERATING SYSTEM IN YOUR POCKET

Today every leader and team member can see the entire 4DX operating system at any moment through the 4DX app. Not only does this powerful technology display progress on the WIG, performance of the lead measures, and the accountability demonstrated following through on commitments, but it allows these metrics to be updated in real time.

HOW TO READ THE REMAINING SECTIONS OF THIS BOOK

As you learned in Part 1, 4DX is an operating system for achieving the goals you must achieve. Keep in mind that 4DX is not a set of suggestions or philosophical ideas that should be merely considered. Instead, 4DX is a set of *disciplines* that will require your finest efforts, but whose payoff will be a team that performs consistently and with excellence. That's why this book contains detailed insights on not only *what to do* but also *how to do it*.

To ensure that your reading of this book is as clear and effective as possible, we'd like to offer some guidance on the remaining sections.

Part 2 is written for leaders of leaders. It explicitly addresses the opportunities and challenges of those who guide leaders of frontline teams as they implement 4DX. If this is your role, Part 2 is critical, because it details the practices and the mindsets necessary for success. We highly recommend that you read (and absorb) Part 2 next. Later, if you'd like to know more, we believe you will find Part 3 to be valuable, because it will enable you to understand the exact process that your leaders of frontline teams will be using.

Part 3 is written for leaders of frontline teams. In this section, you'll find detailed insights into the journey to implement 4DX on the front line. If you are the leader of a frontline team, you'll appreciate its value once you begin. Later, if you'd like to know more, we believe you will find Part 2 to be valuable, because it will enable you to understand the process that your leaders of leaders will be using.

Applying 4DX as a Leader of Leaders

CHAPTER 6

Choosing Where to Focus

Early in our development of 4DX, we interviewed Tim Tassopoulos, who is now President and COO of Chick-fil-A (one of the highest-rated restaurant organizations in the United States). In that interview, Tim offered us an insight that has remained in our minds over the years. He said, "The first thing I want to know when I am talking to a leader is, where has that leader chosen to spend *disproportionate energy*?" Tim knows that if leaders are dividing the energy of their organizations equally between their objectives and priorities, they are probably not moving forward.

Over the years, we have become completely clear that the purpose of 4DX is to *direct focused energy toward a critical breakthrough*. In this chapter, we will dive deeper into the most challenging question for the leader of leaders in 4DX: What should we choose as our Primary WIG for the organization? Or as Tim might say, "Where are we going to spend disproportionate energy?"

As you begin this process, keep in mind the Primary WIG is not an objective you could achieve simply through stroke-of-the-pen moves. It's also not an objective that can be achieved through the existing (life support) activities of the whirlwind.

Your Primary WIG represents a breakthrough result that will require human engagement and a significant change in behavior.

Also keep in mind that the energy required to achieve your Primary WIG is ultimately coming from the frontline teams of the organization. As we said in Chapter 2, it can be helpful to look at the energy of those frontline teams as a form of currency. When you choose a Primary WIG, you are determining how you will spend that currency.

In our consulting work with leaders around the world, we've learned that determining your Primary WIG is not just challenging for you, as a leader of leaders, but is also a task you will likely not complete alone. In our experience, leaders rarely make this choice without careful guidance from a skilled consultant, without rigorous debate and collaboration by an entire leadership team, and with the most senior leader often in a facilitating role and, if needed, making the final decisions.

THE STRATEGY MAP

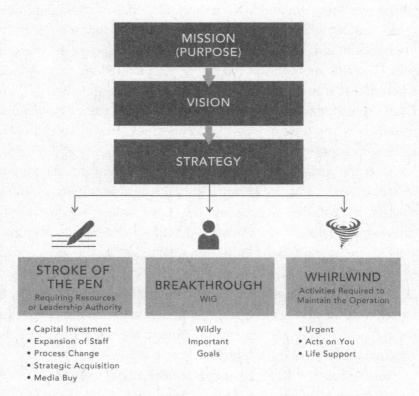

A helpful way we start this conversation with a leadership team is to begin by populating the left and right sections of the Strategy Map with the stroke-of-the-pen aspects of your strategy (or current plan), as well as the key metrics of your whirlwind. This exercise should be relatively straightforward, since your most critical operating metrics are likely well known and any significant stroke-of-the-pen decisions have at least been brought forward for discussion.

As soon as the leadership team can see the stroke-of-the-pen and the whirlwind sections populated, they will have a clearer perspective for identifying candidate Primary WIGs (breakthrough results) that can be placed in the middle section of the diagram. Now your leadership team can focus on where their disproportionate energy should be applied to achieve a breakthrough result.

With this new clarity, elements of your strategy that were initially placed in the stroke-of-the-pen section (left side) or whirlwind section (right side) will often end up repositioned in the center as a candidate for the Primary WIG. The leadership team should also remember that whatever Primary WIG is chosen today, it will one day return to the whirlwind as a normal element of your routine operation, because the team will have formed new habits of performance.

IDENTIFYING YOUR BREAKTHROUGH RESULT

To complete the middle section of the Strategy Map (breakthrough result), you should begin by brainstorming a list of candidate Primary WIGs.

The first question to ask in your brainstorming is "If every other area of our operation remained at its current level of performance, in which *one area* would we most want to achieve significant results?" This question naturally focuses the mind on the result that might represent a breakthrough by holding every other area constant. Our experience with clients has shown that if you can choose only one, that one is most likely to be the area where a breakthrough is needed most. Although this question doesn't produce your final choice (other analytical questions are below), it does create a list of good candidates.

Once you have a list of candidate WIGs, we next discuss how each candidate would be mapped on to the graph below. This exercise is very insightful because it forces your team to assess each candidate

WIG on the two axes of "Impact of Failure" and "At Risk of Failure (Without Significant Change)."

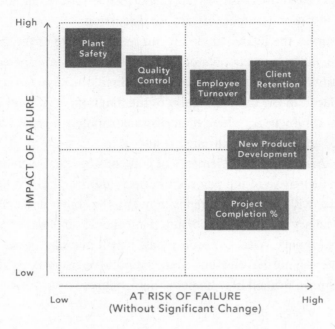

IMPACT OF FAILURE

How mission-critical is the candidate WIG?

While this question might seem straightforward, it can actually require deep thought. Instead of simply focusing on a single short-term objective, evaluating it leads your team to ask the larger questions and to think about the longer-term impact before making a final decision. For example:

- Is this objective so vital to our overall strategy that without it, the strategy may not succeed?
- Is this objective marginally impactful in the near term, but absolutely essential for the future?
- Does this objective move us forward only a little this year, but strengthen the loyalty of our customers or secure our market share from competitors in the event of a downturn?

So far, we have been talking about the WIG as a breakthrough result *for the success of the strategy*. But what if there is no real strategy? Or what if the organization has become financially successful, but is disconnected from its mission and vision? Sometimes a WIG is chosen by a group of leaders for the purpose of getting the organization back on mission, or even for amplifying that mission—in the right circumstances. The greatest failure is failing the mission.

We worked with the new president of a large thrift-store chain just as he was asking himself these questions. His predecessor had put the company on a firm financial and operational footing, updating marketing and advertising, the look and feel of the stores, and the company's accounting procedures. When we got into the WIG discussion, some of his reports thought this emphasis needed to continue. Others wanted more emphasis on hiring more workers with disabilities. Still others argued that their top WIG should be growth. The range of choices was baffling.

To help the team find common ground, the new leader asked everyone to ponder the mission of the organization: "To promote self-reliance among workers with disabilities." Since the company was at this point in a solid financial and operational position, could it be that the area where they now wanted the greatest results might be more directly related to their mission?

Gradually, a WIG began to emerge from this experience, one focused on helping workers with disabilities find jobs outside the organization that could sustain them. While the organization couldn't hire every person with disabilities in their region, it had the operational capacity to train people with disabilities in the retail business and help find better jobs for them so that they could escape from dependency. The new WIG of increasing the number of workers with disabilities placed in sustainable jobs transformed the organization. It also helped the workers become self-reliant and find a new sense of self-worth, while sustaining the day-to-day financial and operational results that made the chain's mission possible. A clear definition of *mission-critical*.

AT RISK OF FAILURE (WITHOUT SIGNIFICANT CHANGE)

Next, we ask a leadership team to consider how "at risk of failure (without significant change)" the candidate WIG may be. In other words, what is the likelihood that without significantly improved engagement and focus, we will fail at this objective?

This second axis for each candidate WIG is easy to overlook, often because leadership teams are reluctant to discuss the possibility of failure of any sort. It's much easier to keep the discussion focused on the comfortable subject of *importance*, rather than on the uncomfortable subject of *risk*. But the decision to define and undertake a WIG is a decision to spend energy not dedicated to the whirlwind—a limited and extremely valuable currency. Waste that currency, and you will likely have lost time and energy that can never be recovered.

Remember, also, that "at risk of failure (without significant change)" doesn't always mean at risk of missing a target, like a projected sales number. It can also mean failing to exploit an opportunity, such as getting a new product to market ahead of your direct competitors or capturing an unexpected rising trend in the buying habits of your customers.

Spending time evaluating "at risk of failure (without significant change)" also helps our clients understand why anything they can achieve satisfactorily from a stroke-of-the-pen decision or handle through the normal (whirlwind) practices of their operation should not become a WIG.

We are not suggesting that your Primary WIG should always be chosen from the candidates that are "high and right" on these two axes. We know that your ultimate choice will come from the careful evaluation of many factors, overlaid by the needs and resources of the business. But we have often found that the exercise of mapping your candidate WIGs on these axes provides valuable insight that can lead to a better final decision.

STRUCTURING WIGS FOR MAXIMUM RESULTS

In Chapter 2, we showed a high-level view of the three ways organizations can structure WIGs to create the focus and alignment needed to achieve the Primary WIG. In the sections that follow, we want to go deeper to illustrate not only the WIG structure, but also the rationale used by the leadership team for choosing it.

Approach A: A Single Primary WIG

When we worked with Covenant Transport, a U.S.-based transportation company, the leadership team chose a single WIG for the entire organization: Reduce driver turnover from 106 to 86 percent per year by December 31.

One of the key reasons this WIG was chosen over other objectives such as "on-time delivery," "total number of shipments," or "improved traffic safety" was that reducing driver turnover would have the ripple effect of impacting many of their other key metrics, effectively multiplying their results. A second consideration was that every team at Covenant could contribute to this WIG in a meaningful way. They *surpassed* their goal by reaching 82 percent turnover (the lowest in company history). They also produced the best financial results they had seen in twelve years, as driver turnover also drove their other key metrics.

Approach B: More Than One Primary WIG

One of our large pharmaceutical clients presented us with twelve strategic imperatives. Predictably, their leadership felt pulled in many directions. After a great deal of discussion, the senior leadership team chose a structure of two Primary WIGs that allowed them to focus on two very different segments of the company.

Their overarching strategic need was to increase their share of market. To do this, they needed the different segments of the company working simultaneously on different outcomes—hence the need for two Primary WIGs. Note here that each segment of the company still had only one focus: the Primary WIG assigned to them. As a result, from the perspective of the teams, it was as though they had only one Primary WIG.

The first Primary WIG was a sweeping process-improvement project to decrease the time required to identify a promising compound, then develop, test, approve, and begin to offer a new drug. They named this Primary WIG "molecule to market." We sometimes label this type of Primary WIG a "Transform WIG" because it requires the organization to do something completely new.

The second Primary WIG was to "increase access to their drugs," which had two Key Battles of its own. The first battle was a massive initiative to educate their prescribers (physicians prescribing the drug) on when and how to use the drug effectively and safely. The second was to streamline the payer side of access to their drugs. This involved working extensively with the people and systems needed to process payments through insurance and health systems around the world.

We often label this type of Primary WIG a "Perform WIG," since the effort is directed toward performing better on existing metrics.

The Transform and Perform WIGs and other variations of this structure are common, particularly in larger-scale strategies where results are achievable only through a significant sustained investment. The diagram below reflects a high-level view of this structure.

Approach C: Multiple Team WIGs With No Primary WIG

TELUS International delivers integrated customer experience and digital-services solutions to some of the world's most disruptive brands. Their overall approach included *four specific strategies* essential to their success:

- Establish leadership in growth industries.
- Deliver sales excellence.
- Prepare organization for growth.
- Drive operational excellence.

Their implementation of 4DX was nontraditional in that it did not include a single Primary WIG. Instead, each team was allowed to create their own Team WIG, so long as it aligned to one of the four strategies. In essence, the four strategies fulfilled the role of the Primary WIG.

During our session their CEO said: "I want these four strategic objectives to guide and direct the teams at the front line as they choose their Team WIG. It's their choice to make, so long as it aligns to one of our four strategies."

So we guided each team toward an essential responsibility: they needed to choose a Team WIG that would not only align to one of the four strategies, but also represent their *greatest possible contribution* to the company's success. With more than four hundred teams involved, driving this selection from the bottom up gave them two distinct advantages:

- It ensured that the choice of a Team WIG was made close to the front line.
- It generated a strong sense of ownership by letting the teams make the choice.

One of our favorite examples is found in the customer-service support team who chose to focus on the strategy of "deliver sales excellence." They set a Team WIG to increase the volume and quality of their outbound calls, which ultimately enabled the company to win a new major account. Another team chose to focus on "drive operational excellence," and created a Team WIG to decrease after-call work (additional work needed after a call) by 50 percent.

These two examples illustrate the precision of the Team WIGs—a rigor enabled by allowing the teams to choose—as well as the engagement required to drive these new behaviors into permanent habits of performance.

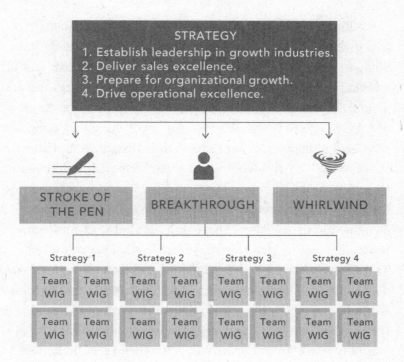

FOUR TRAPS TO AVOID WHEN CREATING WIGS

We want to conclude this chapter by outlining four traps to avoid in the creation of your WIGs. Our experience has taught us that knowing what *not to do* can be the most valuable insight, especially when each "trap" represents a key (and hard-won) lesson from more than two decades in this process.

1. **Creating too many Primary WIGs.** The temptation to create too many WIGs is likely the most seductive of them all. It's also the most destructive. When a leader first understands the potential power of 4DX, they are tempted to apply these powerful practices to *every metric*. The most upsetting calls we receive are the ones in which an excited leader will report with great pride, "We've decided to make *everything* a WIG."

Falling into this trap may seem like an obvious violation of the principle of focus, but that has never stopped leaders from doing it. Remember, the law of diminishing returns is as real in human performance as it is in science. It is also unforgiving and painful. Create enough WIGs, and you will undermine the power of 4DX. In all the years we have been involved in this work, we can't ever remember a client saying in hindsight, "We wish we'd had more WIGs." But we regularly hear, "We wish we'd had more focus."

2. **Choosing a Primary WIG that is too broad**. This is a less obvious trap than the one above, but it's almost as common. We realize that by choosing the term "wildly important," we unknowingly played a part in creating this trap (though it wasn't our intention), influencing leaders to create WIGs that encompass virtually everything the organization does. Part of the challenge is that when leaders hear the words "wildly important," they naturally think "most important." And when they think most important, they think *big*. This leads them to create Primary WIGs like "total profit," "total sales," or "overall market share." As was mentioned in Chapter 2, these "super objectives" do not make good WIGs, mostly because they encompass all the work being done, including all stroke-of-the-pen initiatives and all day-to-day whirlwind activities. While this may feel like focus, it really isn't—a painful reality that will become apparent as soon as you begin trying to identify lead measures in Discipline 2.

One final challenge with Primary WIGs that are too broad is that they often are affected by outside forces that have little if anything to do with your performance. For example, if an organization has chosen "overall market share" as the Primary WIG, they must meet two separate objectives to achieve the goal. First, they must improve their own market share by winning business from their competitors. And second, they must win a larger share than their competitors are winning in the same time frame. In this situation, the organization could achieve their highest-ever growth and still lose to a competitor who grew just a little more. Add in advertising, market trends, pricing, economic volatility, and technological innovation, and you have a Primary WIG that's about much more than *actual performance.* It's also very difficult to hit. We sometimes describe this as "trying to hit a bullet with a bullet." Not impossible, but incredibly unlikely.

3. **Creating a Primary WIG that is aspirational, but not measurable.** Sometimes our clients have a tendency to create a Primary WIG that's so aspirational it actually *can't* be measured. This is an easy trap to fall into because the WIG *sounds* important, even noble. The WIG is inspiring when you say it, but not when you try to achieve it. Bestselling author Tim Ferriss once said, "Life punishes the vague wish, but rewards the specific ask." He couldn't have described this trap more perfectly.

    WIGs such as "Become the preferred provider in our market," "Lead the industry in innovation," and "Earn world-class customer loyalty" are actual examples of falling into this trap. Even when leaders are aware that the Primary WIG doesn't meet the *From X to Y by When* requirement, it's still hard to dissuade them. There are several reasons for this.

    First, leaders might choose to leave the Primary WIG vague because they want *effort toward the outcome,* even if it can't be measured. We run into this a lot, and leaders are the only ones who think this way. Teams never do. The rationale is that since there is no single metric for measuring success, we will just be glad that the WIG has everyone moving in the same direction. Be forewarned: This is a path to failure.

    Clear, measurable targets are the language of execution. Set a vague Primary WIG, and you will quickly learn how impossible it is to execute toward a concept, even when it's a concept you love. Remember, concepts stir the imagination, but targets drive performance.

    Think about the moon shot we discussed in Chapter 2. There were dozens of objectives behind the vague goal of "Lead the world in space exploration," but when President Kennedy set the target of "Put a man on the moon by the end of the decade . . ."

he threw the "Game on!" switch in the mind of every engineer at NASA. It's a beautiful example of 4DX thinking. The target he chose didn't encompass everything NASA was trying to do in the space program, and *it didn't have to*. It was the one breakthrough result that made all the difference—what we call a Primary WIG.

So instead of leaving the Primary WIG vague because it can't be captured in a single metric, we coach our clients to narrow their focus to find the measurable target that, when achieved, will make all the difference in the strategy you are driving.

A second reason they will choose a Primary WIG that is too broad is because they want everyone to feel they are part of the Primary WIG. There's value in this way of thinking and inclusiveness is certainly important, but not if it comes at the price of *clarity*.

If we allow our clients to create a Primary WIG that is too broad simply so they can make everyone feel included, they will unknowingly undermine the real impact of Discipline 1: *focus*. After all, many teams will not be able to directly contribute to the Primary WIG, regardless of what you choose. But this doesn't mean they aren't included. The teams that do not contribute directly can still contribute indirectly by supporting other teams and even by managing the day-to-day whirlwind. They just won't need 4DX to do this. Remember, *all teams are needed to support the strategy, but specific teams (and 4DX) are needed to achieve the Primary WIG.*

4. **Creating WIGs that are not aligned to the mission and vision of the organization.** If you're like most organizations, you have a defined mission (or purpose statement) that clarifies *why* you exist. Once the mission is defined, many leaders then articulate *what* success will look like at some point, usually five or more years into the future. This is your vision. Both your mission and your vision are *aspirational,* meaning they are statements about or ideas of what you want the organization to become. You then naturally create strategy to map out *how* that vision will become a reality.

As our clients dive into the more specific elements of executing the strategy, it's easy for them to forget that their goals exist primarily to fulfill the organization's mission and to realize your shared vision. Forget this, and you will change an organization in the most fundamental way. Your organization can easily become one that achieves its goals, but in the process, loses its soul.

This is why our definitive diagram for illustrating 4DX, the *Strategy Map*, always places the Primary WIG (and all of 4DX) as subordinate to the mission and vision of the organization.

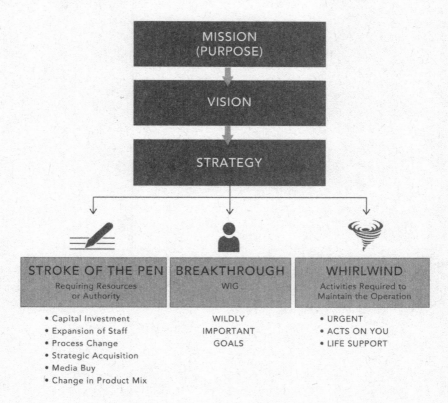

CHAPTER 7

Translating Organizational Focus Into Executable Targets

For the leader of leaders, defining the organization's Primary WIG is the first step in creating focus. However, it's only when you have translated the Primary WIG into Team WIGs at the front line that you have focused the organization. Achieving that level of translation is neither easy nor common. It can, however, create an awesome force for executing a breakthrough.

Execution does not like complexity. In fact, the two best friends of execution are *simplicity* and *transparency*. Translating the Primary WIG into precise targets for each team creates simplicity and transparency beyond anything we have seen.

In Chapter 2, we introduced four rules we enforce for a leader of leaders applying Discipline 1:

Rule 1. No individual focuses on more than one WIG at a time.
Rule 2. The battles you choose must win the war.
Rule 3. Leaders of leaders can veto, but not dictate.
Rule 4. All WIGs must have a finish line in the form of *From X to Y by When.*

While these rules may seem straightforward, even simple, following them requires tremendous commitment and discipline. Creating focus is never simple; it seems simple only once it's been accomplished.

In this chapter, we will show you examples of the work we've done with a number of clients to give you an idea of applying these four rules: first, a large hotel where the teams within the hotel perform *different* functions; second, a large retailer where the store teams perform *the same* function; and finally, a small accounting firm made up of just a few teams who perform different functions (common in small organizations).

THE OPRYLAND HOTEL

When we first met the leaders of the Opryland Hotel in Nashville, Tennessee, the largest convention hotel in the United States outside Las Vegas, they had dozens of urgent priorities, including:

- Introducing new marketing and advertising programs.
- Planning for a 400,000-square-foot expansion of their 2,000-room property.
- Launching several initiatives designed to improve their occupancy rate.
- Controlling expenses to improve their bottom line.
- Engaging in multiple new programs to improve the satisfaction of their guests.
- Revamping their convention services.
- Identifying ways to help their guests more easily navigate the 56-acre property.

As we began the 4DX implementation process with their leadership team, their crucial first step was focusing the entire hotel on the wildly important. This is never automatic, particularly in larger organizations. It takes work, beginning with answering the question "If every other area of our operation remained at its current level of performance, which one area would we want to improve the most?"

As members of the leadership team expressed their ideas about the one area they wanted to see improve the most, guest satisfaction rose quickly to the top. It was both mission-critical and at risk of failure at the highest level. The experience of the guest has an impact on every other result in a hotel, from revenue to market share to profitability.

In addition, corporate leaders also valued that it was a Primary WIG toward which almost every employee could make a contribution.

As their focus became clearer, Arthur Keith, then General Manager, recommended that they agree on "improving guest satisfaction" as the Primary WIG for the hotel. His role at this point in the process was important and timely. During the discussion, leaders should be open to new ideas and should create an open forum in which they listen and explore alternatives, but they may also need to step in *at the right moment* to bring those discussions to a decision. The leader must be ready to play both roles—facilitating the discussion, but also ready to advocate a position.

> *Part of leadership is knowing when to go ahead with a decision that's within your authority because you're really convinced it's the right thing, even if other people don't understand it at that point.*
>
> —Dr. Ingrid Mattson

Selecting a high-level WIG for an entire organization always feels a little like buying a new pair of shoes. You have to walk around in them for a while before deciding if they feel right. Don't force the team to finalize the Primary WIG too quickly. Instead, select the WIG that surfaces most clearly from the discussion, then let the leaders "walk around in it" as they develop supporting WIGs to ensure its achievement. They can always pivot to a different WIG if a better choice emerges.

Another approach we used when applying Discipline 1 for Opryland was identifying the objectives where 4DX wasn't needed—objectives that could be handled by a stroke of the pen or be managed within the whirlwind. For example, there was a planned project to break ground on a new wing of the hotel that would add two hundred new rooms. Within their well-run whirlwind (day-to-day practices), they were deeply experienced in every aspect of running a hotel the size of a small city, from food to power to police—they knew how to drive that project. But when it came to raising guest satisfaction in the midst of that whirlwind, they needed the focus of 4DX to make it happen. Otherwise, it could have been lost amidst all the other competing priorities.

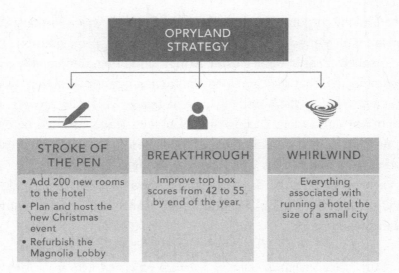

DEFINING WINNING

The measurement system for guest satisfaction at Opryland was a high standard. They tracked only *perfect scores*, 5 out of 5, which they refer to as "top box scores." This was well beyond the normal measures of guest satisfaction we had experienced. Given this, we thoughtfully challenged them to set the highest achievable top box score they could deliver. Their current top box score was 42 percent (meaning 42 percent of their guests gave them a perfect score), while the highest ever recorded score was 45 percent. After much debate, they decided on a Primary WIG to "Improve guest satisfaction from 42 to 55 percent by December 31."

With the Primary WIG set, Opryland leaders next focused on the Key Battles (sub-WIGs to the Primary WIG) that would allow them to concentrate the energy of their teams where it was most needed to ensure victory. This intermediate level of WIGs is not always needed, but in larger organizations, it's vital. To do this, the leaders took a page from the story of NASA and asked, "What is the smallest number of battles necessary to win the war?"

This question has proven to be critical to our process of WIG translation (Primary WIG cascading down to Team WIGs) for two reasons. First, it reminds everyone that the only reason for Key Battles (sub-

WIGs) to exist is to achieve the Primary WIG. Second, and even more critical, it helps leaders pinpoint the Key Battles *most essential* for success by determining the fewest possible battles necessary to win. This is critical for maintaining focus.

Contrast this approach with the way most leaders break a large outcome into smaller objectives. Usually, they begin by trying to identify every deliverable that must be accomplished, with tasks and sub-tasks. And when that effort is complete, it might be impressive, but it's also overwhelming. Having to define the *fewest possible* battles necessary to win forces leaders to think strategically about which victories are absolutely necessary to achieve the primary WIG.

The leadership team at Opryland had never before used this approach. Why? First, because they had never forced themselves to start with a *single* Primary WIG. And second, they were pursuing so many other simultaneous objectives, that they had no insight into the fewest possible battles that would have made the Primary WIG achievable.

Don't think this is easy. Even as the leadership team began to identify the Key Battles needed for winning at guest satisfaction, they had so many candidates, they were still unsure where to begin. It's the rigor of solving for the fewest possible battles that solves the riddle.

After beginning with seventeen candidate battles (sub-WIGs to the Primary WIG), we ended the day with three. What were the fewest possible battles for achieving a top box score of 55? The answer turned out to be winning at arrival experience, problem resolution, and food and beverage quality.

Arrival experience. This battle was essential. Their research had shown that negative opinions of a hotel formed in the first fifteen to twenty minutes were almost impossible to change. Conversely, the higher the quality of that first experience, the better the overall impression of the hotel.

Problem resolution. The leaders knew that, regardless of their efforts, things would still go wrong. Improving guest satisfaction isn't a question of *if* a problem will occur; it's about what you do *when* it occurs. The response of their teams to problems experienced by guests could make or break the guest's entire experience. They wanted their teams to be world-class at resolving problems.

Food and beverage quality. Because Opryland is such a large property, guests are less inclined to travel to restaurants outside the hotel. In addition, most of the hotel's restaurants are considered fine dining and are priced accordingly, leading to higher expectations for food quality and service. Meeting those expectations consistently would significantly raise guest-satisfaction scores.

The leadership team at Opryland believed that if they could put the energy of the entire hotel behind these three critical battles, reaching a top box score of 55 percent was possible. And this is the real power of focusing on the fewest battles: it enables the team to see that their Primary WIG is *winnable.*

Choosing the battles, however, was only half the work. Now each battle had to have a finish line—*From X to Y by When.* This required the answer to two important questions: what was the highest achievable score for each battle, and also, would those scores add up to winning on the Primary WIG of guest satisfaction?

If the battles won't win the war, you haven't created an effective strategy or a winnable game.

We spent an entire day with the Opryland leadership team defining (and refining) the Primary WIG and Key Battles, and setting *From X to Y by When* finish lines for each. When the day was over, Danny Jones, then head of Quality and Guest Satisfaction, said, "Now that we're done, it looks so simple, like something we could have written on the back of a napkin over lunch." He was right, but he also knew that the simplicity and clarity of the plan would be key to its effectiveness.

Danny's thoughts were echoed by Arthur Keith, the General Manager: "This was the most valuable day we've ever spent together as a leadership team. For the first time, we can articulate in just a few sentences the direction and strategic outcomes of the entire hotel."

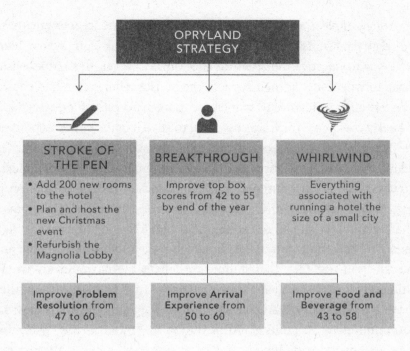

One important caution to keep in mind at this point is that battles (sub-WIGs to the Primary WIG) are *not lead measures*. Arrival experience, problem resolution, and food and beverage quality are lag measures (outcomes). This is sometimes confusing because winning the battles can be thought of as predictive of winning the Primary WIG (one of the two characteristics of lead measures). A lead measure is predictive of goal outcome, but must also be something the team can have direct influence on. At this point, we still have further to go before we get to the lead measures. We will cover this in more detail in Chapter 13, but wanted to ensure there was no confusion here.

Although the excitement of the leadership team at Opryland was a strong endorsement, the real impact of this work was seen in the teams. Seventy-five different operating teams were now able to leverage the clarity and direction the leadership team had provided as we cascaded our working sessions to every team and guided them in choosing their own Team WIG (a process described in Chapter 12).

For example, the battle for a better arrival experience was greatly affected by the results of our session with the front-desk team, whose Team WIG was to improve the speed of check-in. However, this battle wasn't theirs to win alone. In their session, the housekeeping team had chosen a closely aligned Team WIG to increase room availability for guests needing early check-in, which was essential to speeding the check-in process.

The team that caught our attention was the bellstand team. For years, this team had struggled to deliver guest bags more quickly. However, faced with antiquated systems and a massive 56-acre property, they were averaging a delivery time of 106 minutes per guest. That's right: Guests had to wait an hour and forty-six minutes for their bags. The bellstand team knew that even if the room was available and the check-in was fast, their failure to deliver the bags quickly would ultimately hurt the arrival-experience score. In their 4DX session, they chose a challenging Team WIG to reduce luggage delivery time from 106 minutes to 20 minutes. After only a few months, they exceeded their goal by reducing luggage delivery time to a stunning 12 minutes.

The graphic illustrates the 4DX architecture we've just described for winning the battle of arrival experience within the context of the hotel's Primary WIG for guest satisfaction. Keep in mind, we are only showing three of the seventy-five team-level WIGs aimed at the three battles.

As you consider the story of Opryland, remember that each of these teams, while pursuing their Team WIG, still spent *most of their time* on the whirlwind: managing the hotel, serving guests, and responding to dozens of unexpected challenges each day. But now things had changed. As a result of their 4DX sessions, each team had a Team WIG they could focus on in the midst of their day-to-day responsibilities; and for each Team WIG, they had also selected lead measures, created a compelling scoreboard, and were meeting every week to make commitments that would drive those scoreboards.

Their readiness to execute could be measured by two critical questions:

First, had every team chosen a Team WIG that would significantly impact a Key Battle? In other words, had they created a game that mattered?

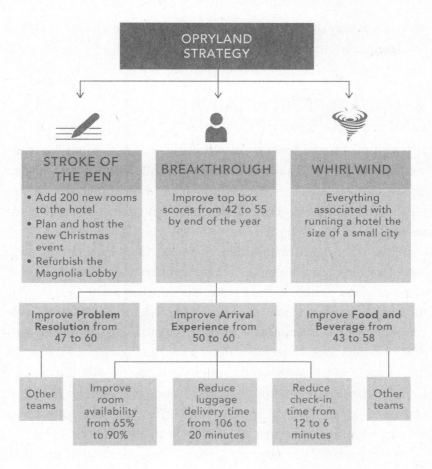

And second, was achieving their Team WIG a winnable game?

When all seventy-five teams answered yes to those two questions, everyone knew that something big was about to happen. And it did.

After nine months, Opryland not only reached a top box guest satisfaction score of 55 percent, but went beyond their goal to hit 61 percent. Remember, they had never before scored higher than 45 percent. Now they had surpassed that previous high mark in nine months. Although Opryland was Gaylord's oldest property, it now led every other Gaylord hotel in guest satisfaction. We were always optimistic, but we never anticipated this level of improvement in this short a time.

For us, the Opryland story serves as a powerful reminder of the untapped talent and potential that exists in even the best-run organizations when they move from a vague strategic intent to a set of specific finish lines.

WHAT IS DIFFERENT ABOUT OPRYLAND'S APPROACH?

It would be easy to look at the Opryland example in hindsight and wonder, "Why would anyone go about this differently? It's so logical." Except that almost every organization *does* do it differently, particularly when it comes to goal achievement. Here are two key differences we often see:

First, when faced with a daunting goal, most leaders find themselves wanting to create either a "master plan" or, in most cases, a lot of small plans. Opryland didn't create *plans,* they created *targets*. The difference between these two approaches is critical. When a leader creates a plan, that leader is telling the organization what needs to be done. Leaders must of course do this when managing both the stroke-of-the-pen and the whirlwind aspects of their strategy. But when it comes to creating a breakthrough result—one that requires the hearts and minds of the people on your team—you must change your approach. By necessity, it must be less of a push and more of a pull.

For instance, if you were the General Manager at Opryland in full planning mode, you might say, "Okay, team, we have over two hundred years of combined hotel experience in this room right now, and I am confident we can fix this guest-satisfaction problem." Then over the next few hours, you and your leaders would decide to launch a lot of great initiatives. You'd get the maintenance engineers trained to perform better preventive maintenance to keep the equipment up and running. You'd renovate the Magnolia Lobby to create a better first impression. You might even adopt some new behaviors like warmly welcoming every guest when they approach the check-in desk. All of these, and dozens of others, would be good things to do. But there is a subtle assumption at work below the surface of this planning paradigm: *We, the senior leaders, are the ones who have all the answers, and our job is to tell the people who follow us what to do.*

When it comes to the stroke-of-the-pen and whirlwind elements of your strategy, you might get away with this approach and even have some success. But that's not so if you want breakthrough results.

When Opryland achieved their breakthrough result, they *did not* start by planning. They used our 4DX implementation process to start by establishing targets—breaking the Primary WIG of top box scores into smaller and smaller targets and assigning specific teams to achieve them. These teams then identified the weekly actions and accountabilities that would best hit those targets. At no point did senior leaders simply tell anyone what to do. A target specifies the outcome you want without dictating how you want the team to do it.

In Discipline 1, we guide leaders to create a set of combined targets designed to achieve the Primary WIG. But these sessions answer nothing but the question of *what.* In Discipline 2, the teams work in their sessions to bring their knowledge and experience to the *how* when they create lead measures. Of course, lead measures are really just smaller (and more influenceable) targets for the actions that will produce results. So the actual *planning* happens when the sessions conclude by implementing Discipline 4—week by week—with the people on the front line identifying the specific commitments that will move the scoreboard. When team members participate in that process, making commitments to one another and being accountable for their follow-through, you get more than engagement—you get *innovation.*

Having team members who are very close to the work making commitments every week to advance a scoreboard is quite different from senior leaders creating a plan for the organization. And because it happens in real time, the teams can adapt and respond to the ever-changing demands of the business—something that could never have been anticipated months earlier if a "master plan" had been developed.

TRANSLATING WIGS THROUGH FUNCTIONALLY SIMILAR ORGANIZATIONS

The seventy-five teams at Opryland were very diverse in their functions, including engineers, housekeepers, front-desk clerks, bellhops, and restaurant teams, as well as support services such as finance, accounting, and human resources.

Other organizations, like retail chains, manufacturing facilities, or sales teams, can consist of many similar units that perform the *same* functions. We apply the same 4DX principles to them; however, in these multiunit organizations, WIGs translate to the front line in a way that looks quite different, as you'll see.

Take our experience implementing 4DX with a large retailer with hundreds of outlets. Just as at Opryland, this retailer's Primary WIG focused on improving the guest experience. But in their case, it was to "increase likelihood to recommend (LTR)," a measure of customer loyalty devised by business strategist Fred Reichheld. Their research had shown a strong correlation between the profitability of their stores and the likelihood that people would recommend them to their friends. With this Primary WIG in place, we spent an entire day with the leadership team defining the *fewest* possible battles necessary to win at the Primary WIG and finally isolated the three most critical:

Improve customer engagement. This was, of course, essential to increasing the willingness of customers to recommend the store. This battle focused primarily on whether their associates were available and eager to help customers find what they needed as soon as they entered the store.

Reduce out-of-stocks. This battle was critical. If a customer wanted a product that was sold out, not only was the sale lost, but the customer was less likely to recommend the store to others.

Increase speed of checkout. In this business, speed makes a huge difference in the experience of the customer. In fact, in the speed-driven world of retailing, getting customers checked out has a *disproportionate* influence. If what customers remember about the store is a frustrating checkout, it will influence their perception of the entire shopping experience.

You might think the battles they chose during our consulting sessions were obvious. But as with Opryland, the leadership team, many of whom had decades in this industry, evaluated dozens of candidate battles before settling on these three. They actually created simplicity out of enormous complexity. It took time, tremendous energy, and a little sparring before they landed on this simple yet powerful plan.

In the end, does the structure of Primary WIG and Key Battles seem simple? Yes. And that simplicity is the key to a successful implementation. Remember, the greatest challenge in execution *is not* in developing the plan. It's in *changing the behavior* of the frontline teams that must execute it.

Now let's see how this multiunit organization translated the Primary WIG to the front line. For the sake of simplicity, we'll describe one region of the company and how they worked in our sessions to translate the Primary WIG and Key Battles to districts, and how each district then translated them to the stores. Unlike the functionally diverse units at Opryland, these units performed *the same functions*; therefore, they adopted the same Primary WIG and Key Battles, even though they were able to customize their *From X to Y by When* finish lines.

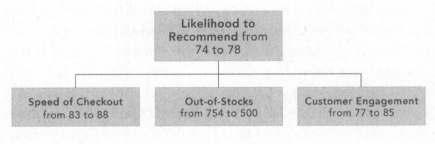

The battles selected to increase the likelihood that customers would recommend the store to others.

In our initial session, the region first chose an overall *From X to Y by When* finish line that was specific to the results expected from their entire region. Then the district leaders, who had helped develop the overall Primary WIG and Key Battles structure, chose unique *From X to Y by When* finish lines for each district in the region. It was critical that the combined results from every district would ensure that the region would hit (or exceed) its target.

Notice in this example that the region leader *did not dictate* the targets to the districts; the district leaders took ownership of this responsibility. Regional leaders were free to ask for adjustments if they didn't agree with the numbers, but ultimately, the district leaders ensured that they defined a winning game for the region.

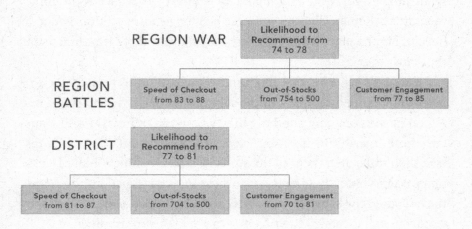

Store WIGs were the same as district WIGs but with a unique *From X to Y by When* measure for each store. However, in our sessions with store leaders, there was a twist. The stores were given the choice, with oversight from the district leader, to choose the battles that represented the greatest opportunities for the store. If a store was already exemplary in out-of-stocks, for example, they could focus on customer engagement and speed of checkout. In this way, two things were accomplished.

- Using the 4DX implementation process, store leaders gained a sense of involvement and choice, and as a result, were naturally more committed to the process.
- They could concentrate their efforts on the battle that needed it most.

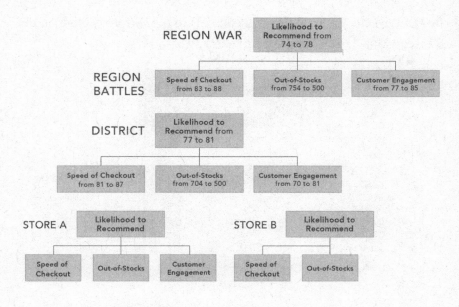

SMALL-COMPANY EXAMPLE

The top six leaders of a fifty-person accounting firm in Sydney, Australia, were working with us at a public event to define their Primary WIG and Key Battles. This team was sitting at one of the tables in a room of two hundred people from different organizations. During one of the exercises, it became obvious they were struggling. When we asked, they dejectedly admitted, "Yeah, we are having trouble."

When we joined them at their table, they shared their struggle. "We know you said not to go too broad with the Primary WIG, and you even used the example of 'total revenue' as something we should avoid because it represents the sum of all we do. But given our current situation, we think the Primary WIG *has* to be revenue. We only have two teams in our company—the people selling our services, and the people who deliver them—and their main focus is driving revenue. Below that, we've identified nine Battle WIGs that are necessary to achieve 'total revenue.' We don't want to give two teams nine Battle WIGs to pursue, so we are not sure what we should do."

We suggested something completely different to them: "Instead of using total revenue as the WIG, just give it a promotion. Move it up from a WIG (in the breakthrough column) to the "Strategy" line on the Strategy Map." (See the diagram below.)

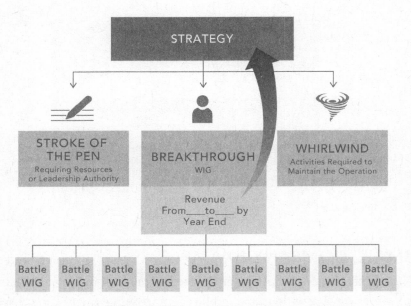

The 9 Battles necessary to achieve the revenue WIG.

When this change was made, they were able to make a fresh beginning on what the Primary WIG should be.

To get started, we asked them if the revenue goal (now at the strategy line) included any stroke-of-the-pen initiatives. Their answer was quick and clear: "We have two new products, and we've hired a new marketing company," they said.

"Is any of that going to contribute to revenue?" we asked. "It better," was the answer. The new products and the hiring of the new marketing company shifted from being battles (where 4DX would be applied) to being stroke-of-the-pen projects (that would not require 4DX).

Next, we asked them to complete a fast calculation of how much revenue they would likely generate from their stroke-of-the-pen initiatives *combined with* their normal performance (whirlwind). They estimated it to be about 85 percent of their (now strategic) total revenue goal. All that was left was to select a Primary WIG that would best close the remaining gap of 15 percent.

We next asked them, "Considering the revenue you produce, is it all equally valuable to the company?" After a moment of thought, they said, "Actually, we love advisory-services revenue. It has our best margins, and when clients buy those services, they end up using every service we offer. Plus, they are our happiest clients." We knew we were almost home.

We then asked, "Could you get enough advisory-services revenue to close that 15 percent gap in your total revenue (strategic) objective?" "Yes, and we would love that!" they practically shouted.

By that point, they could see it. One of the leaders at the table chimed in, "Sounds like our Primary WIG should be aimed at increasing advisory-services revenue." The recommendation was followed by quick agreement and lot of enthusiasm. Once the Primary WIG was narrowed from total revenue to the more focused advisory-services revenue, the leaders had no trouble identifying two Team WIGs that would ensure the success of the Primary WIG:

- **For the sales team**: Increase advisory-services revenue from *new* accounts from X to Y.
- **For the delivery team**: Increase advisory-services revenue from *existing* accounts from X to Y.

There are two valuable lessons in this story worth noting.

First, when we guided the leadership team to keep stroke-of-the-pen and whirlwind elements of the strategy in mind, they saw the scope of the Primary WIG very differently. They realized the Primary WIG didn't need to achieve the overall (strategic) result—only the component that required disciplined focus. And *focus* is the principle on which Discipline 1 is based. 4DX *is not* an effective method for running your entire organization. 4DX is a process for *creating a strategic breakthrough*.

The second lesson demonstrated is that going smaller on your Primary WIG is sometimes the more strategic choice. It's natural to think that bigger goals are more strategic. But it's not always true. In this case, choosing total revenue as the Primary WIG wasn't a strategic choice at all. It was the leadership equivalent of directing your team to "Do everything. Faster."

In these three examples—the large hotel, the national retailer, and the small accounting firm—the same choice was made: to clearly identify the needed *breakthrough result* and then direct focused effort (through 4DX) into a Primary WIG (at the top) and Team WIGs at the front line. This concentration of energy—what we call "breakthrough currency"—was invested to enable each of these organizations to reach a new level of performance. And more important, to ingrain repeatable habits of execution into their operation.

CHAPTER 8

Getting Your
Leaders on Board

*I define a leader as anyone who takes responsibility for finding
the potential in people and processes, and who has the courage to
develop that potential.*

—Brené Brown

The most surprising aspect of our journey with more than three hundred
thousand leaders has always been the human element in 4DX. Unifying
large numbers of leaders around a consistent strategic direction is no
exception. In fact, gaining the full commitment of a leadership team
is just as critical to your success as choosing the right strategy. To help
you succeed in this important objective, this chapter presents the *mind-sets* and *skillsets* that have proven to be most successful.

Although they can be applied anywhere, for simplicity, we will
present these ideas from the point where the leaders of leaders have
already developed a Primary WIG and their Key Battle WIGs. Now they
are ready to engage the leaders of frontline teams who report to them.

In this critical next step, the leaders of leaders have three objectives:

- **Finalize the Primary WIG and the Key Battle WIGs.** These are
  still considered drafts until the leaders of frontline teams can
  give their input. This is the top-down aspect of the process.

- **Develop draft Team WIGs for frontline teams.** WIGs at the team level will be created by the leaders of frontline teams but must be validated by the leaders of leaders. This is the bottom-up aspect of the process.
- **Engage the entire leadership team in a committed effort to win.** The ultimate outcome from this step is a unified team of leaders who are not only clear about their targets at every level, but also committed to achieving them. This type of ownership is created through their active involvement in creating and validating the WIGs at every level.

After guiding so many organizations around the world, we've identified three *leadership mindsets* that are essential if you want to create alignment *and* engagement across an entire leadership team.

TRANSPARENCY MINDSET

While full transparency is not always organizationally possible, the *mindset of transparency* is, and there are few things that develop high trust more rapidly than *authentic transparency*. In fact, our colleague Stephen M. R. Covey in his book *The Speed of Trust* names "Create Transparency" as one of the 13 behaviors of high-trust leaders.

Presenting the draft of the Primary WIG and Key Battle WIGs is a great example. Most leaders can't resist the temptation to present their draft WIGs and then to advocate for them as the "right answer." They do this by emphasizing how "critical these WIGs are to our success" or how these WIGs represent "the only effective option for moving forward." When we prepare leaders for this moment, we coach them to share the logic of how they got to these decisions. We also coach that it's important to outline the other options that were considered and rejected, and any lingering concerns or questions they still have.

Leaders with a transparency mindset share their concerns openly, freely acknowledge that they don't have all the answers, and actively encourage feedback from others no matter where they reside on the organizational chart. Speaking to your fellow leaders with this level of transparency both shows and elicits respect. It demonstrates openness and *invites* others to be open. Don't let your strong desire for unity slip into forced advocacy. Instead, create the kind of involvement that inspires true commitment.

The most visible aspect of a transparency mindset relates to how final decisions are presented. This is critical. Even though leaders of frontline teams are essential and highly valued in the discussion, *final decisions* on the Primary and Key Battle WIGs are made by leaders of leaders. The best approach is to make this clear from the beginning. When you do this, the leaders of frontline teams understand that they are there to gain understanding, as well as offer their insights. But they are not there to be sold on the Primary and Battle WIGs, nor are you going to take a vote or engage in endless debate in an attempt to reach consensus. Showing this level of transparency up front helps build high trust and sets the stage for the leaders of frontline teams to choose their own Team WIGs later in the process.

UNDERSTANDING MINDSET

The key to influence is first to be influenced. An understanding mindset means that the leaders of leaders truly seek to understand the concerns and ideas of the leaders of frontline teams before making a final decision on the Primary WIG and the Key Battle WIGs. When we coach leaders on this mindset, we continually remind them that there is much they do not know, and that feedback from others is necessary for gaining insight and creating the level of buy-in that produces results.

The most effective leaders also understand that a person who is struggling to articulate an idea or who is reluctant to be the first to speak may still have a valuable insight. In this process, your sincere attempt to understand the concerns and ideas from the leaders of frontline teams is essential. Remember, you can understand, even if you don't agree. In fact, it's particularly important on ideas or insights where your first reaction is to disagree. When leaders are unwilling to adopt an understanding mindset, they often project an air of ego or insecurity, neither of which creates the influence you need.

The more you adopt an understanding mindset, the more you will learn, the more you will lower resistance, and the better the decisions you will make.

The greatest need of the human soul is to be understood. In the end, it's far more important to the leaders of frontline teams to feel understood than it is for their ideas to be adopted.

INVOLVEMENT MINDSET

Most conscientious leaders of leaders understand the importance of involvement. What is less understood is *when* and *how* to create that involvement. The following is a simple diagram for the level of involvement leaders of frontline teams have in WIG selection.

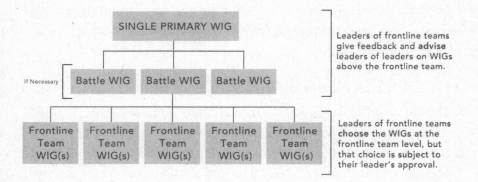

When final decisions are made on the Primary WIG and the Key Battle WIGs, leaders of frontline teams play an essential role in understanding and, if possible, improving these crucial WIGs. But the final decision belongs to the leaders of leaders.

However, when Team WIGs are chosen, leaders of frontline teams make their own decisions, subject only to final validation by the leaders of leaders. In Chapter 2, we gave this rule as "You can veto, but not dictate." What this means is that you don't overtly or subtly let the leader of a frontline team know your preference for their Team WIG, as hard as this may be to resist. You let them choose, and veto only when you have to.

The good news is that when the Primary WIG and Key Battle WIGs are clearly understood, vetoing a Team WIG is seldom necessary. And when this act is called for, the leader of the frontline team is then given an opportunity to rethink their choice and present a new Team WIG for consideration.

One of the most intriguing elements of this work has been observing the reaction of frontline leaders when they are allowed to choose their Team WIG. Where there might have been strong disagreement, even animosity, around the choice of the Primary WIG and Key Battle WIGs, it seems to disappear when the leaders of frontline teams face the same challenges and questions in the choice of their Team WIG.

It's fascinating to see the leaders of frontline teams resisting and debating the choice of a Primary WIG or Key Battle WIGs in one moment, and in the next, fully engaging in the creation of Team WIGs to achieve them. For years we would witness this and wonder, "What just happened? Where did all that animosity go?"

And then we realized that the conversation on the Primary WIG and Key Battle WIGs had simply *ended*. The leaders of frontline teams had offered their best arguments, their most insightful analysis, and the benefit of their own experience. But now that was over. They felt they had been heard, that they were respected, and most important, that they had been understood. In the end, they knew a decision had to be made.

An old maxim could be applied here: "People have to have their say, but they don't have to have their way." But there is something much deeper at work.

Once the leaders of frontline teams created their Team WIGs, they realized their contribution was essential to the success of the entire effort—that they were in essence *partners* with the leaders of leaders. They were also entrusted with the decision of what the most effective Team WIG would be. Even if they disagreed with the overall direction, the invitation created through their involvement was compelling. And the answer to the clear but unspoken request was: "Of course we will help."

Had the leaders of leaders spent their energy trying to convince or control the resistant leaders of the frontline teams, they would have received begrudging compliance at best and open defiance at worst. Instead, they were now on their way to the most powerful outcome of all: willing commitment. Human nature is a curious thing. In the opening of this book, we described execution as a *human challenge*. This example perfectly illustrates what we mean.

FIVE STEPS IN THE 4DX IMPLEMENTATION PROCESS TO FINALIZE WIGS AT ALL LEVELS

Below are the specific steps for applying the mindsets of transparency, understanding, and involvement to the process of finalizing WIGs at all levels. In the 4DX implementation process, we use these steps either as the objectives for a single meeting or for a series of discussions held over several days. However, our experience has taught us that it's critical for all five steps to be understood by everyone before the process begins.

Step 1. Ensure understanding of the Primary WIG and Key Battle WIGs.

As we described above, understanding must precede action if you want results. In the 4DX implementation process, one or more of the leaders of leaders are responsible for sharing not only the draft Primary WIG and Key Battle WIGs, but also how and why they were chosen. The leaders of the frontline teams need to know that just because something has not been defined as a WIG does not mean it is not important. In fact, sustaining performance on all the other metrics and standards needed to run the team's operation is the *enabling force* that makes it possible to focus on the WIGs. We use the chart below as a helpful model for showing the leaders of frontline teams how WIGs work together with stroke-of-the-pen initiatives and day-to-day operations to drive the strategy. In this context, the WIGs (and 4DX) can be seen as simply a special treatment that enables you to put a higher level of focus and discipline toward a critical outcome.

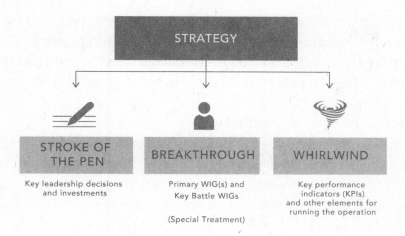

Step 2. Respond to clarifying questions.

In this next step, we often divide the leaders of frontline teams into small groups and then ask them to write down the clarifying questions they'd like to see answered about the Primary WIG and Key Battle WIGs. We are careful to emphasize that we're not asking for feedback yet. For now, we are focusing on ensuring clarity. In these sessions, the leaders of leaders should strive to answer all clarifying questions. This investment of time up front significantly reduces the time needed to address feedback later. In fact, the greater the clarity, usually the less feedback.

We see two things when we elicit clarifying questions from the leaders of frontline teams. First, even though you were clear about not wanting feedback at this point, there will always be feedback. It's natural and predictable. You simply need to remind the leaders of frontline teams that addressing feedback is the next step in the process—one that will be made easier by getting clarifying questions answered first.

Second, there will always be more clarifying questions than you expected, despite your effort to be clear. It never fails. The good news is that every clarifying question reveals an area where confusion could be possible. For example, notice the opportunity for different interpretations of questions such as:

"Is the X to Y showing year-over-year results or year-to-date?"

"Does 'new accounts' also include new accounts within *existing* client organizations?"

157

During this discussion, we coach leaders that the transparency mind-set will be essential, especially when they find themselves saying, "Good question. We actually hadn't thought about that." And when they do, they see the value of specifically addressing clarity before asking for feedback.

Step 3. Be open to feedback.

For this step, we also divide leaders of frontline teams into small groups. The small group enables the leaders of frontline teams to "test out" offering their feedback before they raise it with the larger group. It is also easier to present feedback as part of a small group than as a single individual.

However, we are always clear that the intent of this step in the 4DX implementation process is for the leaders of leaders to *hear and understand* all feedback from the leaders of frontline teams—not to endlessly debate different ideas. The purpose of this feedback is to enable the leaders of leaders to make the best decision possible on the final Primary WIG and Key Battle WIGs.

If you lack an understanding mindset, this step will likely not succeed. To secure this mindset throughout, a great practice is to restate feedback questions or statements before trying to answer them. Restating the feedback both ensures the feedback was heard and demonstrates respect to the person offering it.

Throughout this step, leaders of leaders should be listening for ways to improve the draft Primary WIG and Key Battle WIGs based on the feedback.

Step 4. Make a final decision.

In this step, we meet with the leaders of leaders, without the leaders of frontline teams, to create the final WIGs. If for any reason the leaders of leaders cannot reach agreement, then the most senior leader must step in and make the final decision.

When the final Primary WIG and Key Battle WIGs are presented to the leaders of the frontline teams, we prepare them that there will most likely be feedback that was considered and rejected. As much as possible, we encourage leaders to acknowledge and show appreciation for the investment made in the discussion, and if needed, allow another round of clarifying questions to be offered.

For the best results, the leaders of leaders must offer a thoughtful decision along with real gratitude for the help from the leaders of frontline teams. In the 4DX implementation process, it's too early to expect or seek enthusiasm at this point. The leaders of frontline teams have a lot to think about, and their minds are already busy considering the implications of the final WIGs you've just presented. Enthusiasm will come.

Step 5. Create Team WIGs.

Do you remember the remarkable change in engagement we described in the section on the involvement mindset above? This step in the 4DX implementation process is where it starts to happen. Up to this point, the leaders of frontline teams have been "advisers" to the leaders of leaders, helping them choose the most effective Primary WIG and Key Battle WIGs. Now, the leaders of frontline teams are responsible for creating their Team WIGs that will align with one of the Key Battle WIGs.

During this step, two questions should be foremost in the minds of the leaders of frontline teams.

1. What Team WIG represents the greatest possible contribution our team could make to the Key Battle we're aligned to?
2. Is this Team WIG (with an X to Y) a winnable game?

We will explain this aspect of the 4DX implementation process in greater detail throughout Part 3 of this book.

For now, we want to focus on the corresponding questions that should be foremost in the minds of the leaders of leaders.

1. Can the teams realistically achieve their Team WIGs?
2. Will the achievement of the Team WIGs be sufficient to achieve the Primary WIG?

Inevitably, our consulting session reveal leaders of frontline teams who have "overreached" in setting their Team WIGs or those whose Team WIGs don't align to a Key Battle WIG in a direct enough way. This is normal and correctable. We simply have them try again with a more specific focus. Given a second chance, most will get it.

As the leaders of frontline teams create and then share the Team WIG they have chosen, team optimism grows. A moment comes when they think, "We can do this." Why does this happen? There may be many reasons, but the most obvious is that they finally see the big picture—how all of the Team WIGs concentrate their energy toward the Primary WIG—and in that moment, they know success is possible. This pivotal moment relates to the tendency of teams (and leaders) to operate as silos of competence, despite attempts to facilitate collaboration and break the silos down. This step in the 4DX implementation process underscores how essential each team is to your overall success and instills a unified mindset of *winning*.

There is a scene in the movie *Apollo 13* that captures this feeling perfectly. The engineers at NASA are trying to get three astronauts back to earth in a damaged space capsule when they realize the astronauts are running out of air due to a failed air filter. The leader of an engineering team (a leader of a frontline team) gathers his engineers and says, "Okay. The guys upstairs need us to come through for them."

He then dumps on the table a collection of unrelated parts—items the astronauts would have access to in the capsule—and shows them an example of the defective air filter and an example of a working air filter. He then states the WIG: "We need to turn this [holding up the bad air filter] into this [holding up the good air filter] using nothing but this [pointing to the parts on the table]." There is a moment of silence, and then a dozen engineers dive into the pile of parts. It is one of the most compelling moments in the movie. In that moment, they know that the entire mission, and the lives of the astronauts, depend on their ability to solve this *together*. There's no higher level of ownership or engagement than when frontline teams see that their Team WIG (their piece of the puzzle) might make all the difference.

NOTE TO LEADERS OF LEADERS IN LARGE ORGANIZATIONS

The mindset and the 4DX implementation process discussed in this chapter are also used in our consulting sessions for translating WIGs from the highest level of leadership (e.g., C-level leaders) down to each organizational level of leadership below (e.g., vice presidents, directors, and so forth, all themselves leaders of leaders). However, for the process to be successful, the translation of WIGs to each level must not stop until it ultimately involves the leaders of frontline teams creating Team WIGs for the teams they lead.

CHAPTER 9

Project Execution With 4DX

Over the years, we've been asked many times whether 4DX can be applied to projects, especially when there are already principles of project management being applied. The answer? An emphatic *yes*.

In fact, in our consulting process, 4DX is easily applied to both small and large projects, and the achievement of Project WIGs have contributed to some of our clients' most dramatic results. However, there are differences in how we apply 4DX when the WIG is the completion of a project as opposed to the improvement of an operational (numeric) result. In this chapter, we will share the guidance we offer on determining *if* your project should be a WIG, and if so, *how* to apply 4DX to its achievement.

SHOULD YOUR PROJECT BE A WIG?

There are two situations where we guide leaders to consider choosing a project as their WIG. In one of these, 4DX is ideal; in the other, it's not. In this chapter, we will help you understand which of these situations you are facing, as well as when and how we use the 4DX implementation process when the WIG is a project.

Situation 1. The Project Shop

We use this term to describe a team whose primary role is the management and completion of projects. Some examples are a client software team who is continually creating new applications, a marketing team who is always launching the next campaign, or even a project-management group who is helping various teams around the company in dozens of different projects. If the day job routinely takes the form of projects, this section is designed to help.

If our client's role almost always involves projects, they very likely have some sort of project-management process, whether it's sophisticated and detailed or simply a set of practices they always use. In either case, we need to be clear: the 4DX implementation process we use is not a replacement for a project-management methodology; *it's a discipline for ensuring the project is successful.*

For clients who are project-shop teams, the first insight from our consulting sessions is that the most successful application of 4DX will *not* be on an individual project. Instead, it will be applying 4DX to the running of *all* projects.

For example, if you have a team whose role is to test new software applications and they normally test about twelve new applications every three months, then each of these tested applications can be seen as a project that must be completed. But since these testing projects compete for time and energy, and since some may be more important or urgent than others, the team may struggle with which project they should choose as their WIG. But *this is the wrong approach.*

In our consulting sessions, we do not ask, "Which project should we choose as our WIG?" Instead, we have the project-shop team look at all of their projects as a body of work and ask the 4DX Discipline 1 question: "If everything stayed the same, where do we need to see the most improvement?"

This question leads them to consider:

"Do we need to improve our on-time completion percentage?"
"Do we need to improve being on budget?"
"Do we need to refine our resource-allocation process?"
"Do we need to reduce post-completion rework?"

Often the ideal WIG for a project-shop team originates in one (or more) of these laws of constraints regarding time, quality, or cost of their overall project performance.

Next, we consider Discipline 2 for this same scenario. If the application-testing team chose a WIG (lag measure) of "Improve projects completed on time from 72 to 90 percent by December 31," then one of the most likely sources of predictive lead measures might be their existing methods. For example, if their project-management process had nine critical steps, they might ask questions such as:

"Do any of these steps currently represent a bottleneck that causes delays?"

"If we improved our performance on one of these steps, would it significantly impact our on-time completion?"

"Is there a new step that could be added to the process that would impact on-time completion?"

The diagram below shows two lead measures being chosen from a nine-step project-management process, where the WIG is improving on-time completion. The two steps were chosen because when these are improved, the team believes they have the greatest potential to impact the WIG. Whether your existing process has a few steps or dozens, selecting the one or two that have the greatest potential to impact the WIG is usually a wise choice for your lead measures.

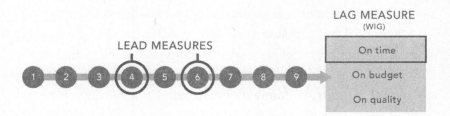

Remember that this is only an example of the 4DX implementation process we use that results in the choice of lead measures. We don't advocate that the WIG always be one of the elements of the law of constraints, nor are we suggesting that the lead measures always need to come out of the existing project-management process. But for project shops, the thought process illustrated here can be helpful.

Situation 2. The Project WIG for Non-Project Managers

In this example, we are focusing on a team whose primary role is *not* running projects, but who *does* have a critical project they are considering as a WIG.

Let's pause for a moment to be sure the differences between Situation 1 and Situation 2 are clear.

- In Situation 1, there are a lot of projects. In Situation 2, there is *one* project.
- In Situation 1, there is a team of people whose *primary role* is to run projects. In Situation 2, running projects is *not* the team's primary role.

While this may seem simple, in almost every situation where we've used the 4DX implementation process for projects, it has been in one of these two scenarios. And without question, it is in Situation 2 where the use of 4DX has been most powerful for driving successful execution on vital projects with our clients.

Remember, 4DX is a process for concentrating energy (not already consumed by the whirlwind), and in Situation 2, the successful completion of a project requires that vital energy. However, as the following example illustrates, the application of 4DX is different.

Mountain Land Rehabilitation is a client who runs thirty-seven physical-therapy practices across the western part of the United States. Through our consulting sessions, they determined that their Primary WIG was to increase the number of practices that achieve their Anchor Level practice of performance—a designation of both specific quality and specific financial performance.

Initially, their WIG was to "Increase Anchor Level practices from three to twelve by the end of the year." They achieved that WIG, and in the next six months, went even further to reach nineteen practices at that level of performance.

However, the functional leaders in the corporate offices who were not directly managing the practice clinics—human resources, information technology, finance, and quality—were initially unsure what *their* WIGs should be to support this effort. After some thought, they created a WIG for the *combined* support-services team they believed would have the biggest impact on helping the practice clinics hit their Anchor Level WIG. It also happened to be a project that had haunted Mountain Land for more than twelve years. Their WIG was to design and develop a comprehensive job-specific training system for the entire company. Most of their leaders believed that not having this training was limiting the company's ability to adopt best practices and increasing the difficulties of both promoting and bringing on new people, since training was always done informally on the job.

"It was always important, but never urgent," said Rick Lybbert, one of the company owners and a champion of the 4DX efforts. "Every year we would decide *again* how important this was, and every year something else always got in the way, even when we had money set aside in the budget to make sure we got it done." By defining this as a Project WIG for the *combined* support-services team, they completed 100 percent of the identified training modules, a grand total of 239, in *less than six months,* with the last two modules completed just before the ball dropped on New Year's Eve.

Let's take a look at a project using 4DX with this example.

Discipline 1

When we are creating the WIG for a project, we emphasize that it requires a little more definition than you need for a numeric operational WIG. The formula of *From X to Y by When* is a great lag measure for numeric WIGs because numbers are objective—something that is not always the case when determining completion of a project. As a result, Mountain Land Rehabilitation needed a bit more information in their WIG definition than "Complete 100 percent of all training modules by December 31." In fact, *percent completion* is one of the least precise measures, since it's seldom objectively measured and since projects tend to suffer from scope creep (an unanticipated expansion of the scope of the project).

We encourage our clients to use the better approach of setting the Project WIG with a clear finish-line date, but to also include the actual products or outcomes the team must produce. Winning is defined by the actual outcomes produced rather than an imprecisely assigned percentage of completion. To do this, your team must become very clear on the definition of "finished."

MOUNTAIN LAND FINAL WIG

Complete 100 percent of the identified training modules by December 31. Each module must . . .

- Include both abbreviated and elaborated learning points.
- Include a post-quiz.
- Receive final completion pass-off by the training committee.

This method enabled the scorekeeping to be based on modules completed, where the current score was always a true representation of progress made toward the final result.

Discipline 2

The lead measures most often chosen for this type of WIG are the defined milestones of the project. However, for milestones to work most effectively, they need to meet certain criteria. For example, if our client selects milestones that are too large, representing major accomplishments, they may be scheduled too far apart to effectively work as lead measures. Alternatively, if they are too granular, they may not allow enough time for the building of execution habits essential to the team. Ideal milestones are usually spaced at intervals of between two and six weeks. For Mountain Land, the lead measures were twelve high-level milestones spaced a week or more apart (see below). At first glance, you might think that twelve lead measures seem to be too many; but remember, the team is focusing on only one or two of them at a time as they work toward completing the project.

LEAD MEASURES (MILESTONES)

June 1	Complete current job descriptions.
June 20	Interview leadership stakeholders on module requests.
July 7	Submit proposed list of training modules for all job descriptions.
July 14	Finalize list of identified training modules.
July 21	Complete guidelines for module format.
July 28	Confirm writers/subject-matter experts (SMEs) for all modules.
Aug. 4	SMEs/writers complete first job description.
Aug. 11	Provide guideline feedback to writers on their first module.
Oct. 18	Complete first third of modules for approval.
Nov. 4	Provide SME/writer feedback on first third of modules.
Nov. 10	Complete second third of modules for approval.
Dec. 15	Complete final third of modules for approval.

Discipline 3

The primary challenge our clients have in creating a scoreboard for a Project WIG is keeping the team focused on the current "active" lead measure (milestone)—the one the team is currently working on.

For example, on June 25, the active lead-measure milestone for the team would be "Submit proposed list of training modules for all job descriptions—due on July 7." That's where the team's focus should be on that date, and as a result, that's the milestone that should be visible on the scoreboard. It's also the milestone team members will focus on when making commitments in Discipline 4 (see below).

While there are several ways we guide our clients to create scoreboards that show these kinds of lead-measure milestones, we will demonstrate Discipline 3 using the 4DX app.

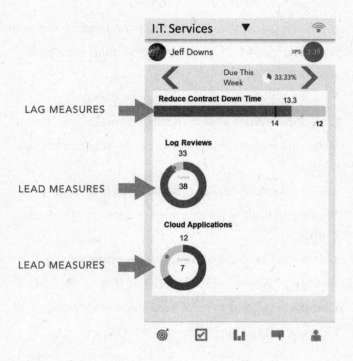

When you enter the lead-measure milestones into the 4DX app, you also specify the activation date when it becomes visible on the scoreboard. Once it's complete, it returns to being invisible. See below.

With this functionality, the team can choose to work on more than one milestone at a time by overlapping activation dates with completion dates. Activation dates can also be modified during the project if necessary.

Also, if the team misses the completion date of an active lead-measure milestone, the next milestone is activated regardless, while the missed milestone is still showing. This often provides an increased sense of urgency for the team.

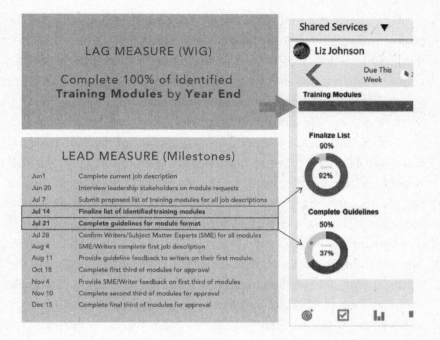

Discipline 4

Implementing Discipline 4 for projects requires us to share only a small adjustment in the question that creates commitments. For Project WIGs, the adjusted question is "What are the one or two things I can do this week that will ensure we meet our next milestone?"

One final thought:

In 2004, we were asked by a major military contractor to take the top fifty developers of the world's most advanced fighter plane through 4DX. This was eight years before the first version of the *4DX* book was published, and the approach was still new. In addition, the leader of our practice, Jim Stuart (to whom this book is dedicated), was not available for the engagement. This left the primary responsibility up to the rest of the team, and the more we prepared to work with these "rocket scientists," the more nervous we became.

One question haunted us: What could we possibly teach the best project managers in the world about execution? We asked Jim Stuart this very question, and after a pause (and an audible sigh of disappointment), he answered us in one sentence: "A project plan is not a scoreboard!" Believe it or not, that was all we needed to hear. We thanked our mentor and got back to work.

Jim's one sentence triggered an entire series of ideas on where we could add real value. Even when a leader is an expert on a particular subject and knows what needs to happen down to the most minute detail, that doesn't guarantee excellence in execution *by the team*. It does not solve the primary challenge with execution—engaging human energy toward nonurgent critical activities in the face of the whirlwind. Jim was right. To deal with that challenge, they would need more than a project plan—they would need a compelling scoreboard. The rocket scientists took to 4DX like a fish to water. They had success on several fronts where they had been stuck for months, and in the end taught us a great deal about applying 4DX in a project world, laying the groundwork for much of the information in this chapter.

CHAPTER 10

Sustaining 4DX Results and Engagement

When leaders define clear ownership and invest in others, they have sown the seeds of success and earned the right to hold people accountable.

—Liz Wiseman

The greatest impact of 4DX is not simply the ability to produce break-through results. It's the ability to *sustain* (and even improve) those results over a significant period of time. This characteristic is rooted in building *habits of execution,* practices that become so ingrained that teams are no longer conscious of them as a requirement for performance. As one of our largest clients remarked, "We don't even think of 4DX as a methodology anymore. It's just the way we execute."

Instilling these habits is the most important outcome for leaders of leaders. Although the Primary WIG will always be the most immediate and most visible target, the greater achievement is your ability to establish a *culture of* execution—one where WIGs can be achieved again and again, regardless of fluctuating conditions.

Achieving your Primary WIG will always be a celebration-worthy outcome, but it simply doesn't prove your team's ability to sustainably execute. After all, achieving your Primary WIG is subject to many forces beyond your team's performance. A rising or falling economy, market trends, surprising innovation by a competitor, legislation and government regulations, currency valuation, technology, and even the weather can inflate or suppress your final results. Because of this, it's a dangerous mindset to accept WIG achievement as the sole indicator that you've created a culture of execution. As a leader of leaders, you need a more definitive measurement.

To help crystallize this focus, we wanted a single indicator that measures not only WIG results but also the habits of execution that drive them—a measure we hope will be the focus for leaders of leaders as you pursue achieving your Primary WIG. The higher this metric, the greater your results *and* the greater your ability to sustain (or improve) them. Over time, we found that aggregating the four most observable elements of 4DX gave us such a metric. We call this metric the Execution Performance Score, or XPS.

UNDERSTANDING XPS

It's important to separate the definition of XPS from how it's used by leaders of leaders. To begin, let's examine the definition. There are four components of XPS:

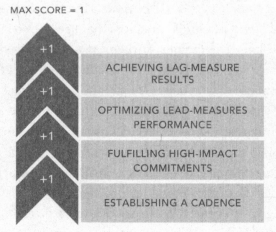

MAX SCORE = 1

+1 ACHIEVING LAG-MEASURE RESULTS

+1 OPTIMIZING LEAD-MEASURES PERFORMANCE

+1 FULFILLING HIGH-IMPACT COMMITMENTS

+1 ESTABLISHING A CADENCE

1. **Establishing a cadence.** This component indicates how well the team has established a cadence of meeting weekly to focus on the scoreboard.

2. **Fulfilling high-impact commitments.** This component indicates how well the team has consistently made commitments and followed through.

3. **Optimizing lead-measures performance.** This component indicates how consistently the lead measures are being performed.

4. **Achieving lag-measure (WIG) results.** This component indicates how effectively the first three components are enabling your team to achieve its WIG.

The calculation of your XPS consists simply of identifying the score for each component and then adding them together. Since each component has a maximum score of 1, a perfect score would be 4. Note that each component of XPS has a maximum value of 1, so overperformance in any one area cannot mask underperformance in another. We were very pleased that the calculation of XPS was simple and straightforward, but also that this calculation is performed automatically in the 4DX app—a tool offered to support our clients as they work with us through the 4DX implementation process.

Your XPS score can then be used to give you insights into your team's performance and the results it is producing.

3.6 to 4.0   **High level of execution excellence.** This score indicates that your team has high adoption of 4DX and is producing results.

3.2 to 3.59   **Good level of execution, but room for improvement.** This score indicates that your team has a good adoption of 4DX, but that there is room for improvement that would produce even greater results.

2.5 to 3.19   **Fair level of execution, along with areas of concern.** This score indicates the need for concerned investigation and, possibly, intervention. Low levels of execution seldom produce acceptable results, but even worse, create skepticism in the team that can lead to disengagement.

0 to 2.49   **Significant level of concern.** This score indicates a team that in reality is not executing at all. Inconsistent effort, low levels of engagement, and the absence of results are all symptoms of a team that is either overwhelmed by their whirlwind or resisting the execution process.

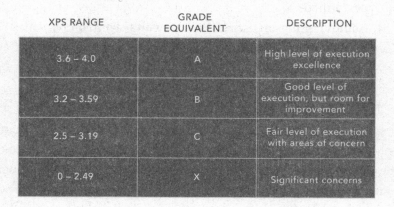

XPS RANGE	GRADE EQUIVALENT	DESCRIPTION
3.6 – 4.0	A	High level of execution excellence
3.2 – 3.59	B	Good level of execution, but room for improvement
2.5 – 3.19	C	Fair level of execution with areas of concern
0 – 2.49	X	Significant concerns

Remember that XPS is an execution score that (through the 4DX App) can be applied to:

- An entire organization, indicating your overall execution capability.
- An individual business unit or team, indicating their execution capability, as well as their ranking against other teams.
- A leadership team, indicating the level at which the leaders of leaders are modeling the execution practices they want their teams to embrace.
- An individual leader, indicating their personal modeling of execution practices.

APPLYING XPS

In our consulting engagements to implement 4DX, we always emphasize that leaders of leaders must do two things. First, they must sustain their current operation (the whirlwind). Second, they must drive future results (the WIG). The whirlwind always seems to have great visibility—lots of measures, maybe even more than we would like. But when it comes to improving on our future results, it can be a different story.

In the absence of definitive measures, the leader often has no objective indicator of whether the teams are really (and regularly) concentrating energy toward the WIG or are simply stuck in the whirlwind of urgent demands. It's one of the most critical questions you will face—one that's seldom easy to answer, leaving you to wonder, "Are they really engaged, or are they just going through the motions?"

This is reminiscent of the days before measurable customer satisfaction was so prevalent—a single comment, positive or negative, could leave you wondering about everything you needed to know with certainty, but didn't. This same dilemma faces leaders of leaders today in knowing how much energy and engagement is being invested in new, breakthrough results, as opposed to handling day-to-day priorities. This is the question XPS answers. As a result, we believe XPS is the *ideal lead measure* for leaders of leaders to use for their own focus (not the focus of frontline teams) in achieving the Primary WIG.

Leaders of leaders have clear and constant visibility into XPS through multiple access points in the 4DX app. The most commonly used is the Executive Scoreboard, a digital dashboard that shows the real-time status of every element of XPS.

Name (leader's name)	Session	Mail	WIG	sub-WIG	Lead	Exclude	Commitments Kept	Commitments Made	Commitments Held	Commitments Index	Commitments Quality
SE TEAM 1	Session		43.24%	--	103.13%		100%	100%	100%	100%	14 days (Corey penniston)
SE TEAM 2	Session		111.4%	--	102.72%		100%	100%	100%	100%	4 days (Shaun Tierney)
Southeast Region	Session		63.99%	10.95%	--		100%	100%	100%	100%	7 days (Corey penniston)
Southeast Quality Control	Session		114.43%	--	100%		100%	100%	100%	100%	--
NE Team 1	Session		97.49%	--	103.26%		100%	100%	100%	100%	16 days (Corey penniston)
NE Team 2	Session		133.63%	--	1742.31%		100%	100%	100%	100%	4 days (Shaun Tierney)
NE Team 3	Session		101.53%	--	96.36%		50%	100%	100%	83.33%	
Northeast Region	Session		143.65%	--	--		92.31%	100%	100%	97.44%	
MW Team 1	Session		180%	--	162.5%		100%	100%	100%	100%	7 days (Shaun Tierney)
MW Team 2	Session		156.64%	--	108.42%		87.5%	100%	100%	95.83%	7 days (Don Schmidt)
Midwest Region	Session		96.12%	157.32%	--		30.47%	100%	100%	98.49%	7 days (Corey penniston)
PAC TEAM 1	Session		127.5%	--	113.13%		50%	100%	100%	83.33%	7 days (Don Schmidt)
PAC TEAM 2	Session		146.89%	--	93.75%		100%	50%	100%	83.33%	4 days (Shaun Tierney)
PAC TEAM 3	Session		107.96%	--	106.88%		75%	100%	100%	91.67%	7 days (Ed Knott)
PAC TEAM 4	Session		150.39%	--	107.5%		100%	100%	100%	100%	7 days (Ed Knott)
Pacific Region	Session		111.61%	--	--		84%	90%	100%	91.33%	14 days (Don Schmidt)
ABC Corporation	Session		20.74%	--	--		93.75%	100%	100%	97.92%	
AVERAGES:			100.91%	67.9%	320.28%		91.83%	97.14%	100%	96.22%	7 days

Through this view, the leader of leaders can monitor the XPS elements *of every team*, including:

- WIG (lag measure) results
- Lead-measure performance
- Commitments kept
- Commitments made
- WIG Sessions held

In the remainder of this chapter, we will use XPS as the framework for sharing insights on how leaders of leaders produce sustainable results over the long term through 4DX.

ESTABLISHING A CADENCE

The most fundamental practice in 4DX is the weekly WIG Session (or WIG Huddle for some frontline teams), defined in Discipline 4. This meeting, which lasts no more than twenty to thirty minutes, sets the basic rhythm of accountability for the team, as we have discussed in previous chapters and will cover in detail in Part 3. It's also the first *tactical standard* implemented in 4DX. Often leaders who express great confidence in their level of discipline find that they struggle to consistently hold this weekly meeting without disruption, distraction, or rescheduling. This is a lesson in humility that also brings insight. If you consistently allow the day-to-day urgency of the whirlwind to interrupt or abort this meeting, you've come face-to-face with the real challenge of execution: remaining focused on the WIG in spite of your whirlwind.

For leaders of leaders, establishing a weekly cadence of accountability is the clearest indication to their teams that the Primary WIG (and its achievement) is critically important. And when leaders of leaders model this discipline, the leaders of frontline teams soon follow. Unfortunately, the opposite is also true. If you regularly cancel, reschedule, or delegate this meeting, you will soon find the same decisions being made by the leaders of frontline teams. And when the cadence stops, so do the results.

If you want to improve the organization, you have to improve yourself and the organization gets pulled up with you. I wouldn't ask anyone to do anything I wouldn't do myself.

—Indra Nooyi

When we are implementing Discipline 4 with leaders of leaders, we encourage them to remember that their frontline teams are facing their own whirlwind, and the easiest (and most familiar) decision they can make is to give in to its urgent demands. And from their perspective, this can even feel like the right thing to do. In those critical moments when the whirlwind is raging and it's time for the WIG Session, the example set by leaders of leaders is their strongest influence to hold to the discipline.

Naturally, if you are ill, on vacation, or facing a true emergency, you can delegate the running of the meeting to a member of your team, *but the meeting always happens.* The message you send to the team by holding this standard is that "emergencies happen, but execution continues." This same standard applies to beginning on time, restricting the discussion solely to actions and results related to the WIG, and holding one another accountable for follow-through on commitments—topics that will be covered later in this chapter.

For now, think of this first element of XPS like the foundation of a house—everything that follows will be built on top of it. Establish a strong foundation by modeling a high standard, and it will be the basis for a strong execution culture. Establish a weak or flawed foundation through inconsistency or low accountability, and you are unlikely to succeed. As a result, your XPS on "Establishing a Cadence" for leaders of leaders should always be 100 percent.

FULFILLING HIGH-IMPACT COMMITMENTS

The second element of XPS that leads to sustainable results is making and fulfilling commitments. In 4DX, leaders make weekly commitments. No exceptions. But the weekly commitments made by leaders of leaders are designed to support or enhance the frontline team's ability to execute. That's why we refer to them as "second-level commitments."

The leader of a frontline team makes commitments that are designed primarily to raise the lead measures that move the Team WIG. This will be discussed in detail in Part 3. In contrast, leaders of leaders make commitments that are designed to have a larger impact and often raise the performance of the entire team.

Let's take the example of Susan, one of our clients, who is a Vice President of Sales over two different sales teams. Each frontline sales team has its own leader, as well as a Team WIG driven by two lead measures, as illustrated in the diagram below.

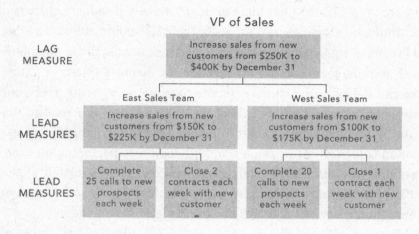

In a given week, the leaders of the frontline sales teams (East and West) would make commitments designed to move the lead measures of "calls to prospects" and "closing contracts," such as:

- *This week I will listen to ten calls made by team members and offer feedback on how they can improve.*
- *This week I will coach two team members who are struggling to close new contracts.*

Susan, as the leader of leaders, would make commitments at a higher level of impact (i.e., second level), such as:

- *This week I will review our criteria for qualifying prospects and make any needed changes to ensure higher quality.*

- *This week I will identify a training program to build skill in prospecting for our entire sales team and get it scheduled for next quarter.*
- *This week I will review our contract language with the legal team and make changes to simplify the closing process for new clients.*
- *This week I will send an email thanking or congratulating an individual contributor who has a high XPS score and makes and keeps clear commitments.*

Remember that through the Executive Scoreboard in the 4DX app, Susan can see the XPS performance of every team she leads and can target her commitments to those teams where her help is most needed and where she can have the greatest impact.

These simple examples illustrate how leaders of leaders would work "on the system" to impact results on a broader scale, while the leaders of frontline teams would work "in the system" by making commitments to drive lead measures.

The next aspect of this XPS element is keeping the commitments you make. The most precisely targeted commitment will mean nothing if you don't follow through. That's why *fulfilling* commitments is equally weighted with *making* commitments. You must do both to raise your XPS and drive results.

The context of this entire chapter is building a *culture of execution* based on the forming of habits, and no habit has more impact than following through on the commitments you make. In terms of performance, second-level commitments have a measurable impact on the results your teams produce. But in terms of leadership, no other action builds trust and respect faster than the simple act of doing what you say you will do, every time. Model this standard consistently, and the leaders of frontline teams will soon follow. It doesn't take long to build what one CEO referred to as "performance swagger"—an outward reflection of inner confidence that comes from knowing that whatever your team commits to do will absolutely happen. Your XPS standard for fulfilling commitments should be 90 percent (or higher).

OPTIMIZING LEAD-MEASURES PERFORMANCE

One of the most powerful aspects of 4DX is the *principle of leverage*. The idea of concentrating the energy of your teams on the few actions that produce the greatest results is simple but surprisingly powerful. In more than two decades, we've almost always seen two team dynamics at play:

- Every team feels that they are working at maximum capacity.
- Every leader feels the team has capacity that is untapped.

Interestingly, both are often true. The leader feels that the true capabilities of the team are not fully reflected in the team's results, but without *insight* into what the team should do differently, the leader has to attribute the deficit to insufficient *effort*. In contrast, the team sees that their current efforts are not producing adequate results, so they resist the push to simply do more of what's already not working. The solution to both perspectives is something we address in-depth when we are coaching clients through the 4DX implementation process: *optimizing your lead measures*. This is why it's the next element of XPS and consists of two important aspects:

- *Is the team acting on the right lead measures?*
- *Are the lead measures sufficiently raising the lag measure (WIG)?*

In our coaching on lead measures, we want to be very clear. It is the responsibility of the leaders of frontline teams to ensure their teams create and perform lead measures that drive the Team WIG. But leaders of leaders are responsible for ensuring that teams act on lead measures that *provide leverage* for moving the WIG.

This is a critical area of focus—one where small changes can lead to significant improvements. And nowhere is this more visible than when *good* lead measures are optimized into *great* lead measures.

Here are a few examples that illustrate the value of optimizing your lead measures:

- The surgical team in one of our leading clients, a large inner-city hospital, changed their lead measure from *Audit the surgical tray before every surgery* to *Audit the surgical tray and complete a verbal confirmation of every procedure.* The result was a 17 percent reduction in perioperative accidents.
- The front-desk team in one of the largest hotels in the United States (an organization where we've implemented 4DX in almost two thousand hotels) changed their lead measure from *Warmly welcome every guest* to *Make eye contact, smile, and welcome every guest within seven feet of the front desk.* The result was a 38 percent increase in the "guest-satisfaction rating on arrival" experience.
- The stocking team in a major home-improvement retailer changed their lead measure from *Restock all shelves by 8 a.m. opening* to *Every associate will walk every aisle twice per day and fill all empty shelf spaces.* The result was a significant reduction in out-of-stocks, which led to increased sales.

Each of these examples may seem undeniably simple, even subtle, but to the teams who acted on them, the results were dramatic—a large return on a very small change, or in their language, a way of working *smarter*, not *harder*. As our clients move through the 4DX implementation process, we remind them often that their role as a leader of leaders is not to identify changes on individual lead measures—only the frontline teams can do that. Your role is to ensure that every leader of a frontline team is regularly evaluating and challenging their team's lead measures, and where needed, modifying (or replacing) them. XPS becomes a lens through which you can see this clearly.

In our consulting sessions, we ensure your teams are using the most effective lead measures by showing them how to assess the answers to these five optimizing questions:

1. **Is the lead measure directly predictive of impacting the lag measure?** This is the most common area of confusion in lead measures—choosing a lead measure that is "good to do" rather than an action that directly moves the lag-measure result.

2. **Is the level of performance set high enough?** The team may have identified the right lead measure but is not performing it often enough to move the score.

3. **Is the scorekeeping credible?** It's not unusual for a team to become "casual" in their scorekeeping by simply estimating the score. If the scorekeeping is not credible, no real assessment can be made of the predictiveness of the lead measure.

4. **Is it a quality problem?** Very often, a team may be performing the lead measure at the specified level but failing to perform it well enough. Thus, they may have consistency but not quality. If a team is simply going through the motions, then even the most well-chosen lead measure will not perform at its maximum impact.

5. **Is it a team game or a leader's game?** Leaders of frontline teams will sometimes create lead measures that are solely their responsibility: quality leaders will perform quality audits, housekeeping leaders will perform inspections, shift leaders (in manufacturing) will limit overtime, etc. These are important responsibilities and may even impact the WIG. The problem is that they are actions performed solely by the leaders, not by the team—resulting in lower impact and even disengagement.

These questions, if thoughtfully considered, will reveal the vast majority of opportunities to improve lead measures—either by altering the lead measure or by replacing it with a new one. Whenever a frontline team is performing their lead measures without seeing a resulting change in their Team WIG, it's the role of the leader of leaders to ensure that the leaders of frontline teams ask the right questions and then make the right changes to enhance results. As a leader of leaders, you should hold frontline teams to the expectation of performing their lead measures at 90 percent (or more) of the target, every week.

ACHIEVING LAG-MEASURE (WIG) RESULTS

Without question, the first three components of XPS (establishing a cadence, fulfilling high-impact commitments, and optimizing lead-measures performance) are major drivers of success on your WIGs and are areas of critical focus. But when we are coaching leaders of leaders through the 4DX implementation process, we emphasize that there are two additional areas that are equally meaningful:

- Holding others accountable with respect.
- Recognizing high performance.

Holding Others Accountable With Respect

Accountability is one of the most powerful drivers of human behavior. When used effectively, it enables individuals and teams to reach higher performance, while building trust and respect at every level. You can see it at work in almost every aspect of human endeavor: athletes rise to the expectations of a great coach; military personnel rise to the spirit of service their oath demands; doctors and nurses give their all for patients even when great sacrifice is required, to name only a few. Certainly, there are many forces at work in each of these examples. But the common thread running through them is accountability—accountability to a commitment, to a standard, and most important, to one another. When a leader of leaders builds this type of accountability into their teams, almost nothing can stop them.

Accountability at this level is not a lofty ideal; it's a pragmatic reality. And it can be created by holding others accountable through consistency, authenticity, and respect. To illustrate this, let's again use the example of Susan, the Vice President of Sales mentioned earlier in this chapter, as she holds her weekly WIG Session with the leaders of her two frontline teams, Bianca (leading the East Team) and Marcus (leading the West Team).

Susan's team is beginning their second quarter in pursuit of their Primary WIG: *Increase sales from new customers from $250,000 to $400,000 by December 31.*

The East Team (led by Bianca) is on track to achieve their Team WIG: *Increase sales from new customers from $150,000 to $225,000 by December 31.* However, the West Team (led by Marcus) is struggling. They've fallen behind the pace needed to reach their Team WIG: *In-*

crease sales from new customers from $100,000 to $175,000 by Decem-ber 31. Let's watch how Susan uses accountability, authenticity, and respect to drive performance with the leaders of frontline teams.

SUSAN: Good morning, everyone. It's 8:15; let's get started.

[Review the scoreboard.]

As you can see, we've made good progress on our WIG of revenue from new customers, but we're not quite on pace to reach our goal. I'd like for us to focus today on what we can do as a team to get back on track.

Overall, we're at $92,000 to begin the quarter against our target for this point of $100,000. Bianca, congratulations on the East Team being slightly ahead at $57,000 against a target of $55,000. Well done. Marcus, the West Team has had some good results, but as you know, you're at $33,000 against a target of $43,000.

Susan's review of the numbers is candid and clear—as is her mes-sage emphasizing that they are in this *as a team*, winning or losing together. There's no shame or blame in her comments, but there's a clear message: *We must find a solution.*

[Report on last week's commitments.]

SUSAN: Now, for my commitments, last week I committed to attend the quarterly review meeting with one of our largest clients and to facilitate the discussion on revised pricing. The meeting went well, and we came to a great conclusion, adding two additional business units as new customers.

I also committed to review the language in our contract and to find ways to simplify it so that new customers are more willing to sign. I completed that review and sent you a new draft version by email last night.

For next week, I've committed to make three visits with

Marcus, all with potential new customers. We hope to sign at least two of them.

Susan begins by leading through example—she reports on her commitments, as well as her follow-through. She makes herself accountable to her team. This earns her the ability, not just by title but by respect, to then hold her team to the same standard. It's also important to note the type of commitments made by Susan—streamlining the contract and helping to close new customers—are second-level commitments that *help the entire team*. She's working "on" the system.

BIANCA: Thanks, Susan, especially for the work on the contract. It's really going to help. We're happy to be slightly ahead of pace on our target, but as we all know, it can disappear quickly. So my commitment this week was to review our lead measures with the team and identify any ideas for improvement that might enable us to produce more results. Out of this review, we developed a new script for our prospecting calls that we believe will be more effective. We'll be using it this week, and I'll report next week on our progress.

As a leader of a frontline team, Bianca has focused her commitments on improving lead-measures performance. With improved language, the calls made to prospects should help win new customers. She's working "in" the system.

BIANCA: My commitment for next week is to personally coach our newest team member, Jeff. He's been struggling to make his prospect calls and I want to help him establish a better daily process.

SUSAN: What do you think is the basic issue with Jeff?

BIANCA: I'm not sure. He's smart, and his communication skills are good, but he doesn't seem to be engaged.

SUSAN: That's a concern, especially for someone who's new. We'll want to know how your time with him goes and what insights you have next week. Please be ready to share. I also want to be sure that we are fair but clear with Jeff. If there's an issue where we can help him, let's do it. We need him on our team, and we care about him as an individual. But let's also be clear—in his position, hitting the target is a critical element of performance. Good luck in the meeting. If I can help, just ask.

Susan's response is supportive but firm. Bianca is expected to understand the issue and, if possible, resolve it by next week. And she knows she'll be reporting during the next meeting. While Susan's hope for Jeff to succeed is authentic, she's also clear that performance is a requirement. It's a message that balances accountability with respect, for both Bianca and Jeff.

MARCUS: Well, as we've said, my team is behind target. The mystery to me is that everyone is working very hard, but we just can't seem to keep up. I wonder if we've set the goals too aggressively. I wasn't even able to keep my commitments for last week because I decided to just make prospecting calls myself to help make our numbers. I know the numbers are all that really matter.

SUSAN: Marcus, I know this is a tough moment for you. It is for all of us. Targets were increased for every team this year, and the pressure is high. But I also know what I've seen you do in the past, how you've found an answer and always lifted your team to a higher level. I know you can do that again, and I'm committed to help you. You aren't facing this alone.

In this moment, Susan knows she has a problem—a leader of a frontline team, one who has performed well in the past, is now overwhelmed and turning negative. She needs to address the issue, but first, she makes sure Marcus knows he has her respect and that she hasn't forgotten how well he's done in the past. On this foundation of respect, she can now hold him accountable in a way that will challenge Marcus to rise to a higher level of leadership.

> SUSAN: But I also need to be clear, Marcus. I am concerned that your mindset is part of the problem and may be affecting your team and their performance. I need to know that I can count on you to figure out what's missing for your team. I'd like for you to give this some thought, and then let's spend some time together this week to discuss it.

Susan knows that these words said in front of his peers will have an impact on Marcus. She's careful and respectful, while still being completely aboveboard: *something has to change.*

> MARCUS: I hate to admit it, but I know you're right. I'm committed to be a better leader than I have been these past few weeks, but I'm still uncertain what to do for my team.

> SUSAN: Thank you, Marcus. Why don't you and I meet this week to review your lead measures? We can use the five optimizing questions to brainstorm an adjustment, or a replacement, that will produce more leverage for your team.

> BIANCA: Marcus, I can also send you our new script for prospecting calls. It might be worth having both teams try it out. And if it's okay, I'd also like to join your meeting and go over the lead measures with you and Susan. There might be improvements that would help both teams.

Susan now has the entire team pulling together to reach a new level of performance. But more important, she's demonstrated that:

- They can trust her to be authentically clear.
- She will treat them and their teams with respect.

- She will consistently hold the entire team, and herself, to a high level of accountability.

This is leadership that produces results.

RECOGNIZING HIGH PERFORMANCE

At the heart of every team's performance, there are two fundamental forces at work: accountability and engagement. Accountability, as we've discussed, is the key driver of *what* people do and how they do it. It's the force that makes things happen in a team. Engagement, alternatively, is the key driver of *why* we do what we do. It affects the quality of the team's performance. Accountability leads to immediate and purposeful action. Engagement fuels the ability to sustain that performance over the long term.

Accountability is almost always present in a team (in some form), but true engagement is rare. When the influence of a leader of leaders is predominantly based on accountability, it creates teams that are highly compliant; they will do what they are told to do. Often the problem is that this is *all* they will do, nothing more. But when leaders of leaders combine accountability with genuine engagement, they create teams that are not only willing but *committed*. That's why coaching around recognition is a major emphasis in our 4DX implementation process.

Genuine recognition, based on performance, is one of the most powerful drivers of human performance. A Gallup survey found that 82 percent of employees say recognition, not rewards, motivates them to improve their job performance.[15] While no one is saying rewards aren't important, it's stunning to see such a high percentage saying *recognition matters more*.

We've said from the beginning that execution is, at its core, a human challenge. And every leader has seen (or sensed) the need for recognition in the people they lead, both as an indication of quality work and as a validation of the individual who performed it.

One of the greatest examples of engaged leadership we've encountered came from Dave Grissen, former President of the Americas for

Marriott International. Highly regarded as a strong, pragmatic leader of leaders, Dave brought no lack of intense accountability to his teams. And the results were evidence of how well his teams responded. But what is not widely known (outside of Marriott) is that he used the power of recognition to both drive performance and instill a sense of loyalty and worth in individuals at every level. Each week, Dave composed multiple notes to housekeepers, chefs, maintenance engineers, and baggage handlers on two continents—some were based on his personal interactions and others were based on what he learned from the people around them.

Dave's notes are now the stuff of legend. People *treasure* them. Some are framed, hanging on the wall in the office or at home. Others are photographed and shared on social media with friends and family with great pride. These notes *matter*, not just because they came from the President, but because they communicated that *the individual mattered to Dave*.

Leadership is communicating to people their worth and potential so clearly that they come to see it in themselves.

—Stephen R. Covey

This is what every note from Dave conveys: that he sees worth and value in them, and even more important, that he *appreciates* all they are doing to make the company great. The level of engagement he created is a direct result of a team who knows their worth is seen and their contribution is valued.

Keep in mind that the type of recognition we're advocating isn't grand or formal. Formal recognition has a place in most organizations and is valuable. But you don't need a company meeting or a crystal statue every time you want to convey this message. In fact, it's actually better if it's spontaneous, informal, and authentic. Whether your style is to pen a handwritten note, send an email, voice your appreciation during a meeting, or simply have a private conversation, recognition is one of the most powerful tools you possess as a leader of leaders.

Over the years, we've been able to distill the key attributes that make this type of recognition such a powerful driver of performance and to make them a definitive focus in the 4DX implementation process. If you're new to this practice or looking to raise your game, here's a high-level view of what we teach:

- **Be credible.** Acknowledge the performance you are recognizing. Avoid platitudes ("great job," "wonderful contribution," etc.), and instead include enough specifics that your message has credibility.
- **Be brief.** Resist the temptation to write a dissertation or give a speech. Focus instead on the contribution being recognized and your appreciation for the individual.
- **Be personal.** Avoid formal language or "leader speak."
- **Be authentic.** Say only what you mean and mean everything you say. Recognition that lacks sincerity can create *disengagement* and erode trust.

In closing this chapter, we want to briefly recap the 4DX implementation process we use in working with our clients. In essence, this is the "playbook" we offered, using XPS as a performance framework:

1. **Establishing a cadence.** The key to this element is consistency. The discipline to hold strongly to the cadence of a weekly WIG Session, regardless of the urgent demands of your whirlwind, is the foundation of an execution culture.
2. **Fulfilling high-impact commitments.** The key to this element is in making "second-level commitments"—commitments that work "on the system"—and setting a high standard for follow-through.
3. **Optimizing lead-measures performance.** The key to this component is challenging the lead measures of frontline teams through thought-provoking questions and being prepared to make changes or replacements when a lead measure isn't sufficiently moving the lag measure (WIG).
4. **Achieving lag-measure (WIG) results.** The key to this component is respectfully holding the leaders of frontline teams

accountable for performance and results, and authentically recognizing performance in a meaningful (and memorable) way.

We've highlighted Marriott in this chapter as our largest worldwide 4DX implementation. At this time, more than 70,000 leaders within the company have become formally certified in 4DX and have used XPS and the principles offered in this chapter to sustain performance *for more than a decade*. These leaders have made more than 7 million weekly commitments and followed through at a rate above 97 percent—where every commitment was focused on improving the experience of their guests. This is the level of focus that led them to become one of the largest and most respected hospitality companies in the world.

These core metrics illustrate that simple practices, in the hands of committed and engaged leaders, will produce results that not only represent a breakthrough, but can also be sustained (and improved) indefinitely.

As we quoted from our client in the beginning of this chapter, "We don't even think of 4DX as a methodology anymore. It's just the way we execute." This is the true definition of a *culture of execution*.

PART 3

Applying 4DX as a Leader of a Frontline Team

CHAPTER 11

What to Expect

As you learned in Part 1, 4DX is an operating system for achieving the goals you must achieve. Keep in mind that 4DX is not a set of suggestions or philosophical ideas that should be merely considered—4DX is a set of *disciplines* that will require your finest efforts, but whose payoff will be a team that performs consistently and with excellence.

In Part 2, you learned the key practices that drive 4DX as a leader who will lead other leaders in implementing 4DX. If you're a leader of a frontline team who will be implementing 4DX with *your own team*, you'll find a detailed insights from our experience in Part 3. Think of it as a valuable map with all the information we use with our clients to ensure their success.

THE BIG PICTURE

In Greek mythology, Sisyphus is a man whom the gods punish by requiring him to push a boulder up a mountain. Each time he reaches the peak, the stone rolls back down, and he has to push it back up the mountain all over again, for eternity! This is a little like leaving work at the end of an exhausting day without being able to point to a single significant accomplishment and knowing that tomorrow you'll push that boulder all over again.

Jim Dixon, the General Manager of Store 334 in a large grocery chain, felt very much like Sisyphus every day. Store 334 had the worst financial performance of the 250 stores in the division. People didn't want to shop there, and they didn't want to work there either.

Every day when Jim came to work, he would do what he called the head slap over the same old problems. Shopping carts and trash all over the parking lot. Broken bottles in the aisles. Big gaps in products on the shelves. Nothing in that store happened until Jim told somebody to do it or he did it himself. Midnight often found him stocking shelves or mopping up spilled milk. Not only had he hired people to do these things, he had hired people to *hire* people to do these things.

Like Sisyphus, Jim felt he was pushing the same boulder up the hill every day just to watch it roll down again. He never had time or energy to move the store forward in a significant way.

Jim had been considered a high-potential leader when he was put in charge at Store 334. Now he seemed to be a low-potential micromanager. We met Jim when we were engaged to use the 4DX implementation process to try and help Jim and his team succeed. At that point he'd been working sixteen days straight and hadn't taken a vacation in over a year. Sales were way down while employee turnover was up. The vice president of human resources confided to us, "Jim's either going to quit, or we're going to have to let him go."

With all he had to do, you can imagine how delighted Jim would be to go to a *4 Disciplines* work session on top of everything else. And in December too, which is the busiest time of the year for the grocery business.

For Jim and his department heads, the Wildly Important Goal was no mystery. If they didn't meet the year-over-year revenue figure, the store itself was in danger of closing. Nothing else mattered. However, the tricky problem was determining their lead measure. What could they do differently that they weren't doing already? What would have the most impact on driving up store revenues?

In our consulting session with Jim and his team, they were sure that if store conditions improved, revenue would improve. A clean, attractive, fully stocked store should draw more customers. So, we worked with the leader of each department to individually come up with the two or three most important things to measure for that department, and they decided to score themselves daily on a 1-to-10 scale.

For the meat department, fresh cuts in a crystal-clear display.

Shelves in the produce department fully stocked by five in the morning.

For the bakery, hot, fresh bread on the racks every two hours.

At the end of this stage in the 4DX implementation process, Jim and his team felt that they had a plan! They would start executing immediately, and the assistant manager and the department heads would update the scoreboard daily. The bet was that as store conditions improved, so would year-over-year revenue. It felt like it might work.

That morning they posted the scoreboards, and that night the employees tore them down. Despite their discouragement, the leaders in the store put the scoreboards back up again, but the whirlwind of day-to-day pressures sucked the department heads right back to where they had been before. After two weeks, the five departments were averaging thirteen out of fifty on a scale they'd created themselves! Jim was frustrated, and the Wildly Important Goal was in trouble.

It just wasn't working.

One day, for example, Jim found only day-old bread on the bakery racks and nothing but cookie crumbs in the display case.

"Yolanda!" He called the bakery manager. She appeared, covered with flour and simmering mad when he pointed at the scoreboard.

"I have too much to do to worry about that scoreboard," she retorted, hands on hips. "I got a big catering order that'll take all day. And I've got to do something about inventory 'cause I'm running out. There's just no time. I'm understaffed."

Sisyphus was alive and well. Despite the effort that had been exerted in choosing the WIG, the lead measures, the scoreboards, nothing had changed in the store. We pinpointed the reason.

In their rush to succeed, they'd forgotten Discipline 4. It was completely missing, and as a result, there was no cadence of accountability.

There was no regular weekly accounting to say, "Here's what I did *last* week, and here's what I'm going to do *this* week, to move that score." So we pleaded with Jim to meeting with his staff and asking each one this simple question: "What is the one thing you can do *this week* that would have the most impact on the scoreboard?"

Jim held his first WIG Session the next day. He promised it would take only a few minutes around the store scoreboard. When the department heads gathered, Jim started with the bakery manager.

"Yolanda, what is the one thing, just *one* thing, you could do that would have the biggest impact on the store-conditions scoreboard this week?"

Surprised by Jim's earnest look, Yolanda asked, "You want *me* to choose?"

Jim nodded . . . and waited.

"I guess I could get the back room cleaned out."

"Okay. And how would that move the score on store conditions?"

"Well, it's kind of cluttered. I've got a lot of extra racks out on the floor. If I can get the back room cleaned up, I can get some of that stuff off the floor. It'd look better."

"Great. Just that one thing, Yolanda. That's it." Then he turned to the seafood manager. "Ted, what's the one thing you could do this week that would have the biggest impact on your score?"

"I have a big promotion this week," Ted replied. "I'll be focused on the lobster special we are preparing for. That's what I'm doing."

"That's great, Ted. I know that's important, and you need to do that, but how is that going to move the scoreboard?"

"Oh, I see what you're getting at." Something clicked for Ted. The special, while important, wouldn't by itself contribute to improving store conditions—the *Wildly* Important Goal. "Yeah, okay. Bobby's been here three weeks and doesn't know how to set up the displays in the morning . . . I'll get him trained, and he can back me up."

"Perfect!" Jim responded.

Ask yourself—who was coming up with these ideas? Jim or his department heads? Do you think that makes much of a difference?

Was Jim micromanaging now? No! The staff members themselves were choosing what to do to move the score. He *had* been micromanaging, not because he wanted to be an overbearing boss, but because he didn't know what else to do!

So Jim's staff met every week around the scoreboard, committing to one another to do just *one* thing to move the score. As the team started working in rhythm, in a cadence of accountability to one another, their attitudes changed, and the store changed.

After ten weeks, the average score on store conditions rose from 13 to 38 on the scale of 50. Furthermore, their strategic bet paid off. As the scores on store conditions went up, so did the revenue.

Store 334—the worst of 250 stores—went on to outproduce the rest of the zone in year-over-year sales!

A few months later, we conducted a debrief meeting with the president of Jim's division to hear Jim report on the progress of the store.

He told them, "Things are going so well, I didn't even have to go in this morning."

The divisional president asked him, "What has this change meant to you personally?"

Jim replied, "I was going to carry this store on my back until I could get a transfer. Now you can leave me there as long as you want."

Jim Dixon and his team now knew how it felt to win at a Wildly Important Goal. They didn't need external motivation.

Deep down, everyone wants to win. Everyone wants to contribute to goals that matter. It's so disheartening to push day in and day out and wonder if you're making a difference. That's why 4DX is so vital. The people at Store 334 learned that. The disciplines make the difference between pushing that rock up the hill forever or taking it over the top.

THE FIVE STAGES OF CHANGE

Because changing human behavior is such a big job, many leaders face challenges like these when installing 4DX. In fact, we've found that most teams go through five stages of behavior change. In this chapter, we hope to help you understand and manage your way through these stages.

Stage 1: Getting Clear

STAGE 1: Getting Clear

The leader and the team commit to a new level of performance. They are oriented to 4DX and develop crystal-clear WIGs, lag and lead measures, and a compelling scoreboard. They commit to regular WIG Sessions. Although you can naturally expect varying levels of commitment, team members will be more motivated if they are closely involved in the *4DX* work session.

Let's follow Marilyn, leader of the surgical nursing unit at a large inner-city hospital, as she installs 4DX with her team. She and her team face a whirlwind like no other, as lives literally depend on how well they execute dozens of surgeries every day.

Marilyn's team had recently seen a sharp rise in *perioperative* incidents—things that go wrong in surgery. Despite the raging whirlwind of an operating room, the team shared a passion for reducing such incidents.

In a *4DX* work session, they translated this focus into a Wildly Important Goal: Increase surgeries without perioperative incidents from 89 to 98 percent by December 31.

The team then carefully reviewed the factors that caused the most incidents, as well as those that created the greatest risk to patients, and isolated two lead measures that would give them the greatest leverage: Achieve 100 percent compliance on all presurgery audits at least thirty minutes before surgery, and double-count surgical items following 100 percent of surgeries.

Now that Marilyn and her team had a Wildly Important Goal (Discipline 1) and two lead measures (Discipline 2), they designed a simple scoreboard (Discipline 3) for tracking their performance and scheduled a weekly WIG Session to hold themselves accountable for continuous progress (Discipline 4).

As they closed the team meeting, Marilyn looked forward to the launch the next week. She had never felt clearer about a goal and a plan. The rest, she thought, would be easy.

Of course, she was underestimating the task. It is inherently difficult to change human behavior in the midst of a raging whirlwind. Success starts by getting to crystal clarity on the WIG and the 4DX implementation process. Remember your key actions in implementing 4DX:

- Be a model of focus on the Wildly Important Goal(s).
- Identify high-leverage lead measures.
- Create a players' scoreboard.
- Schedule WIG Sessions at least weekly and *hold* them.

Stage 2: Launch

STAGE 2: Launch

Now the team is at the starting line. Whether you hold a formal kickoff meeting or gather your team in a brief huddle, you launch the team into action on the WIG. But just as a rocket requires tremendous, highly focused energy to escape the earth's gravity, the team needs intense involvement from the leader at this point of launch.

Marilyn launched the 4DX process beginning with the first surgery of the week: Monday morning at seven. By noon, the team was already struggling. The lead measure required the nurses to do equipment audits twenty minutes earlier than normal, but the schedule change and a new checklist confused everyone.

With a full surgical schedule and a nurse home sick, Marilyn was stretched and her team was scrambling. That first morning taught her about the problems of executing in the midst of the whirlwind.

Marilyn also noticed that some were more willing to change than others. Her top performers were succeeding, and although it wasn't easy, they relished the challenge. However, two of her most senior nurses still wondered why the change in the audit routine was needed and complained about the added stress. Furthermore, Marilyn saw that the newer nurses, who were not yet confident in their roles, were actually slowing down the audit.

That week, Marilyn realized that what was simple to plan was very difficult to launch. She faced not only a whirlwind but a team with mixed motivations.

The launch phase of 4DX is not guaranteed to go smoothly. You will have your Models (those who get on board), your Not Yets (those who struggle at first), and your Nevers (those who don't want to get on board). Here are some keys to a successful launch:

Recognize that a launch phase requires focus and energy— especially from the leader.

Remain focused and implement the 4DX process diligently. You can trust the process.

Identify your Models, Not Yets, and Nevers (more on these groups below).

Stage 3: Adoption

Marilyn worked hard to maintain focus on the WIG. Her team adjusted their schedules and refined their methods of scorekeeping. She trained and coached her Not Yets. She counseled the Nevers about the need for change.

> ## STAGE 3: Adoption
>
> Team members adopt the 4DX
> process, and new behaviors drive
> the achievement of the WIG.
> You can expect resistance to
> fade and enthusiasm to increase
> as 4DX begins to work for them.
> They become accountable to
> each other for the new level of
> performance despite the
> demands of the whirlwind.

Each week, they worked at the lead measures, and they slowly improved. When they met in their weekly WIG Sessions, they first reviewed their scoreboard and then individually made commitments to move the needle on the scores.

Before long, Marilyn sensed the team finding its rhythm, and the incident rate declined. As the team saw that the lead measures were working, their excitement grew. For the first time in many months, they felt that they were winning.

Recognize that adoption of the new 4DX process will take time. Adherence to the process is essential to your success on the WIG. Be respectful but diligent about sticking with the process. Otherwise, the whirlwind will quickly take over. These are the keys to successful adoption of 4DX:

- Focus first on adherence to the process, then on results.
- Make commitments and hold one another accountable in weekly WIG Sessions.
- Track results each week on a visible scoreboard.
- Make adjustments as needed.
- Invest in the Not Yets through additional training and mentoring.

- Respond straightforwardly to issues with Nevers, and clear the path for them if needed.

Stage 4: Optimization

> ### Stage 4: Optimization
>
> At this stage, the team shifts to a 4DX mindset. You can expect them to become more purposeful and more engaged in their work as they produce results that make a difference. They will start looking for ways to optimize their performance—they now know what "playing to win" feels like.

Over the next eight weeks, Marilyn was pleased with her team's progress and with the steady though small decline in surgical incidents. But the team would have to pick up the pace to reach the WIG by the end of the year, and she wasn't sure what more they could do.

In the WIG Session later that day, her nurses surprised her by proposing changes to the lead measures. First, they wanted to reposition the equipment trays in the operating room so they could do their audits more quickly and accurately. Second, if they audited the operating rooms for both first and second surgeries simultaneously at the beginning of the shift, they could stay ahead of schedule the rest of the day. Third, they suggested the patient-transport team notify them as soon as the patient was on the way to surgery, giving them time to cross-check the operating room a final time.

Marilyn was pleased and surprised that her team had found these ways to optimize their performance. It struck her that if she had proposed these things herself, the team probably would have resisted the extra work. But because the ideas came from them, they were not only willing but excited to carry them out.

Marilyn had created a game that mattered, and now her team was playing to win.

The nurses took ownership of the process. They kept coming up with new ways to move the lead measures, and the lag measure continued to rise. Their weekly commitments were precise and their follow-through excellent. The WIG Sessions were tightly focused on results.

However, what really fascinated Marilyn was the new level of engagement and an energy she had never seen before.

If you're consistent about 4DX, you can expect team members to begin optimizing it on their own. Here are keys to making the most of this stage:

- Encourage and recognize abundant creative ideas for moving the lead measures, even if some work better than others.
- Recognize excellent follow-through, and celebrate successes.
- Encourage team members to clear the path for one another, and celebrate this when it happens.
- Recognize when the Not Yets start performing like the Models.

Stage 5: Habits

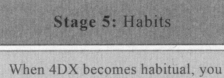

Stage 5: Habits

When 4DX becomes habitual, you can expect not only to reach the goal, but also see a permanent rise in the level of your team's performance. The ultimate aim of 4DX is not just to get results, but to create a culture of excellent execution.

Eleven months prior, Marilyn had been facing a crisis—the rising incident rate could have impacted her job and, much more important, the lives of her patients. Now she and her team were recognized for having exceeded their goal and for the lowest incident rate in the hospital's history.

Marilyn knew that the change in her team went far beyond the achievement of their goal; they had fundamentally changed the way they performed and, in the process, had developed habits of execution that would ensure future success. The behavior changes that had been so hard to make were now standard performance for her team. In essence, the practices that reduced surgical incidents were now a normal component of her whirlwind, but because of them, her whirlwind had become far more manageable.

As a result, she knew the team could sustain a whole new level of focus and commitment; and as they turned to a new WIG, they were on a winning track.

4DX is habit-forming. Once the new behaviors become ingrained in the day-to-day operation, you can set new goals and execute with excellence again and again. Here are keys to help the team make 4DX habitual:

- Celebrate the accomplishment of the WIG.
- Move immediately to new WIGs in order to formalize 4DX as your operating system.
- Emphasize that your new operating standard is sustained superior performance on lead measures.
- Help individual team members become high performers.

One example of great performance is Erasmus University Medical Center near Rotterdam in the Netherlands. As in the rest of the world, European hospitals face a disturbing increase in lethal hospital-acquired infections (HAIs), which are estimated to account for two-thirds of the 25,000 hospital deaths each year on the Continent.

At Erasmus MC, infections were still within acceptable limits, but administrators were determined to wipe them out. To achieve their

WIG, they adopted a set of lead measures they called *search and destroy,* which eliminated nearly all HAIs within five years. To their credit, the entire hospital system of the Netherlands followed their lead.[16]

By definition, hospitals are filled with sick people. Germs abound. And most hospitals seem content with infection rates within accepted norms. However, for a high-performance team like the administrators of Erasmus University Medical Center, the only acceptable infection rate is *zero.*

Within a matter of months, vulnerable patients stopped getting sick and dying.

In our experience—whether with hospitals, grocery chains, engineering firms, hotels, software companies, power plants, government contractors, or multiunit retail operations—the outcome is almost always the same: a new culture of high performance along with consistent results.

Getting there isn't easy and doesn't happen overnight. It takes focus and discipline *over time* to implement 4DX and to make it stick. The pattern to expect usually looks like this.

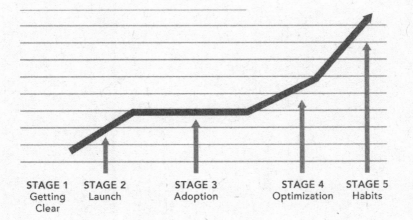

| STAGE 1 | STAGE 2 | STAGE 3 | STAGE 4 | STAGE 5 |
| Getting Clear | Launch | Adoption | Optimization | Habits |

Initially, results improve quickly, but we've noticed a plateau period as the team works to adopt the new mindset. Once team *members* become habituated to 4DX, it starts to pay real dividends.

We began this book by pointing out that possibly the single greatest challenge you will face as a leader is driving a strategy that depends on changing human behavior. 4DX is a proven system for meeting that challenge, not just once, but again and again.

In the following chapters, we will take you carefully through each discipline.

CHAPTER 12

Applying Discipline 1: Focus on the Wildly Important

In our 4DX implementation process, superb team performance begins with selecting a single Team WIG during our initial consulting sessions. Focusing on a single breakthrough goal is the foundational principle of 4DX. Without it, your team will get lost in the whirlwind.

Many teams have multiple goals—sometimes dozens, all of which are Priority One. Of course, that means nothing is Priority One. A client of ours put it best: "When you work on that many goals, you actually work on none of them, because the amount of energy you can put into each one is so small, it's meaningless."

Selecting the right WIG is crucial. Leaders often hesitate to narrow their focus because they worry about the consequences of choosing the wrong WIG or failing to achieve it. Still, when you choose a WIG, you're starting a game that matters—one where the stakes are high, and the team can make a real difference. Discipline 1 is necessary if you're going to play to win.

To illustrate, imagine being the principal of a school serving the poorest students in one of the poorest cities in one of the poorest counties in California. The school had an enrollment of over seven hundred students, of which close to 90 percent were economically disadvantaged, and that percentage was rising. What was *not* rising was the students' statewide standardized assessment performance. Such was the situation for Carmel Elementary Principal Craig Gunter.

During a working session with FranklinCovey, Craig was introduced to the 4 Disciplines of Execution (4DX). As a seasoned educator, Craig was well versed in goal setting, but something about 4DX struck Craig as different. 4DX appeared to be a way to actually *execute* his written goals. It was something much more than simply writing a goal and hoping for results, or writing a huge School Improvement Plan burdened with too many strategies to manage. Craig believed 4DX could be their solution.

Working with FranklinCovey, he set WIGs at the student level, and then Carmel established schoolwide scoreboards to represent progress on their reading WIG. Students had common lead measures: read thirty minutes per night, and after completing an Accelerated Reader book, achieve 85 percent on the comprehension assessment. Celebrations occurred when students met their point and accuracy goal. The result? Carmel went from 240 students meeting their Accelerated Reader accuracy goal one year to over 600 students meeting their goal the following year.

STEP 1. CONSIDER THE POSSIBILITIES

The 4DX implementation process used by our consultants begins by brainstorming possible WIGs. Although you might feel you already know what the WIG should be, you might end this process with entirely different WIGs. In our sessions, this happens often. The brainstorming proceeds differently, depending on the kind of organization you belong to and the role of your team.

Before we begin, we note that if your organization does not have a Primary WIG (4DX), then we substitute an existing element of the company's strategy (profitability, revenue, quality, customer satisfaction, etc.). Your Team WIG should always align to an outcome that drives the company's strategy forward.

IF ➡	THEN
The team is part of an organization with many goals ➡	Gather ideas on which of the organizational goals are more crucial than others.
The organization has already designated WIG(s) at the top level ➡	Gather ideas on how to contribute to the established WIG(s).
The team is the organization (e.g., a small business or nonprofit) ➡	Gather ideas that will have the most impact on achieving the mission or growing the organization.

Getting Input

For most of our clients, there are three options for the consulting sessions we conduct:

1. You can brainstorm with peer leaders, especially if you are all focusing on the same Primary WIG for the organization. If you're concerned that your peers might not understand your team's operation, we want to assure you that their outside perspective will still be valuable, particularly if you depend on them or they depend on you.
2. You can brainstorm with your team or with a representative subset of the team. Obviously, if the team is involved in selecting the WIG, they will take ownership of it more readily.
3. You can brainstorm alone. You will still be able to validate the WIG with your team when you introduce it to them later.

Top-Down or Bottom-Up?

Should WIGs come from the leader or from the team?

Top-down: A leader who imposes WIGs without input from the team might have problems getting team ownership. If they drive accountability mostly through their authority, they probably won't develop a

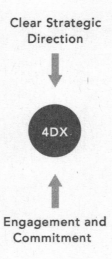

Clear Strategic
Direction

4DX

Engagement and
Commitment

With the 4 Disciplines, leaders provide top-down strategic direction in defining the
WIG, while team members provide active input that increases their engagement and
commitment to the WIG.

high-performance team and will pay a price in low retention and limited creativity and innovation.

Bottom-up: WIGs that come exclusively from the team might lack relevance to the overall WIG. Without strong direction, the team could lose valuable time and energy in getting consensus on every move.

Top-down *and* **bottom-up:** Ideally, both the leader and the team participate in defining the WIGs. Only the leader can clarify what matters most. The leader is ultimately responsible for the WIG but should actively engage team members in the process. To reach the goal and transform the team, team members must be able to provide active input in defining the WIG.

Discovery Questions

In our consulting sessions, we've found these three questions to be useful in discovering the WIG.

"Which one area of our team's performance would represent our greatest contribution to the Primary WIG of the organization?" This question is more useful than "What's the most important thing we can do?"

"What are the greatest strengths of the team that can be leveraged to ensure the Primary WIG is achieved?" This question will generate ideas in areas where your team is already succeeding, but where they can also take their performance to an even higher level.

"What are the areas where the team's poor performance most needs to be improved to ensure the Primary WIG is achieved?" This question will generate ideas around performance gaps that, if not improved, represent a threat to achieving the Primary WIG.

Our consultants emphasize that you shouldn't settle for a few ideas for the Team WIG. Gather as many ideas in the session as you can reasonably capture. Our experience shows that the longer and more creative the list of possible Team WIGs, the higher-quality the final choice.

Think what, not how. We guide our clients to avoid the common mistake at this point of shifting their focus from the Team WIG itself to how to achieve it. The how is the new and better behavior (lead measures) that will lead to the WIG. That discussion comes later in Discipline 2.

One of our clients, a five-star hotel chain, had this Primary WIG: Increase total profit from $54 million to $62 million by December 31. In our consulting sessions with them, the various departments in one hotel brainstormed ideas for their Team WIGs:

Housekeeping	Clean guestrooms like they've never been cleaned before. We're already the best—let's get better!
Restaurant	Make alliances with local sports and culture venues.
Valet Parking	Ensure no one waits for their car.
Reception	Move guests through the system more quickly. No more queues at the registration desk.

Let's look at the actual list of ideas from one department: Event Management. Since this group can impact profit by both increasing revenue and reducing expenses, they brainstormed ideas to do both.

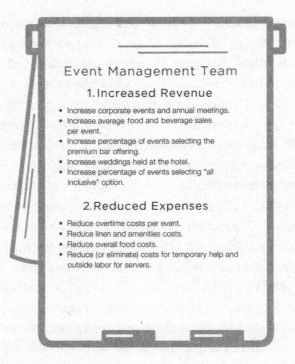

Event Management Team

1. Increased Revenue

- Increase corporate events and annual meetings.
- Increase average food and beverage sales per event.
- Increase percentage of events selecting the premium bar offering.
- Increase weddings held at the hotel.
- Increase percentage of events selecting "all inclusive" option.

2. Reduced Expenses

- Reduce overtime costs per event.
- Reduce linen and amenities costs.
- Reduce overall food costs.
- Reduce (or eliminate) costs for temporary help and outside labor for servers.

STEP 2. RANK BY IMPACT

When our clients are satisfied with their list of candidate Team WIGs, they're ready to identify the one that promises the greatest potential impact *on the Primary WIG*.

Calculating the impact of a Team WIG depends on the nature of the Primary WIG:

If the overall WIG is	Then rank the WIG in terms of
A financial goal	Prospective revenues, profitability, investment performance, cash flow, and/or cost savings.
A quality goal	Efficiencies gained, cycle times, productivity improvements, and/or customer satisfaction.
A strategic goal	Service to the mission, competitive advantages gained, opportunities captured, and/or threats reduced.

Serena, who runs the Event Management team in the hotel, is responsible for meetings, banquets, and special events. In step 1 of our session, they identified Team WIGs that would contribute to the Primary WIG of profit.

To narrow this list, they then calculated the financial impact of each idea. It wasn't hard to identify the ideas that would generate the most profit for her team, but that was not the right focus.

The real challenge was to rank the ideas in terms of impact *on the overall organizational WIG*—in other words, to isolate those that would generate the most profit for the *entire hotel*. When we guided them to this different ranking, corporate events and weddings rose to the top because they generated revenue beyond the event itself, through rooms booked by out-of-town guests, restaurant meals, even spa services.

In the 4DX implementation process, we caution leaders to avoid the trap of selecting WIGs that improve the team's performance but might have little to do with achieving the overall WIG.

In the end, Serena and her team chose two candidate WIGs that would clearly have the greatest impact on the overall WIG:

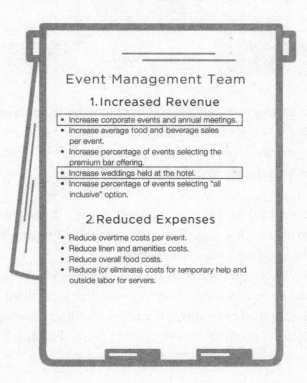

Event Management Team

1. Increased Revenue
- Increase corporate events and annual meetings.
- Increase average food and beverage sales per event.
- Increase percentage of events selecting the premium bar offering.
- Increase weddings held at the hotel.
- Increase percentage of events selecting "all inclusive" option.

2. Reduced Expenses
- Reduce overtime costs per event.
- Reduce linen and amenities costs.
- Reduce overall food costs.
- Reduce (or eliminate) costs for temporary help and outside labor for servers.

STEP 3. TEST TOP IDEAS

Once they've identified a few Team WIG candidates, we take our clients through the process of testing four specific criteria:

1. Is the Team WIG aligned to the overall WIG?
2. Is it measurable?
3. Who owns the results—our team or some other team?
4. Who owns the game—the leader or the team?

Is it aligned? The 4DX implementation process requires that there be an unbroken line of sight between the candidate Team WIG and the Primary WIG. To create meaningful Team WIGs, you should have a clear line of sight between your team (in the center) and the WIGs of the overall organization (if they can be identified).

Although this test may seem obvious, many teams become so excited about an idea, that they forget achievement of the overall WIG is the top priority. If the idea fails this test, eliminate it and choose the next most high-impact idea from the list.

Is it measurable? As one of our clients put it, "If you're not keeping score, you're just practicing." A game without a clearly measurable score will never be a game that matters.

A Team WIG requires that a credible measurement be in place *from the day you begin executing.* If significant effort is required before you begin measuring—for example, if you need to build a system to track results before you can begin—it should be crossed off for now. Once the system is running, reconsider it, but time invested in a game without a score is time lost.

Who owns the result? Does the team have at least 80 percent ownership of the result? This test is about eliminating significant dependence on other teams. The conceptual measure of 80 percent can help you determine how much your team will have to depend on other teams to achieve the WIG.

If it's less than 80 percent, neither team will take responsibility and accountability will be lost.

Of course, if two teams own the same WIG, joint ownership can be a powerful driver of performance, so long as both teams, and both leaders, understand that they win or lose together.

Who owns the game—leader or team? Is it a leader's game or a team game? This final test is more subtle than the others, but equally important. The question is whether results are driven by the performance of the leader or the performance of the team.

If the WIG depends too much on functions that only the leader performs, the team will quickly lose interest in the game. The Team WIG should depend primarily on what the team does, not just the leader.

These tests may seem straightforward, but our consultants take great care in each of the answers.

Failure to pass any of these tests means you must reevaluate the idea you're considering. Don't ask the team to play a game that's flawed; under the pressure of accountability, those flaws will quickly become apparent.

STEP 4. DEFINE THE WIG

Once our clients have tested their ideas and selected a final Team WIG, we work to make it as clear and measurable as possible. We define the Team WIG according to the following rules:

- Begin with a verb.
- Define the lag measure in terms of *From X to Y by When*.

- Keep it simple.
- Focus on what, not how.

Begin With a Verb

Simple verbs focus the mind immediately on action. Almost all multi-syllabic verbs have simple equivalents.

Long, overwrought introductions are also unnecessary. Just state the WIG:

THIS	NOT THIS
Cut costs... Grow revenue... Raise customer-satisfaction score... Add one plant... Launch product...	In order to drive increased value to our shareholders, enhance the careers of our employees, and remain true to our fundamental values, we will be implementing a Wildly Important Goal this year to...

Define the Lag Measure

Lag measures tell you if you've achieved the goal. They mark a precise finish line for the team. We then write the lag measure in the format *From X to Y by When,* as these examples show.

Current Result (From X)	Desired Result (To Y)	Deadline (By When)
11% error rate	4% error rate	July 31
8 inventory turns per year	10 inventory turns per year	fiscal year-end
12% return on investment per year	30% return on investment per year	within 3 years

Our client's resulting WIG looks like this:

- Decrease routing error rate from 11 to 4 percent by July 31.

- Raise annual inventory-turn rate from 8 to 10 by fiscal year-end.
- Increase our average ROI from 12 to 30 percent within three years.

Keep It Simple

Earlier, we shared the startling fact that 85 percent of our client's team usually cannot state from memory their team's most important goal. Most organizational goals are vague, complex, and pretentious.

THIS	NOT THIS
Raise our customer-loyalty score from 40 to 70 by December 31.	"We are committed to enhancing and enriching our relationships with our customers."
Increase customer utilization of our investment counseling service by 25% this fiscal year.	"Our principal aim for the coming fiscal year is to facilitate investment, infrastructure, and access growth through effective coordination."
Launch three $10 million bio products within five years.	"We hope to foster industry innovation by addressing needs for bio-based resources through biotechnology."

Focus on What, Not How

Many teams define a clear Team WIG but then complicate it by adding a lengthy description of how the goal will be achieved.

THIS	NOT THIS
Increase guest retention from 63% to 75% over the next two years.	Increase guest retention from 63% to 75% over the next two years through providing exceptional customer experiences.

We help our clients avoid this by identifying *how* they plan to achieve the Team WIG when they develop lead measures in Discipline 2. Their WIG should focus exclusively on *what* the team plans to achieve.

MAKE SURE THE WIG IS ACHIEVABLE

We often encounter leaders who believe in setting goals that are far beyond anything their team can achieve, while privately acknowledging that they'll be satisfied if they get 75 percent of the goal. This type of gamesmanship can significantly undermine your ability to drive engagement and results.

We want to be very careful here. We're not advocating goals that are easy to reach. We guide our clients to set a goal that challenges the team to rise to their highest level of performance but not beyond it. In other words, create a WIG that is both *worthy* and *winnable*.

THE DELIVERABLE

The deliverable from our consulting session for Discipline 1 is a Team WIG with *From X to Y by When* (lag measure).

You now know that the simplicity of a WIG is deceptive—it will be *challenging* to achieve. However, the team now has a clear focus on what matters most, a focus that can be sustained beyond the day-to-day requirements of the team's operation. Like a compass, the Team WIG provides clear, consistent direction toward a result that's *wildly important*.

WIG Builder

1. Brainstorm ideas for the WIG.
2. Brainstorm lag measures for each idea (From X to Y by When).
3. Rank in order of importance to the organization or to the overall WIG.
4. Test your ideas against the checklist on the following page.
5. Write your final WIG(s).

Ideas for the WIG	Current Result (From X)	Desired Result (To Y)	Deadline (By When)	Rank

Final WIG(s)

_____

_____

_____

_____

Did You Get It Right?

Check off each item to ensure your Team WIGs and lag measures meet the standard:

☐ Have you have gathered rich input both top-down and bottom-up?

☐ Will the Team WIG have a clear, predictable impact on the overall organizational WIG or strategy, not just on team performance?

☐ Is the Team WIG the most impactful thing the team can do to drive achievement of the overall WIG?

☐ Does the team clearly have the power to achieve the WIG without heavy dependence on other teams?

☐ Does the WIG require the focus of the entire team, not just of the leader or a subgroup?

☐ Is the lag measure written in the format "From X to Y by When"?

☐ Can the WIG be simplified any further? Does it start with a simple verb and end with a clear lag measure?

CHAPTER 13

Applying Discipline 2: Act on the Lead Measures

Great teams invest their best efforts in those few activities that have the most impact on the Team WIG: the lead measures. This insight is crucial and distinctive, yet so little understood that we call it the secret of excellence in execution. Unlike lag measures (*From X to Y by When*), which tell you if you *have* achieved your goal, lead measures tell you if you are *likely* to achieve your goal. You will use lead measures to track those activities that have the highest leverage on the Team WIG.

Lead measures must be both *predictive* of achieving the Team WIG and *influenceable* by the team, as these examples show:

Team	Lag Measure	Lead Measure
Hospital Quality-Improvement Team	Decrease mortality rate in the hospital from 4% to 2% this year.	Evaluate susceptible patients twice a day against pneumonia prevention protocols.
Shipping Company Dispatching Team	Reduce trucking costs by 12% this quarter.	Ensure 90% of trips are with fully loaded trucks.
Restaurant	Increase average check amount by 10% by year end.	Suggest the specialty cocktail of the day to 90% of tables.

Each of these lead measures is both predictive and influenceable. The team can manageably act on the lead measure, which in turn will move the lag measure.

Acting on lead measures is essential to superb performance, but it is also the single most difficult aspect of the 4DX implementation process we lead with our clients.

There are three reasons for this:

Lead measures can be counterintuitive. Most leaders focus on lag measures, the bottom-line results that ultimately matter. This focus is only natural. But you cannot *act* on a lag measure because it's in the past.

Lead measures are hard to track. They are measures of new and different behaviors, and tracking behaviors is much harder than tracking results. Often there is no readily available system for tracking lead measures, so you might have to invent such a system.

Lead measures often look too simple. They demand a precise focus on a certain behavior that might look insignificant (although it isn't), particularly to those outside the team.

For example, a retail store chose this lead measure for driving a Team WIG of increasing sales: Limit out-of-stocks on top items to twenty or fewer per week. Can this very common measure really make an important difference? And shouldn't they be doing that already? But if this simple lever is applied inconsistently, customers who can't find what they want will not return.

Often lead measures simply close the gap between knowing what to do and actually doing it. Just as a simple lever can move a big rock, a good lead measure provides powerful leverage.

TWO TYPES OF LEAD MEASURES

Before you and your team develop lead measures, we want you to understand more about the types and characteristics of these powerful drivers of execution. To begin, there are two types of lead measures that can be developed through the 4DX implementation process: small outcomes and leveraged behaviors.

Small outcomes are lead measures that focus the team on achieving a weekly result but give each member of the team latitude to choose their own method for achieving it. "Limit out-of-stocks to twenty or fewer per week" is a small-outcome lead measure where a variety of actions could be applied. Whatever actions they choose, with a small-outcome lead measure, the team is ultimately accountable for producing the result.

Leveraged behaviors are lead measures that track the specific behaviors you want the team to perform throughout the week. They enable the entire team to adopt new behaviors at the same level of consistency and quality, as well as provide a clear measurement of how well they are performed. With a leveraged-behavior lead measure, the team is accountable for performing the behavior rather than producing the result.

Both types of lead measures are *equally valid* applications of Discipline 2 and are powerful drivers of results.

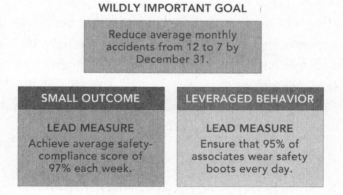

WILDLY IMPORTANT GOAL

Reduce average monthly accidents from 12 to 7 by December 31.

SMALL OUTCOME

LEAD MEASURE
Achieve average safety-compliance score of 97% each week.

LEVERAGED BEHAVIOR

LEAD MEASURE
Ensure that 95% of associates wear safety boots every day.

This example is drawn from the 4DX implementation process at Younger Brothers Construction, where the Team WIG was a lower accident rate. They chose the small outcome of compliance to safety standards, which involved driving multiple new behaviors. If they had believed that their team would be unsuccessful focusing on six behaviors, they could have chosen to begin with a single leveraged behavior of, say, wearing safety boots (one of the six safety standards) and, over time, incorporate the additional behaviors as new habits for the team.

WILDLY IMPORTANT GOAL

Increase average weekly sales
from $1 million to $1.5 million
by December 31.

SMALL OUTCOME	LEVERAGED BEHAVIOR
LEAD MEASURE	**LEAD MEASURE**
Limit out-of-stocks on top items to 20 or fewer per week.	Complete 2 additional shelf reviews each day, filling all holes on top items.

This example is drawn from the 4DX implementation process with a large grocery chain, where one of the most powerful drivers of the Team WIG of increased sales was ensuring that the top-selling products were always available to customers. They chose to focus on a leveraged behavior, "Complete two additional shelf reviews every shift," in which every member of the team could participate.

We want you to see from these examples that both types of lead measures give your team leverage for achieving the Team WIG. It's not a question of *which* is a better lead measure. It's a question of which is a better lead measure *for your team*.

Here are the steps for arriving at high-leverage lead measures utilized in the 4DX implementation process.

STEP 1. CONSIDER THE POSSIBILITIES

We begin our consulting session by brainstorming possible lead measures. In these sessions, we encourage our clients to resist the temptation to choose quickly. Our experience has taught us that the greater the number of ideas generated, the higher the quality of the lead measures.

We've found these questions useful in discovering lead measures:

- What could we do that we've never done before that might make all the difference to the Team WIG?

- What strengths of this team can we use as leverage on the Team WIG? Where are our "pockets of excellence"? What do our best performers do differently?
- What weaknesses might keep us from achieving the Team WIG? What could we do more consistently?

For example, a grocery store once chose this Team WIG: "Increase year-over-year sales by 5 percent." Here are some candidate lead measures we helped them create:

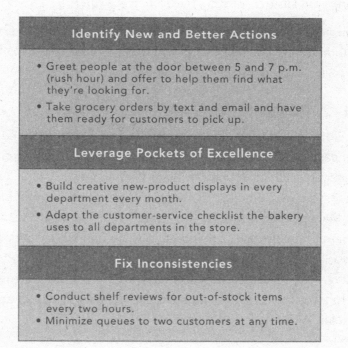

Identify New and Better Actions

- Greet people at the door between 5 and 7 p.m. (rush hour) and offer to help them find what they're looking for.
- Take grocery orders by text and email and have them ready for customers to pick up.

Leverage Pockets of Excellence

- Build creative new-product displays in every department every month.
- Adapt the customer-service checklist the bakery uses to all departments in the store.

Fix Inconsistencies

- Conduct shelf reviews for out-of-stock items every two hours.
- Minimize queues to two customers at any time.

Stay solely focused on ideas that will drive the Team WIG. Don't drift into a general discussion of good things to do rather than things that will impact the Team WIG, or you will end up with a long list of irrelevancies.

A famous example of a productive lead measure is the 15 percent rule at the 3M Company. For decades, this great company has held out the strategic WIG of creating a flow of great new products that never stops. To drive this goal, they adopted the lead measure of requiring their research teams to devote 15 percent of their time on projects of their choice. Author Jim Collins comments:

> No one is told what products to work on, just how much to work. And that loosening of controls has led to a stream of profitable innovations, from the famous Post-it Notes to less well-known examples such as reflective license plates and machines that replace the functions of the human heart during surgery. 3M's sales and earnings have increased more than forty-fold since instituting the 15 percent rule.[17]

The ideal lead measure, like 3M's 15 percent rule, is extremely fruitful in driving the WIG and is within the control of the team.

STEP 2. RANK BY IMPACT

When both we and the client are satisfied with the list of candidate lead measures, they're ready to identify the ideas that promise the greatest potential impact on the Team WIG.

In service of the hotel's Primary WIG to increase profitability, the Event Management team set this Team WIG: Increase revenue from corporate events from $22 million to $31 million by December 31.

In a 4DX work session, we helped Serena and her team in brainstorming lead measures for this Team WIG. We then narrowed the focus to three ideas that would have the greatest impact on achieving their Team WIG:

1. *Increase the number of site visits.* Serena's team knew from experience that whenever they could influence a customer to visit the hotel, their success at winning the contract for the event was significantly higher.
2. *Upsell the premium bar package.* Since margins were highest on products in the premium bar package, every event that upgraded to this option increased not only revenue but profitability.
3. *Generate more high-quality proposals.* The proposal was the last step

Event Management Team

WIG: Increase revenue from corporate events from $22 million to $31 million by December 31.

Lead-Measure Ideas

- Increase the number of site visits we conduct.
- Develop contacts at new local corporations.
- Explore additional opportunities for events with existing clients.
- Attend trade shows for corporate events.
- Develop and implement a new marketing program.
- Improve our banquet food options.
- Upsell our premium bar package.
- Upsell our expanded audio-visual package.
- Generate more high-quality proposals.
- Join meeting-planner associations and attend meetings.
- Contact former clients lost to other hotels and win them back.

in the sales process, so the more often prospects advanced to this stage, the more likely they would buy. The idea was to make sure each proposal went through a checklist of winning quality standards.

Watch Out

After producing the list of candidate lead measures, we often hear team members say, "We need to do all of these things." No doubt they are all good things to do, but the more you try to do, the less energy you have to give to any one thing.

Additionally, narrowing the focus to a few lead measures permits stronger leverage. As we often say, "A lever must move a lot to move the rock a little." In other words, the team must press hard on the lead measure to move the lag measure. Too many lead measures, and you dissipate that pressure.

STEP 3. TEST TOP IDEAS

Once we identified a few high-leverage lead-measure ideas, we then helped the team test them against these six criteria:

- Is it predictive?
- Is it influenceable?
- Is it an ongoing process or a "one-and-done"?
- Is it a leader's game or a team game?
- Can it be measured?
- Is it worth measuring?

Is the Measure Predictive of Achieving the Team WIG?

This is the first and most important test for a candidate lead measure. If the idea fails this test, even if it's a good idea, eliminate it and choose the next most impactful idea from the brainstorming list.

Can the Team Influence the Measure?

By asking if the team can influence the measure, we mean to ask if the team has at least 80 percent control over it. As in Discipline 1, this test eliminates significant dependencies on other teams.

These are candidate lead measures Serena's Event Management team might have proposed as an alternative to uncontrollable lag measures:

Uninfluenceable Lag Measures	Influenceable Lead Measures
Raise food-and-drink profitability by 20%.	Upsell premium bar package and improve banquet options.
Win back former clients.	Contact former clients lost to other hotels and generate persuasive proposals to re-sign.
Book more conventions.	Participate actively in the convention-planning association's monthly meetings.

Remember, the ideal lead measure is an action that moves the lag measure and that the team can readily take *without significant dependence on another team.*

Is It an Ongoing Process or a "One-and-Done"?

The ideal lead measure is a behavior change that becomes habitual and brings continuous improvements to the lag measure. Although an action taken once might bring temporary improvement, it is not a behavior change and has little effect on the culture of the team.

Here are some examples that might have been used by Serena's team that illustrate the important differences this test reveals:

Ongoing Process (Do This)	One-and-Done (Not This)
Ensure that every client is aware of our audio-visual capabilities and receives a customized setup.	Upgrade our entire audio-visual system.
Maintain 100% compliance to the banquet table-setting checklist.	Hold a training session on the standards for setting up banquet tables.
Attend Chamber of Commerce meetings and contact companies opening new locations in our city.	Join the Chamber of Commerce.

Although the one-and-done ideas can make a temporary difference—possibly a big one—only the behavioral habits the team develops can drive permanent improvement. This is one of the greatest insights in the 4DX implementation process.

Is It a Leader's Game or a Team Game?

The behavior of the team must drive the lead measure. If only the leader (or one individual) can move the lead measure, the team will quickly lose interest in the game.

For example, a quality initiative requires the leader to audit the process frequently, and an outcome is continuously improving audit results. If the proposed lead measure is more frequent audits, it fails this test because only the leader can do audits. But if the proposal is to respond in a timely manner to all audit findings, it becomes a team game. The actions to drive an audit score involve everyone on the team.

In the same way, candidate measures such as filling open positions, reducing overtime hours, or improving scheduling are usually examples of a leader's game in most organizations. Remember, lead measures connect the team to the WIG, but only if it's the team's game to play.

Can It Be Measured?

As we've said, data on lead measures is hard to get, and most teams don't have systems for tracking these. But success on lag measures absolutely requires successfully tracking the lead measures.

If the Team WIG is truly wildly important, you must find ways to measure the new behaviors.

Is the Lead Measure Worth Measuring?

If it takes more effort than its impact is worth or it has serious unintended consequences, it fails the test of a lead measure.

For example, one large fast-food retailer hired inspectors to visit each franchise regularly to measure compliance with the company's standards. The inspectors were widely considered to be spies. Team members felt disrespected. To the direct cost of hiring this army of inspectors, company leaders could also add the cost of mounting distrust and sinking morale.

Ultimately, the lead measures developed by Serena's Event Management team passed all the tests. In the testing process, they discovered that nearly every site visit they conducted resulted in a successful proposal. So they decided to focus on conducting more site visits and upselling the premium bar package.

STEP 4: DEFINE THE LEAD MEASURES

The next step in the 4DX implementation process is to answer these questions to put the lead measures in final form:

Are We Tracking Team or Individual Performance?

This choice will affect our client's scorekeeping, the design of their scoreboard and, ultimately, how the team is held accountable. Tracking results for individual performers creates the highest level of accountability, but it's also the most difficult game to win because it demands the same performance from everyone. Alternatively, tracking team results allows for differences in individual performance while still enabling the team to achieve the outcome.

Individual Score	Team Score	
Engage 20 customers per associate per day with a warm greeting and offer assistance.	Engage 100 customers per day as a team with a warm greeting and offer assistance.	Measured Daily
Engage 100 customers per associate per week with a warm greeting and offer assistance.	Engage 700 customers per week as a team with a warm greeting and offer assistance.	Measured Weekly

Are We Tracking the Lead Measures Daily or Weekly?

To reach the highest level of engagement, team members need to see the lead-measure scores moving at least weekly; otherwise, they will lose interest fast. Daily tracking creates the highest level of accountability because it demands the same performance from every associate every day, whereas weekly tracking allows for varying performance each day, as long as the overall result for the week is achieved.

Here is an example of the *same lead measure* with individual and team scoring, as well as daily and weekly tracking.

In the 4DX implementation process, we guide our clients to consider these questions in their decision making:

Individual Score	Team Score	
• Every team member must achieve the lead measure. • Personal accountability is very high as tracking is done by person. • Scorekeeping is very detailed.	• The team can win, even when individual members underperform. • Results from high performers can mask those from low performers.	Measured Daily
• Individuals can win for the week, even if some daily goals are missed. • The team wins only when every member performs. • Scorekeeping is detailed.	• The team can win for the week, even when daily goals are missed. • Results from high performers can mask those from low performers. • The team wins or loses together.	Measured Weekly

What Is the Quantitative Standard?

In other words, "How much/how often/how consistently are we supposed to perform?"

At Younger Brothers, the lead measure was 97 percent compliance with six safety standards. How did they arrive at 97 percent? How would you?

You decide based on the urgency and importance of the Team WIG. Remember that the lever has to move a lot to move the rock a little. If safety compliance is only 67 percent, going for 97 percent will move the rock a lot—and if lives and limbs are at stake, that rock *needs* to move dramatically. Choose numbers that challenge the team without making it an unwinnable game.

For example, in the Netherlands, every patient admitted to a hospital is swabbed for infection, a key lead measure for wiping out HAIs. Obviously, swabbing every patient consumes time and resources, but it can be managed. Other countries with a higher tolerance for HAIs or perhaps less of a problem with them might screen some but certainly not all patients. For them, zero HAIs is not a WIG.

Sometimes you discover the numbers through trial and error. A building-materials client sent two email blasts out every week before a sale, but got little response from the blasts. When they experimented with sending out three emails, they were flooded with business. There was something magical about three emails instead of two. Who knew?

If you'll be measuring an activity your team already does, the level of performance must go up significantly beyond where it is today. Otherwise you'll be playing out a familiar definition of insanity: *doing the same things you've always done but expecting different results.*

What Is the Qualitative Standard?

In other words, "How *well* are we supposed to perform?"

Not all lead measures have to answer this question. Still, the most impactful lead measures set the standard not only for how often or how many, but also for how well the team must perform.

At Younger Brothers, the six safety standards were the qualitative component of the lead measure. For a team in a lean manufacturing facility, it might be compliance with value-stream maps.

Does It Start With a Verb?

Simple verbs focus the mind immediately on action.

WIG	Lead Measure
Make $2 million in new revenue by quarter end.	*Complete* 500 more outbound calls per week.
Raise our win rate on bids from 75% to 85% this fiscal year.	*Ensure* proposals achieve 98% compliance with our quality writing standards.
Improve customer-loyalty score from 40 to 70 within two years.	*Achieve* 99% server availability each week.
Increase inventory turns from 8 to 10 this year.	*Send* 3 emails to contacts for every special offer.

Is It Simple?

In the 4DX implementation process, we guide our clients to state their lead measures in as few words as possible. Eliminate opening explanations such as "In order to achieve our WIG and to exceed the expectations of our customers, we will . . ." What comes *after* the words "we will" is the lead measure, and it's all you need to say. A clear WIG statement captures most of what you would say in a prefacing statement anyway.

SPECIAL NOTE ABOUT PROCESS-ORIENTED LEAD MEASURES

Another way we identify powerful lead measures is to ask our clients to look at their work in the form of process steps, particularly if they already know that their Team WIG comes out of a process. (Examples would be a sales-revenue Team WIG from a sales process, a quality Team WIG from a manufacturing process, or a project-completion Team WIG from a project-management process.)

The example here is a basic eleven-step sales process.

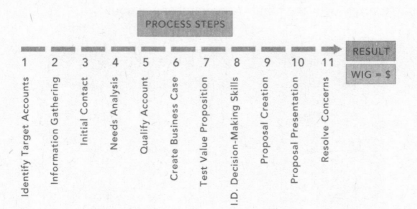

Processes always present the same challenges: Is the process getting us results? Are we even following the process? Do we have the right process?

Somewhere in every process there are leverage points—critical steps in the process where performance falters. If these leverage points become lead measures, the team can apply concentrated energy against them.

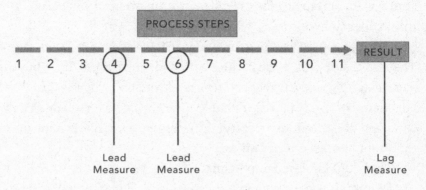

In this chart, the team has decided that a significantly better job on needs analysis (step 4) and business cases (step 6) would have the greatest impact on their results. They have made their bet.

In the 4DX implementation process, the team now defines lead measures for these leverage points. In our sessions, they'll ask, "How do we measure whether a good needs analysis has taken place?" "How do we know we have a good business case?" These kinds of lead measures are vastly more effective than proposing to improve the entire process all at once. In that case, the leader would spread their energy pushing change across the whole process, and the team would never break the old habits.

4DX gives a leader the ability to lock down the most critical points of a process and then move on to the next most critical points.

THE DELIVERABLE

In the 4DX implementation process, our deliverable for Discipline 2 is a small set of lead measures that will move the lag measure on the Team WIG.

The final lead measures for Serena's team were clear—and challenging:

- Complete two quality site visits per associate per week.
- Upsell our premium bar package to 90 percent of all events.

Discipline 2 provided Serena with a clear, concise, and measurable strategy for improving her team's performance *and* delivering great results for the hotel.

Discipline 2 is exciting for many teams, and with good reason. They have not only a clear WIG with a defined finish line, but also some carefully constructed lead measures for achieving the Team WIG. For many, it is the most *executable* plan they've ever made. They're confident they've done everything necessary to make it happen and that from here on out, it's all easy.

They could not be more wrong.

Despite the beautiful game they've just designed, it will disappear into the whirlwind within days of the launch unless they go on to Discipline 3.

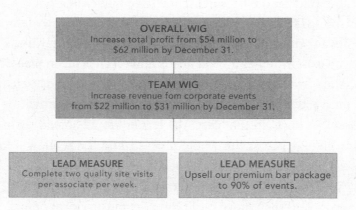

Lead Measure Builder

1. Insert the Wildly Important Goal and lag measure in the top box.
2. Brainstorm ideas for lead measures.
3. Brainstorm methods for measuring those ideas.
4. Rank in order of impact on the WIG.
5. Test your ideas against the checklist on the following page.
6. Write your final lead measures.

Ideas for Lead Measures	How to Measure?	Rank

Final Lead Measures

_____

_____

_____

Did You Get It Right?

Check off each item to ensure your Team WIG and lead measures meet the standard:

☐ Have you have gathered rich input both top-down and bottom-up?

☐ Will the Team WIG have a clear, predictable impact on the overall organizational WIG or strategy, not just on team performance?

☐ Is the Team WIG the most impactful thing the team can do to drive achievement of the overall WIG?

☐ Does the team clearly have the power to achieve the WIG without heavy dependence on other teams?

☐ Does the WIG require the focus of the entire team, not just of the leader or a subgroup?

☐ Is the lag measure written in the format "From X to Y by When"?

☐ Can the WIG be simplified any further? Does it start with a simple verb and end with a clear lag measure?

CHAPTER 14

Applying Discipline 3: Keep a Compelling Scoreboard

Discipline 3 is the discipline of engagement. Even though you've defined a clear and effective game in Disciplines 1 and 2, the team won't play at their best unless they are emotionally engaged—and that *happens* when they can tell if they are winning or losing.

The key to engagement is a visible, continually updated scoreboard that is compelling to the players, whether it's a digital scoreboard in the 4DX app or a physical board constructed by the team. Why do we put so much emphasis on the scoreboard?

In a recent FranklinCovey survey of retail stores, we found that 73 percent of the top performers agree with this statement: "Our success measures are visible, accessible, and continually updated." Only 33 percent of the bottom performers agreed with the statement. Top performers are thus more than twice as likely to see and interact with some form of compelling scoreboard so they can see if they are winning or not. Why is this so?

Recall three principles.

1. PEOPLE PLAY DIFFERENTLY WHEN THEY ARE KEEPING SCORE

People give less than their best and finest effort if no one is keeping score—it's just human nature. And note the emphasis: People play differently when *they* are keeping score. There's a remarkable difference between a game where the leader scores the team and a game where the players own the outcome. It means that the team takes ownership of the results. It's their game to play.

2. A COACH'S SCOREBOARD IS NOT A PLAYERS' SCOREBOARD

A coach's (or a leader's) scoreboard is complex and full of data. A players' scoreboard is simple. It shows a handful of measures that indicate to the players if they are winning or losing the game. They serve different purposes.

3. THE PURPOSE OF A PLAYERS' SCOREBOARD IS TO MOTIVATE THE PLAYERS TO WIN

If the scoreboard doesn't motivate energetic action, whether physical or in the 4DX app, it's not compelling enough to the players. All team members should be able to see it and watch it change moment by moment, day by day, or week by week. They should be discussing it all the time. They should never really take their minds off it.

CREATING A PHYSICAL SCOREBOARD

As you will soon learn, the 4DX app provides a real-time digital scoreboard that is compelling, simple, and always available to you and your team. We will cover this in detail at the end of this chapter.

For some teams, in the 4DX implementation process, there is an added benefit to allowing the team to construct a physical scoreboard uniquely their own. In this section, you'll learn how we involve the team in creating a compelling scoreboard. You'll also see how different scoreboard designs drive different behaviors.

We've found that the more the team is involved in designing the scoreboard, illustrated in this graphic by giving the team more distinct responsibilities, the more the scale is tipped to instill their ownership.

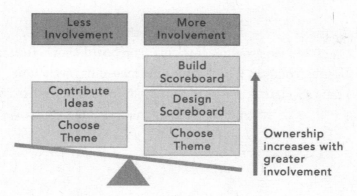

Here are the steps we use to complete this important outcome:

STEP 1. CHOOSE A THEME

In our consulting sessions, we begin by having the team choose a theme for their scoreboard that displays clearly and *instantly* the measures they are tracking. Our clients have several options.

Trend Lines

By far the most useful scoreboards for displaying lag measures, trend lines easily communicate *From X to Y by When*.

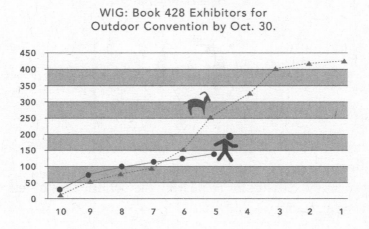

BEAT THE GOAT

WIG: Book 428 Exhibitors for Outdoor Convention by Oct. 30.

Speedometer

Like an automobile speedometer, this scoreboard shows the status of the measures instantly. It's ideal for time measures (cycle time, process speed, time to market, retrieval times, etc.). Consider other common gauges such as thermometers, pressure meters, rulers, or scales.

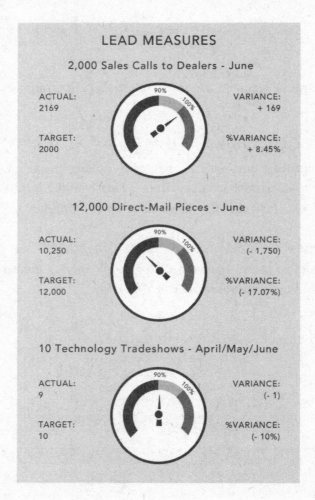

Bar Chart

This scoreboard is useful for comparing the performance of teams or groups within teams.

LEAD MEASURES

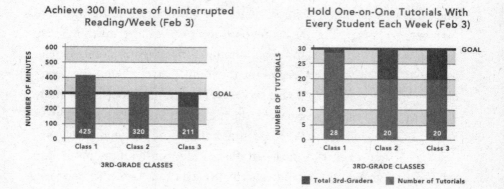

Achieve 300 Minutes of Uninterrupted Reading/Week (Feb 3)

Hold One-on-One Tutorials With Every Student Each Week (Feb 3)

Andon

An Andon chart consists of colored signals or lights that show a process is on track (green), in danger of going off track (yellow), or off track (red). This kind of scoreboard is useful for showing the status of lead measures.

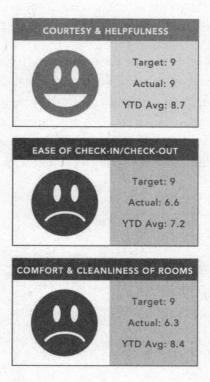

Personalized

The next step in the 4DX implementation process is guiding the team members to personalize the scoreboard to make it more meaningful to them. They can add a team name, photographs of team members, cartoons, or other items that represent the team. Personalizing the scoreboard is of course fun, but it also serves an important purpose—the more the team feels it's *their* scoreboard, the more they will take ownership of the results. Achieving the WIG becomes a matter of personal pride.

We've seen even the most serious-minded individuals jump into this effort. Cardiac nurses put surgical instruments on a scoreboard, engineers set up flashing lights, motorcycle-riding chefs add leather chaps. When the scoreboard becomes personal, they become engaged.

STEP 2. DESIGN THE SCOREBOARD

Once they've determined the theme or type of scoreboard they want, the teams should design the scoreboard with these questions in mind:

Is it simple?

We encourage our clients to resist the temptation to complicate the scoreboard by adding too many variables or supporting data such as historical trends, year-over-year comparisons, or future projections. Don't use the scoreboard as a communication board to post reports, status updates, and other general information that distracts the team from the results they need to see. In the midst of the whirlwind, simplicity is the key to keeping the team engaged.

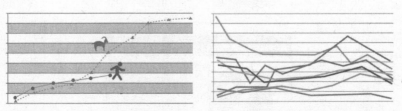

THIS   **NOT THIS**

Team members can immediately see if they're winning from the scoreboard on the left, but they would have to study carefully the scoreboard on the right to understand it—there are too many variables to interpret.

Can the team see it easily?

When it's finished, we have the team post the scoreboard where they will see it often. The more visible the scoreboard, the more the team will stay connected to the game. If you want to motivate the team even more, post it where *other* teams can see it as well. If your team is dispersed geographically, you'll want to use the scoreboard provided in the 4DX app.

Does it contain both lead and lag measures?

Include both actual results and target results. The scoreboard must answer not only *Where are we now?* but also *Where should we be?*

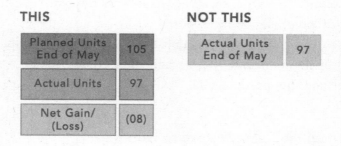

THIS

Planned Units End of May	105
Actual Units	97
Net Gain/ (Loss)	(08)

NOT THIS

Actual Units End of May	97

If the team can see only the units they produce each month, they can't tell if they're winning or losing. They need to see the number of units planned—it also helps to do the math for them and show if they're up or down on the goal (net gain or loss).

Include both the WIG lag measure and the lead measures. Include legends and other minimal labels to explain the measures. Don't assume everyone knows what they are. (Remember, 85 percent of team members we surveyed could not name their most important goals!)

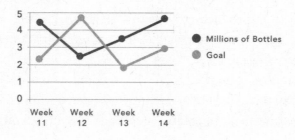

Week	Unit 1	Unit 2	Unit 3	Unit 4	Unit 5	Unit 6	Unit 7	Unit 8	Unit 9
11		✓							✓
12	✓	✓		✓	✓		✓	✓	✓
13	✓	✓	✓	✓		✓	✓	✓	✓
14	✓	✓		✓	✓	✓	✓	✓	✓

This team's WIG was to produce a certain number of bottles of water each week. The lead measure was to do maintenance on the bottling units on a strict schedule. As long as the bottling units were up and running, they could meet the goal.

When they noted a correlation between a drop in maintenance and a drop in production, they became more consistent about the lead measure and shot past the goal.

Can we tell at a glance if we're winning?

We show our clients how to design the scoreboard so that in five seconds or less, the team can determine whether they are winning or losing. This is the true test of a players' scoreboard.

STEP 3. BUILD THE SCOREBOARD

Let the team build the scoreboard. The greater their involvement, the better—they will take more ownership of it if they build it themselves.

Of course, the size and nature of your team will make a difference. If they have very little discretionary time, the leader needs to take more of a role in producing the actual scoreboard. Still, most teams embrace the opportunity to create their own scoreboard and often volunteer their own time for it.

Finally, it doesn't matter much what medium you use for the scoreboard. You can put up an electronic sign, a poster, a whiteboard, or even a chalkboard, as long as it meets the design standards discussed here.

STEP 4. KEEP IT UPDATED

The design of the scoreboard should make it easy to update at least weekly. If the scoreboard is hard to update, you'll be tempted to put it off when the whirlwind strikes—and your Wildly Important Goal will disappear in the noise and confusion.

The leader should make very clear:

- Who is responsible for the scoreboard.
- When it will be posted.
- How often it will be updated.

AN EXAMPLE

Let's follow Serena's Event Management team as they design and build a scoreboard during a session in the 4DX implementation process.

Applying Discipline 1, they set a Team WIG to increase revenue from corporate events from $22 million to $31 million by December 31. They then applied Discipline 2 to identify two high-impact lead measures:

- Complete two quality site visits per associate per week.
- Upsell our premium bar package to 90 percent of events.

With the game clearly defined, Serena and her team were now ready to build a scoreboard. They began by defining clearly on the scoreboard the WIG and lag measure:

WIG

Increase revenue from corporate events from $22 million to $31 million by December 31.

$31

$22

1 2 3 4 5 6 7 8

Next they added Lead Measure 1 with a detailed graph for tracking individual performance.

Finally, they added Lead Measure 2 and a bar graph to track upsell attempts.

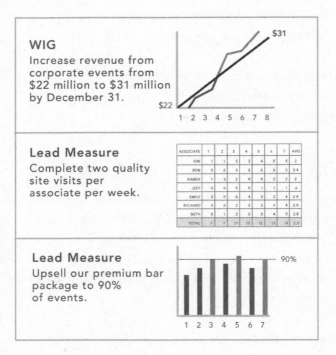

With the WIG on top and the lead measures clearly charted, Serena's scoreboard easily meets the design standards.

It's simple, not overloaded with data. It has only three major components, and each component is crystal clear and quantifiable.

It's visible, with large, dark fonts and easily grasped visuals.

It's complete. The entire game is shown. The Team WIG, its lag measure, and the lead measures are clearly defined. The team's actual performance against the target is clear. The scoreboard is motivating because the team can see their actual results in relation to where they should be for each week. The darker target line makes that possible.

WIG

Increase revenue from corporate events from $22 million to $31 million by December 31.

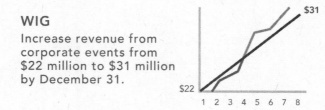

In this case, the lag measure is a straightforward financial goal based on the organization's WIGs. With other possible WIGs such as increased customer satisfaction or improved quality, there might not be a predetermined way to measure progression. In such cases, draw the target line subjectively based on your expectations and knowledge of the team's performance.

But whether formally budgeted or subjectively determined, *a target line must be visible on the scoreboard.* Without it, the team can't tell day by day whether they're winning or not.

For lead measures, the target line is usually set as a single standard for performance (for example, the 90 percent bar in the graph on the left). That standard must be not only reached but sustained. In some cases, you might draw a ramp-up target, indicated by a diagonal line, followed by the horizontal line indicating sustained performance (in the graph on the right).

Lead Measure
Upsell our premium bar package to 90% of events.

Lead Measure
Upsell our premium bar package to 90% of events.

The lead measure to complete two quality site visits per associate per week required that the team's performance be reported individually. Each team member was recorded on the scoreboard with their own results each week.

ASSOCIATE	1	2	3	4	5	6	7	AVG
KIM	1	1	2	2	4	X	X	2
BOB	2	2	3	2	X	X	3	2.4
KAREN	1	3	2	X	X	2	2	2
JEFF	0	0	X	X	1	1	1	.6
EMILY	3	X	X	4	3	2	4	2.8
RICHARD	X	X	2	2	2	4	4	2.8
BETH	X	1	2	5	2	4	X	2.8
TOTAL	7	7	11	15	12	13	14	2.3

(1) Associates track their own performance.

(2) Associates update the scoreboard.

(3) Leader audits performance vs. scoreboard and coaches where needed.

To ensure the credibility of the scoreboard, the leader periodically audits the performance of the team to validate that the scores being recorded match the level of performance observed. The rule here is trust but verify.

Because every graph displays both actual results and target results, team members can instantly tell whether they are winning or losing on each lead measure as well as on the WIG. The colors green and red, when used, can make it even easier to tell how they're doing.

WIG
Increase revenue from corporate events from $22 million to $31 million by December 31.

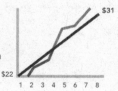

$31

$22

1 2 3 4 5 6 7 8

Lead Measure
Upsell our premium bar package to 90% of events.

90%

1 2 3 4 5 6 7

Note that with the Lead Measure below the team wins only when every member performs. The team truly wins when everybody completes two or more site visits that week.

ASSOCIATE	1	2	3	4	5	6	7	AVG
KIM	1	1	2	2	4	X	X	2
BOB	2	2	3	2	X	X	3	2.4
KAREN	1	3	2	X	X	2	2	2
JEFF	0	0	X	X	1	1	1	.6
EMILY	3	X	X	4	3	2	4	2.8
RICHARD	X	X	2	2	2	4	4	2.8
BETH	X	1	2	5	2	4	X	2.8
TOTAL	7	7	11	15	12	13	14	2.3

THE DELIVERABLE

In the 4DX implementation process, the deliverable for Discipline 3 is a scoreboard that keeps the team engaged.

There's a huge difference in performance between a team that knows about WIGs and measures *as a concept*, and a team that actually knows the score. As Jim Stuart said, "Without clear, visible measures, the same goal will mean a hundred different things to a hundred different people." If the measures aren't captured on a highly visible scoreboard and regularly updated, the WIG will disappear into the distraction of the whirlwind. People disengage when they don't know the score.

It's the sense of winning that drives engagement, and nothing drives results more than a team that is fully engaged—you'll see that every time you update the scoreboard.

By completing Disciplines 1, 2, and 3 in the 4DX implementation process, our clients have designed a team game that is clear and winnable, but that game is still on the drawing board. In Discipline 4, they learn to put that game into action as everyone becomes accountable—to one another—for high performance.

Scoreboard Builder

Use this template to create a compelling scoreboard. Test your ideas against the checklist on the facing page.

Team WIG	Lag Measure
Lead Measure 1	Graph
Lead Measure 2	Graph

Did You Get It Right?

Check off each item to ensure that the team scoreboard is compelling and will drive high performance:

☐ Has the team been closely involved in creating the scoreboard?

☐ Does the scoreboard track the Team WIG, lag measures, and lead measures?

☐ Is there a full explanation of the WIG and measures along with the graphs?

☐ Does every graph display both actual results and the target results *(Where are we now? Where should we be?)*?

☐ Can the team tell at a glance on every measure if they're winning or losing?

☐ Is the scoreboard posted in a highly visible location where the team can see it easily and often?

☐ Is the scoreboard easy to update?

☐ Is the scoreboard personalized—a unique expression of the team?

CHAPTER 15

Applying Discipline 4: Create a Cadence of Accountability

Discipline 4 is the discipline of accountability. Even though you've designed a game that's clear and effective, without consistent accountability, the team will never give their best efforts to the game. You might begin well, your team may have the best of intentions to execute, but before long, the whirlwind will pull you back into a consuming cycle of reacting to the urgent.

Author John Case described this perfectly in an article in *Inc.* magazine:

> Managers began putting up whiteboards, chalkboards, and corkboards. They cranked out data on defects per 1,000, average time spent on hold, and dozens of other performance measures. It was hard to walk into a plant, warehouse, or office without seeing a metric or two charted on the wall.
>
> For a while, the numbers on the charts improved. People paid attention to the boards and figured out how to improve their performance. But then something funny happened. A week might go by without anyone updating the scoreboard. Or maybe a whole month. Somebody did finally mark in the new numbers and noticed there hadn't been much improvement—which meant that nobody was eager to update the board the

next time, either. Before long, the boards fell into disuse. Soon they were taken down.

With hindsight, that outcome isn't so surprising. The real truth about human nature is that what gets measured does get done—but only for a while. Then other human reactions are likely to cut in, such as "Why are they always measuring us?" and "Who really cares if we make those numbers, anyway?"[18]

As the next step in the 4DX implementation process, Discipline 4 breaks this cycle by constantly reconnecting team members to the game. More crucially, it reconnects them in a *personal* way. Because they are frequently and regularly accountable to one another, they become invested in the results and play to win.

When leaders hear about Discipline 4, they are understandably skeptical: "*Another* meeting—every week?" "Can you really accomplish that much in such a short meeting?"

After only a few weeks, these same leaders often tell us, as our biggest client did, "I thought another meeting was the last thing we needed. Now it's the one meeting we won't cancel because it's the most important thing we do."

Discipline 4 asks teams to meet frequently and regularly in WIG Sessions, in which each member of the team makes *personal* commitments to drive the lead measures.

Because a WIG Session might sound like just another quick meeting, you might see nothing much new about it. You're about to see that the cadence of accountability requires real skill and a degree of *precision* if you want your team to perform at the highest level.

WHAT IS A WIG SESSION?

A WIG Session is unlike any other meeting you will ever attend. It has a singular purpose: to refocus the team on the WIG despite the daily whirlwind. It takes place regularly, at least weekly, and sometimes more often. It has a fixed agenda, as illustrated in the model below:

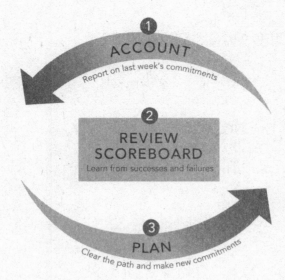

A WIG Session is a short, intense team meeting devoted to these three—and only these three—activities. The purpose of the WIG Session is to account for prior commitments and make commitments to move the WIG scoreboard.

1. *Account: Report on last week's commitments.* Each team member reports on the commitments to move the lead measures they made the prior week.
2. *Review the scoreboard: Learn from successes and failures.* The team assesses whether their commitments are moving the lead measure, and whether the lead measure is moving the lag measure. They discuss what they've learned about what works and what doesn't, and how to adapt.
3. *Plan: Clear the path and make new commitments.* Based on this assessment, each member of the team makes commitments for the coming week that will raise the lead measures to the required level of performance. Because team members create the commitments themselves, and because they are publicly accountable for them to each other, they go away determined to follow through—it becomes *personally important.*

Although this cadence of accountability is simple in concept, it takes focus and discipline to maintain in the midst of the whirlwind.

WHY HOLD WIG SESSIONS?

WIG HUDDLES

Some teams, such as the emergency-room team in an inner-city hospital with little to no discretionary time will need to hold an alternative meeting called a WIG Huddle.

WIG Huddles take place once each week for five to seven minutes with the entire team in a circle around the scoreboard where they do three things:

1. **Review the Scoreboard** – reinforcing their accountability for results.
2. **Report on Last Week's Team Commitment** – making a single team commitment to raise their performance.
3. **Make New Commitments for the Coming Week**

The sessions keep the team's focus on the WIG, despite the constant whirlwind of other urgent demands.

The sessions enable team members to learn from one another about how to move the lead measures. If one person succeeds, others can adopt their approach. On the other hand, if a course of action isn't working, the team finds out early.

The sessions give team members the help they need to keep their commitments. If someone runs into a barrier, the team decides how to clear the path.

The sessions enable the team to adapt on the fly to the changing needs of the business. The session ends with a just-in-time plan that addresses challenges impossible to foresee through annual planning.

The sessions provide an opportunity to celebrate progress, reenlist the energies of the team, and reengage everyone.

We started thinking hard about WIG Sessions after learning from successful business leader Stephen Cooper. When Cooper took over a little company called Etec in Silicon Valley, it was generating $1 million in red ink every month. Cooper set the WIG to increase revenues tenfold within seven years. To achieve that WIG, he asked each team to identify a few enabling goals with metrics and to reduce their plan to a single sheet of paper.

This exercise provided clarity for each team, but the real key to Cooper's ultimate success was his weekly reviews. He instituted three rules to keep those reviews fast and focused. "People should limit their status reports to four minutes. For each goal, people should cover objectives, status, issues, and recommendations. Finally, the reviews should encourage joint problem solving rather than just reporting."

One of Cooper's team leaders said of these weekly sessions, "[They] stop problems from becoming crises. . . . People have time to react in a comfortable manner instead of a chaotic manner. Each manager takes a few minutes to present and review progress charts, surface problems, and try to solve them. These routines help you to keep your eye on the ball. People move forward with a minimum of direction. It gives everyone their marching orders."[19]

Inspired by Cooper, we experimented for years with different formats for the WIG Session. Today it's a sleek and highly developed concept used by hundreds of organizations to advance their most important priorities.

WHAT HAPPENS IN A WIG SESSION?

To illustrate how a WIG Session should work, let's look in on Serena's Event Management team.

Remember that they have defined a Team WIG—to increase revenue from corporate events from $22 million to $31 million by December 31—and two high-impact lead measures:

- Complete two quality site visits per associate per week.
- Upsell our premium bar package to 90 percent of events.

And they have built a compelling scoreboard.

As Serena and her team begin their WIG Session on Monday morning, they have just completed their third month of execution and their scoreboard is up to date.

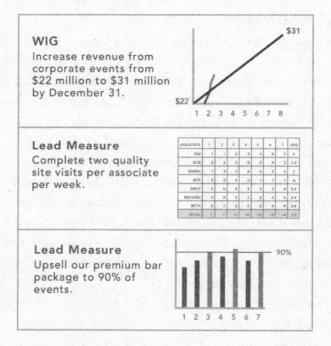

SERENA: Good morning, everyone. It's eight-fifteen. Let's get started by reviewing the scoreboard.

[Review the scoreboard.]

We have good news today. We've just completed our third month of execution, and we are above target for our Team WIG of increasing revenue from corporate events! Our lag measure score for last month is $14 million against a target of $10.4 million. Congratulations, everyone.

As you can see, last week we raised our site visits on Lead

Measure 1 to a total of 14, our highest result in the past seven weeks. Congratulations to our top performers, Emily and Richard, who each completed four site visits.

In addition, we hit our highest percentage of upselling so far on Lead Measure 2, with 95 percent of events having been offered our premium bar package, but we've missed our percentage goal four out of the last seven weeks. While I know we're pleased with last week's percentage, we have work to do to demonstrate that we can sustain it.

[Report on last week's commitments.]

Now, for my commitments, last week I committed to work with Kim and Karen for twenty minutes each on improving their upselling scripts for our bar package, as well as practicing their delivery. I completed this.

I also committed to attend the Chamber of Commerce meeting and capture at least three new corporate contacts that are not currently holding events at our hotel. I was very pleased to come back with contacts for five organizations, which I'll pass over to several of you this afternoon.

For next week, I'll complete the final review of our new marketing materials for our premium bar package. Also, I'll interview three candidates for the open position on our team and make an offer to the one that best meets our requirements.

KIM: Last week I committed to have face-to-face meetings with two companies that have just opened new offices downtown, and I did this. Good news—one of them is scheduled for a site visit next week!

On the scoreboard, I completed two site visits, but had an upsell conversation with only one of them, for a score of 50 percent, which I will improve next week.

For next week, I will have a conversation, by phone or in person, with two of my clients who held their annual meeting with us last year, but haven't committed yet for this year. I want to schedule site visits for them to see our new banquet room and, hopefully, convince them to sign up for this year.

BOB: My commitment last week was to create a special upsell experience for our premium bar package with the three clients that were scheduled for site visits, since they represent large-event opportunities. I did this by getting the chef to create a wine-tasting display, along with light hors d'oeuvres for each client. It went over well, and all three of them upgraded to the premium bar package for their events!

On the scoreboard, I had three site visits and had upsell conversations with all of them for a score of 100 percent.

For next week, I only have one site visit scheduled so far, so I will contact at least five new prospective clients by the end of the day Monday and have at least one of them commit to making a site visit before the end of the week.

KAREN: My commitment last week was to send a memories packet to ten of my clients who held events with us last year. In each packet, I inserted two or three photos from their event, plus the banquet menu they used, along with a handwritten note from me saying how much I hoped to see them again this year. I completed this and am pleased to report that four of them called to thank me for the photos, and two have agreed to site visits to see the new banquet room.

On the scoreboard, I had two site visits and discussed our premium bar package with both of them for a score of 100 percent.

For next week, I'm going to create memories packets for five more clients from last year and send them out.

Serena's WIG Session continues this way until each member of the team finishes reporting. Note that they are accounting not only to Serena, but to one another for their follow-through and for their results.

MAKE NEW HIGH-IMPACT COMMITMENTS FOR THE COMING WEEK

The effectiveness of the WIG Session depends on the consistency of the cadence, but the *results* on the scoreboard depend on the *impact* of the commitments. You'll need to guide the team in making commitments that have the highest possible impact.

Start with this question: "What are the one or two most important things I can do this week to impact the team's performance on the scoreboard?"

Let's break down this question so you understand its significance to the WIG.

One or two: In Discipline 4, following through on a few high-impact commitments is far more important than making a lot of commitments. You want the team to do a few things with excellence, not a lot of things with mediocrity. The greater the number of commitments, the less likely follow-through becomes. In this context, it's better to make two high-impact commitments and fulfill them exactly than to make five commitments and keep them badly.

Most important: Don't waste time on peripheral activities. Focus your attention and effort on those commitments that will make the biggest difference.

I: All commitments made in a WIG Session are *personal responsibilities*. You're not committing other people to do things; you're committing to things *you* will do. Although you'll be working with others, commit to be accountable for only that part of the effort you can be personally responsible for.

This week: Discipline 4 requires at least a weekly cadence of accountability. Make only those commitments that can be completed *within the coming week* so that accountability can be maintained. If you commit to something four weeks in the future, then for three of those weeks you're not accountable. If it's a multiweek initiative, commit only to what you can do this coming week. Weekly commitments create a sense of urgency that helps you stay focused when your whirlwind is raging.

Performance on the scoreboard: This is most critical. Every commitment must be directed at moving the lead and lag measures on your scoreboard. Without this focus, you'll be tempted to make commitments to the whirlwind. While they might be urgent, these commitments will contribute nothing to the WIG.

If everyone answers this question precisely in every WIG Session, the team will establish a regular rhythm of execution that will drive results.

Serena's WIG Session produced commitments that will make that kind of difference:

"Work with Kim and Karen for twenty minutes each on improving their upselling scripts for our bar package, as well as practicing their delivery."

"Attend the Chamber of Commerce meeting and capture at least three new corporate contacts who are not currently holding events at our hotel."

"Complete the final review of our new marketing materials for our premium bar package."

"Interview three candidates for the open position on our team, and make an offer to the one that best meets our requirements."

"Complete face-to-face meetings with two companies that have just opened new offices downtown."

"Create a special upsell experience for our premium bar package with the three clients that were scheduled for site visits."

"Send a memories packet to ten of my clients who held events with us last year, along with a handwritten note."

Team members are more likely to take ownership of commitments they come up with themselves. Still, the leader should make sure the commitments meet the following standards:

Specific. The more specific the commitment, the higher the accountability for it. You can't hold people accountable for vague commitments. Commit to exactly what you will do, when you will do it, and what you expect the outcome will be.

Aligned to moving the scoreboard. Make sure the commitments move the scoreboard; otherwise, you're just committing more energy to the whirlwind. For instance, the week before your annual budget is due, you might be tempted to make a commitment to complete the budget because it's both urgent and important. However, if the budget has little to do with the lead measures, it won't affect the WIG, no matter how urgent it seems.

Timely. High-impact commitments must be completed within the coming week, but they should also impact the team's performance *in the near term*. If the real impact of your commitment is too far in the future, it won't help to build the weekly rhythm of winning.

This table illustrates the differences between low- and high-impact commitments:

LOW-IMPACT COMMITMENT	HIGH-IMPACT COMMITMENT
I will focus on training this week	I will work with Kim and Karen for 20 minutes each on improving their upselling scripts for our bar package, as well as practicing their delivery.
I will attend the Chamber of Commerce meeting	I will attend the Chamber of Commerce meeting and capture at least three new corporate contacts not currently holding events at our hotel.
I will do some interviews	I will interview three candidates for the open position on our team and make an offer to the one that best meets our requirements.
I will reach out to new clients this week.	I will complete face-to-face meetings with two companies that have just opened new offices downtown.
I will call on old clients	I will send a "memories" packet to 10 of my clients who held events with us last year, along with a handwritten note.

Note the great strength of commitments specifically aligned to moving the lead measures.

269

WATCH OUT

Avoid these common pitfalls that undermine the cadence of accountability.

Competing whirlwind responsibilities. This is the most common challenge you and your team will face when you begin applying Discipline 4. Don't mistake whirlwind urgencies for WIG commitments. An effective question for testing a commitment is "How will fulfilling this commitment impact the scoreboard?" If you struggle to answer the question directly, the commitment you're considering is likely focused on your whirlwind.

Holding WIG Sessions with no specific outcomes. The cadence of accountability will collapse without disciplined adherence to the WIG Session agenda. Every WIG Session needs to account specifically for prior commitments and result in clear commitments for the future.

Repeating the same commitment more than two consecutive weeks. Even a high-impact commitment, if repeated week after week, becomes routine. You should always be looking for new and better ways to move the lead measures.

Accepting unfulfilled commitments. The team must fulfill their commitments regardless of their day-to-day whirlwind. When a team member fails to keep a commitment, regardless of all the work you've done to install 4DX, you face *the moment that matters most.*

If you can instill the discipline of accountability in your team, they will beat the whirlwind every week. However, if you're casual about accountability for commitments as well as for results, the whirlwind will overwhelm the Wildly Important Goal.

Let's see how Serena handles this important moment in the WIG Session.

SERENA: Jeff, you're next.

JEFF: Thanks, Serena. Well, I had committed to contact several of my clients from last year about a site visit, but as you all know, I also had a major event taking place in the hotel last week. Since this was my largest group of the year, I wanted to be sure that it was successful, so I gave them a lot of personal attention. And when the projector in the main ballroom crashed, I had to scramble to get another one. I spent a lot of time making sure the client wasn't upset and that things were back on track. Before I realized it, the week was gone and there just wasn't time.

In essence, Jeff is saying that he couldn't keep his commitment because of his whirlwind; what's more damaging, Jeff believes that he *shouldn't* be held accountable for his commitment if his whirlwind is significant enough. This is where execution breaks down.

Most commitments we make are conditional. For example, when a team member says, "I'll have that report to you by nine Tuesday morning," what they mean is "Unless something urgent comes up." But something urgent *always* comes up—it's the nature of the ever-present whirlwind.

If you let the whirlwind overwhelm your commitments, you'll never invest the energy needed to progress. The execution discipline starts and ends with keeping your WIG Session commitments.

That's why Serena's job as the leader, particularly in the first few WIG Sessions, is to set a new standard: Commitments are *unconditional*. As a client of ours says, "Whenever we make a commitment on our team, we know we have to find a way to make it happen, no matter what."

How should Serena respond?

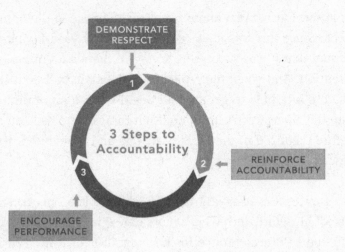

STEP 1. DEMONSTRATE RESPECT

SERENA: Jeff, I want you to know that the event last week was a huge success, and without you, it could have been a disaster. Everyone on this team understands how hard you worked and how important this client is to us. Thank you for everything you did.

In this crucial first step, Serena shows Jeff that she respects him as a team member, but she also shows the team that she *respects the whirlwind*. If she skips this step, she'll send two incorrect messages: that Jeff is not valued, and that the whirlwind is not important.

STEP 2. REINFORCE ACCOUNTABILITY

SERENA: Jeff, I also want you to know how important your contribution is to this team. Without you, we can't reach our goal. This means that when we make a commitment, we have to find a way to fulfill it no matter what happens during the week.

This is a challenging moment for both Jeff and Serena; but because Serena has made it clear that she respects Jeff and the demands of the whirlwind, Jeff should be able to see the importance of doing his best *for the team.*

STEP 3. ENCOURAGE PERFORMANCE

SERENA: Jeff, I know you want to help us follow through. Can we count on you to catch up, by fulfilling last week's commitment as well as the one you were planning on making for next week?

Serena gives Jeff the opportunity to report with pride that all commitments have been fulfilled.

Bringing this important interaction to a successful close is very important. It's important to Jeff because he can now keep his commitment to the team. It's important to the leader because the team sees she's committed to the 4DX discipline. And it's important for the team to know that a new standard for performance is expected.

Without unconditional commitments, you can't drive the black into the gray. The gray whirlwind will simply fill in the black commitments. That's the story of execution breakdown.

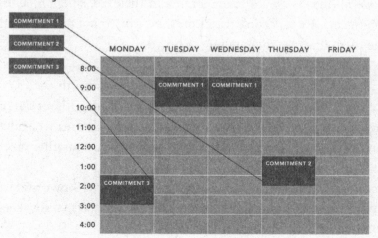

273

Hyrum Smith, one of the founders of FranklinCovey, said, "If your entire paycheck was based on this one commitment, two things would happen automatically. You would be more careful in making the commitment, and you would be absolutely certain to follow through." This is the purpose of the WIG Session: to make commitments intelligently and with the determination to keep them regardless of the whirlwind.

KEYS TO SUCCESSFUL WIG SESSIONS

In the 4DX implementation process, we emphasize these keys to success in Discipline 4:

Hold WIG Sessions as scheduled. Keep WIG Sessions to the same day at the same time in the same place every week (including electronically), regardless of the whirlwind. If you're gone, delegate leadership of the session to another team member.

Keep the sessions brief. Maintain a brisk and energetic pace. A rule of thumb: Sessions shouldn't run more than twenty to thirty minutes. Take too long, and the session risks turning into a whirlwind meeting.

Set the standard as the leader. Begin every WIG Session by reviewing the overall results on the scoreboard and then *reporting on your own commitments.* By reporting first, you show you're not asking anything of the team that you're unwilling to do yourself.

Post the scoreboard. Update the scoreboard before the session, and make sure it's present. You can't hold a WIG Session without the scoreboard. It reconnects the team to the game and indicates what's working and what isn't. Without it, the WIG Session is just another meeting.

Celebrate successes. Reinforce commitment to the WIG by congratulating both the team and individual members on successfully keeping commitments and moving the measures.

Share learning. Through the week, people will discover what does and doesn't move the lead measures. They will also discover that some measures work better than others. Everyone needs this information.

Refuse to let the whirlwind enter. Limit discussion to commitments that can move the scoreboard. Defer dialogues about the whirlwind, the weather, morning traffic, or sports for other settings.

Clear the path for one another. Remove obstacles for one another. Clearing the path does not mean passing a problem to someone else, but leveraging the strengths of the team. If you agree to clear the path for someone, it becomes one of your commitments for the week and requires the same follow-through as any other commitment.

Execute in spite of the whirlwind. Hold team members unconditionally accountable for their commitments regardless of the whirlwind. If a commitment is missed one week, it must be accounted for the following week.

THE DELIVERABLE

In the 4DX implementation process, the deliverable for Discipline 4 is a regular, frequent WIG Session that moves the lead measures.

But far beyond this, the ultimate outcome of Discipline 4 is a cadence of accountability that produces not only reliable results again and again, but also a high-performance team.

Discipline 4 requires real skill and a degree of precision in making and keeping important commitments.

Discipline 4 keeps your team in the game every week, as the members connect their personal contributions to the most important priorities of the organization. With this comes not only the awareness that they are winning on a key goal, but that they have become a *winning team.*

Which is the ultimate return on the investment you make in 4DX.

WIG Session Agenda

Distribute this agenda electronically or on paper at the beginning of the WIG Session. After you hold the session, check it against the criteria on the facing page.

WIG SESSION AGENDA			
Where		**When**	
WIG(s)			
Individual Reports	Team Member	Commitment	Status
Scoreboard Update			

Did You Get It Right?

Check off each item to ensure that the WIG Session will drive high performance:

☐ Are you holding WIG Sessions as scheduled?

☐ Are you keeping the sessions brief, brisk, and energetic (less than twenty minutes)?

☐ Is the leader the model for reporting and making commitments?

☐ Do you review an updated scoreboard?

☐ Do you analyze why you're winning or losing on each measure?

☐ Do you celebrate successes?

☐ Do you hold each other unconditionally accountable for your commitments?

☐ Does each team member make specific commitments for the coming week?

☐ Do you clear the path for each other, finding ways to help team members who encounter obstacles to keeping their commitments?

☐ Do you keep the whirlwind out of the WIG Session?

The Missing Ingredient

Throughout this book, we've offered both the principles and the practices that create breakthrough results. However, there is one final ingredient—what we often see as the "missing ingredient"—without which execution never reaches its highest level: the *personal* characteristics of the leaders themselves. In this final chapter, we want to share the four most impactful of these characteristics with you. It's important to note here that we're not just referring to the leadership characteristics that drive execution. We're using *execution* as a lens to share what we have learned about *great leadership*.

HUMILITY

It's a paradox that the leaders who taught us the most about humility are not those who you would likely describe as "humble people." This is partly because they are leaders who refuse to portray false humility. They are also unimpeded by self-doubt or an inability to act. They are leaders who make their impression on us through *humility in action*, more than words, and it comes in two forms:

- First, these leaders have a clear-eyed respect for the magnitude of the execution challenge they face.
- Second, they are willing to do whatever is necessary to overcome it.

Leaders who excel at execution aren't looking for shortcuts, rah-rah programs, or surface-level changes. They're not anxious to delegate the "execution stuff" so they can be free to think "big thoughts."

And most important, they *do not* cast themselves as the hero of the story. In fact, they intentionally stay out of the story so that their teams get the recognition.

Watch these leaders, and you'll see that they spend significant time *listening* to the people who follow them, understanding the complexity and the nuances of their challenges, and looking for ways to help them succeed. These leaders aren't interested in a conceptual understanding of 4DX. They are hungry (and humble) enough to *go deep*, and are willing to think about, and wrestle with, everything our experience has taught us, even though their professional achievements far outweigh ours.

A great example of this is Mike Crisafulli, a Senior VP running the IT organization in one of America's largest companies and a brilliant implementer of 4DX. We met him when he first applied 4DX to a problem with systems and application downtime that had plagued his company for years. Four months into the effort, which included launching 4DX with forty-six functional teams focused on the downtime issue, his early results were very favorable.

We met with Mike to congratulate him on his early success, but were surprised by his response: "Am I happy with the results?" he said candidly. "Honestly, no. Because I don't really understand them. If our results turned bad tomorrow, I wouldn't understand why, and I can't manage what I cannot understand."

This is the type of humility we are describing. Most leaders are quick to embrace any results that are favorable (and even accept credit for them), but not Mike. He and his top leaders had all forty-six teams report individually to them on their results and what they had learned. At the conclusion of those meetings, Mike and his team understood *exactly* what was driving the new level of performance and how to sustain it. But it was the humility to listen to forty-six different teams that paid the biggest dividends. They finished that year with an achievement that was *three times greater* than the original goal.

DETERMINATION

Execution has always been about discipline. But if personal discipline does not come naturally to you (and it rarely does to anyone), then success with 4DX will require you to have *determination*. For example, if the urgent demands of leading confront you with dozens of distractions every day, you'll need determination to remain focused on the things that matter most. The 4 Disciplines of Execution won't *give* you determination, but they will *demand* it. This is especially true when your highest level of determination is needed *before* the results are visible. In the end, 4DX generously rewards those who are determined, but does little for those who are not.

Beverly (BJ) Walker is a dramatic example of this level of determination. She began 4DX during the most difficult time in her career—a time when she focused her entire team on a goal of great significance: "Reduce by 50 percent the incidents that lead to death and serious injury" (as described in detail in the foreword to this book).

In the midst of enormous pressure, both public and political, BJ remained determined to hold a 4DX WIG Session with her division directors every week—directors who were seasoned government leaders unaccustomed to this level of focus and accountability. It wasn't easy, but BJ's determination was never in question—they were going to stay *accountable* for this goal. Not only did this meeting happen each week without exception, the local media was invited to attend. If there were questions for BJ or her leaders, they could be asked after every WIG Session.

No public relations campaign could ever have generated the level of respect in the media created by seeing these high-level government officers report personally on commitments they had made, each and every week. More important, it sent a shock wave of accountability through those agencies that resulted in full adoption of 4DX, and ultimately, profound results.

Another significant example of determination is Michael Stengel, when he was General Manager of the Marriott Marquis in Times Square, New York. His commitment to the 4DX process was so strong that even when he was in China, Michael got up at 2:00 A.M. (Beijing time) to attend the weekly WIG Session by phone with the leaders in his hotel. Mike and his leadership team showed their determination to execute, and it resulted in an intense level of engagement throughout the hotel. That year, the Times Square Marquis achieved its highest revenue, highest profitability, and highest guest satisfaction in the twenty-year history of the hotel.

COURAGE

Courage is always present in strong executers—not the absence of fear, but simply the willingness to act in spite of it. For example, it takes real courage to designate a single result as "wildly important" and to then invest disproportionate energy into achieving it. It might (at first) seem far safer to invest a little energy in lots of outcomes, at least until the law of diminishing returns proves once again that the more you focus on, the less you achieve.

There's also the courage of explicitly stating the *From X to Y by When* of a goal up front, making you accountable for both the final result *and* the date by which your team will achieve it. Fail at *either* and you've missed the goal. Defining a finish line and a deadline is a high standard—one that is always accompanied by great uncertainty. To do it, a leader must have the courage to override their fear of the many variables that are beyond their control.

Finally, there is the courage (even the audacity) of committing to a WIG that represents a true breakthrough—reaching a level that has never been reached before. In 4DX, commitment always precedes accomplishment, and can't be fully implemented without the characteristic of courage.

We see this dynamic play out in more subtle ways all the time. For example, when the political winds in a large company shift, how does a leader respond? When they inherit a challenge that seems insurmountable, do they hide and play it safe, or do they rise?

When LeAnn Talbot inherited the Chicago Region of Comcast, it was both the largest *and* the lowest-performing in the company. She worried that her new team had become accustomed to losing, and she wanted to break that mindset by enabling them to experience early wins. She began with small pilots, sometimes without permission. But as the results increased, she was able to get her leadership team, and eventually her entire region, to adopt 4DX. Within three years, the Chicago Region became the top-performing region in all of Comcast.

Were the stakes high for LeAnn? Of course. But because she had the courage to take on the challenge, she transformed a discouraged team into winners and produced a great result for her company.

LOVE

The final characteristic we want to offer is love.

If the word "love" feels too personal or too soft, feel free to substitute "sincere concern for the individual." But we'll stay with "love," because it's the only way to really describe how these leaders feel about the people who follow them.

Think of it like the love you might see in a great parent or mentor—one that combines genuine care for the person with a belief in their potential and a commitment to support them. It's the kind of love that has the power to affect people deeply—personally and professionally. When a leader sees more potential in you than you see in yourself and helps you to grow and develop, it's beyond encouraging, it's *transformational*.

Wegmans grocery stores are known around the world for their extraordinary level of quality, service, and innovation. Their customer loyalty is so high, it's not uncommon to find people camping out in their parking lots before a grand opening. In 2016, Wegmans was voted number two in the USA for "best company to work for" (just behind Google) and number two in the USA for "most respected company" (just behind Amazon). It's a stunning achievement.

Colleen Wegman took over for her father, Danny, as CEO in 2018, after being involved in nearly every aspect of the business her entire life. We didn't have to be around her long to recognize her humility, determination, and courage. But what really comes across from Colleen is love—that combination of sincere concern and incredible belief in the people she leads. It's a characteristic that permeates the entire organization, and it isn't limited to Wegmans employees. We recognized it even as outside consultants. It created a level of loyalty in us so intense that we would have done anything to avoid disappointing them.

Leaders with this characteristic don't talk about it often. It's not in the employee handbook, and you'll never find it in the marketing message. You have to *see* it—the leaders showing care and concern in a hundred different ways throughout the year and then spending Christmas Eve in a van driving from store to store giving out gifts. Then one day you get it. *This* is how they make everyone feel. They *love* their people.

Intent is more important than technique.

—Mahan Khalsa

This book contains everything we know about successfully executing on your Wildly Important Goal, and we hope you find value in every chapter. But in the end, we believe love will be the greatest determiner of your success. And that's a legacy that can't be measured.

We wish you the best of luck.

Glossary

4DX: An abbreviation for the 4 Disciplines of Execution.

4DX app: An online tool for managing (1) adherence to the 4 Disciplines across the organization and (2) achievement of team and organizational WIGs.

4 Disciplines of Execution: An orderly pattern of conduct that leads to achievement of an organizational goal with excellence. The 4 Disciplines are based on deep research and field work, as well as fundamental principles of human behavior, and are proprietary to FranklinCovey.

Accountability: The ability to report progress or lack of progress using numbers.

Battle: Within the context of the 4 Disciplines, an enabling or supporting WIG owned by a lower-level team. The principle is to identify the fewest possible battles to win the war.

"Beating the Goat": The point at which a lead measure on a scoreboard is "on target" (i.e., where it should be, according to plan). The expression comes from a scoreboard created by a 4DX practitioner on which the symbol of a goat is used to represent a lead measure.

Behavioral-Change Strategy: A strategy that requires people—sometimes many people—to do things that are new and different. Because of the difficulty of changing human behavior, such a strategy is usually much more difficult to execute than a stroke-of-the-pen strategy (see entry).

Cadence of Accountability: A recurring cycle of planning and accounting for results. Disciplined execution of WIGs requires a cadence—a rhythm of planning, follow-through, and reporting. This cycle takes the form of a WIG Session at least weekly.

Champion: The organizational sponsor of the 4 Disciplines process.

Clearing the Path: Taking ownership of and resolving a problem or an obstacle to achieving the WIG; helping another team member to accomplish an objective. One of the purposes of the Team WIG Session is to plan how to clear the path to execution.

Coach: A person well versed in the 4 Disciplines who acts as a resource to managers installing the 4 Disciplines in their teams.

Commitment: Within the context of the 4 Disciplines, an individual team member's weekly contribution to achieving a WIG.

Dashboard: A collection of scoreboards by which senior leaders can readily gauge progress on key organizational measures and adherence to the 4 Disciplines.

Discipline: A consistent regimen that leads to freedom of action. Without consistent discipline, the team loses the ability to achieve WIGs with precision and excellence, thus losing influence and scope for action.

Discipline 1: Focus on the Wildly Important: The practice of defining crucial goals and narrowing the team's focus to those goals. Work teams who practice Discipline 1 are totally clear on a few WIGs and the lag measures (see entry) for those goals.

Discipline 2: Act on the Lead Measures: The practice of consistently carrying out and tracking results on those high-leverage activities that will lead to achievement of WIGs. Work teams who practice Discipline 2 are clear on the lead measures (see entry) of their goals and track them carefully.

Discipline 3: Keep a Compelling Scoreboard: The practice of visibly tracking key success measures on a goal. Work teams who practice Discipline 3 are continually preoccupied with moving the measures on the scoreboard.

Discipline 4: Create a Cadence of Accountability: The practice of regularly and frequently planning and reporting on activities intended to move the measures on the WIG scoreboard. Work teams who practice Discipline 4 make individual and collective commitments and account for those commitments in weekly WIG Sessions.

Execution: The discipline of getting things done as promised—on time, on budget, and with quality. What "executives" are hired to do!

Execution Gap: The gap between setting a strategy or a goal and actually achieving it. This gap is expressed in terms of *From X to Y by When* (see lag measure).

From X to Y by When: The formula for expressing lag measures, tracking movement from a current X to a better or more desirable Y within a certain time frame. This formula is essential to understanding exactly what it means to "win," to achieve the WIG.

Goal: Any target expressed in terms of lag measures (see entry) that represents improvement in the organization's performance.

Important Goal: A goal with significant consequence and value. Compare to Wildly Important Goal (see entry).

Lag Measure: The measure of goal or WIG achievement. A historical measure of performance (e.g., end-of-year revenue, quality scores, customer-satisfaction numbers). Lag measures are typically easy to measure but difficult to influence directly. A lag measure is always expressed in terms of *From X to Y by When*.

Lead Measure: The measure of an action planned and taken as a means to achieving a WIG. Unlike lag measures, lead measures are influenceable by the team and predictive of the goal. Good lead measures are the highest-leverage activities a team can engage in to ensure execution of the WIG; therefore, lead measures are carefully tracked on the team scoreboard. The lead measures constitute the team's "strategic bet" that if they take these measures, they will execute the goal with excellence. Thus, one purpose of the execution process is to test the lead measures to determine as quickly as possible if the bet is a good one.

Line of Sight: The relationship between goals at each level of an organization (e.g., the link between the daily tasks of a frontline worker and the overall strategy of the organization). Teams in a well-executing organization have clear line of sight at all levels.

Manager Certification: A process in which managers gain the documented ability to lead a team to achieving a WIG by implementing the 4 Disciplines of Execution.

Manager Work Session: A session in which peer managers are oriented to the 4 Disciplines of Execution and draft WIGs and measures for the teams they manage.

Mission: The organization's or team's predefined purpose or reason for being. A WIG is often a goal essential to carrying out the organization's mission or strategy (see entry).

Project: A planned undertaking involving defined steps, milestones, and tasks. A project may be undertaken in order to achieve a WIG, but the project itself is not a WIG.

Scoreboard: A mechanism for tracking progress on lead and lag measures for a WIG. It should be visible to the entire team and consistently and regularly updated. A scoreboard is compelling if it indicates quickly and clearly whether the team is winning or not, thus motivating action.

Strategic Bet: The hypothesis that certain high-leverage activities will drive the achievement of a goal. This hypothesis must be proven through execution (see lead measure).

Strategy: A plan or method for achieving the mission of the organization or team. A WIG is a goal essential to carrying out the organization's strategy.

Stroke-of-the-Pen Strategy: A strategy that leaders execute just by ordering or authorizing it to be done and that generally does not require a lot of people to do things differently. Contrast this with behavioral-change strategies, which require people to do new and different things.

Summit: A periodic report to senior management on progress on WIGs. It provides the team an opportunity to be recognized and to celebrate their success.

Team: A group of people specifically designated to achieve a WIG. A team may or may not be aligned with a formal organizational chart.

Team Work Session: A work session in which teams finalize their goals and measures and commit to maintaining a cadence of accountability for their goals.

War: Within the context of the 4 Disciplines, a synonym for the highest-level organizational WIG. Compare to battle (see entry). Also called the overall WIG.

Whirlwind: A metaphor for the enormous amount of time and energy required to keep the organization at its current level of performance. The whirlwind is the main threat to the execution of WIGs; therefore, one of the recurring tasks of the work team is to plan how to clear the path through the whirlwind of demands on everyone's time.

WIG: Acronym for Wildly Important Goal (see entry).

WIG Session: A team meeting held at least weekly to account for commitments, review WIG scoreboards, and plan how to improve the scores on the scoreboards. The regular WIG Session is essential to maintaining the cadence of accountability, which is key to executing WIGs.

Wildly Important Goal (WIG): A goal essential to carrying out the organization's mission or strategy. Failure to achieve this goal will render all other achievements secondary. Compare to important goal (see entry).

Work Session: A meeting in which WIGs, measures, and scoreboards are developed for carrying out key organizational strategies.

Notes

Chapter 1. The Real Problem With Execution

1 Patrick Litré, David Michels, Ivan Hindshaw, and Parijat Ghosh, "Results Delivery: Busting Three Common Myths of Change Management," Bain & Company, August 2, 2018; http://www.bain .com/publications/articles/results-delivery-busting-3-common-change -management-myths.aspx.

2 See Rafael Aguayo, *Dr. Deming: The American Who Taught the Japanese About Quality* (New York: Touchstone, 1991), 57–63.

3 Tim Harford, "Trial, Error, and the God Complex," TED.com, July 20, 2011; http://www.ted.com/talks/tim_harford.html.

Chapter 2. Discipline 1: Focus on the Wildly Important

4 Marcia Blenko, Eric Garton, and Ludovica Mottura, "Winning Operating Models That Convert Strategy to Results." Bain & Company, December 10, 2014; https://www.bain.com/insights/winning-operating-models-that-convert-strategy-to-results/.

5 Quoted in Adena Hodges, "Multitasking Dangers Reversed Through Meditation," Meditate on Me, February 20, 2017; https:// meditateonme.com/multitasking-dangers-reversed-through-meditation/.

6 Dan Frommer, "Apple COO Tim Cook," *Business Insider,* February 23, 2010; http://www.businessinsider.com/live-apple-coo-tim-cook-at-the -goldman-tech-conference-2010-2.

7 Cited in Steven J. Dick, "Why We Explore," http://www.nasa.gov /exploration/whyweexplore/Why_We_29.html.

8 "Text of President John F. Kennedy's Rice Moon Speech," September 12, 1962; https://er.jsc.nasa.gov/seh/ricetalk.htm.

Chapter 3. Discipline 2: Act on the Lead Measures

9 Quoted in Aguayo, *Dr. Deming,* 18.

Chapter 4. Discipline 3: Keep a Compelling Scoreboard

10 Teresa M. Amabile and Steven J. Kramer, "The Power of Small Wins," *Harvard Business Review,* May 2011.

Chapter 5. Discipline 4: Create a Cadence of Accountability

11 Jack Welch, Suzy Welch, *Winning* (New York: Harper Business, 2005), 67.

12 From Atul Gawande, *Better: A Surgeon's Notes on Performance* (New York: Metropolitan Books, 2007).

13 Patrick Lencioni, *The Three Signs of a Miserable Job* (San Francisco: Jossey-Bass, 2007), 136–37.

14 Edward M. Hallowell, *Crazy Busy* (New York: Random House Digital, 2007), 183.

Chapter 10. Sustaining 4DX Results and Engagement

15 Jim Harter, "U.S. Employee Engagement Reverts Back to Pre-COVID-19 Levels," Gallup.com, October 2020, https://www.gallup.com/workplace /321965/employee-engagement-reverts-back-pre-covid-levels.aspx.

Chapter 11. What to Expect

16 Margreet C. Vos et al., "5 years of experience implementing a methicillin-resistant Staphylococcus aureus search and destroy policy at the largest university medical center in the Netherlands," *Infection Control and Hospital Epidemiology* 30, no. 10 (2009): 977–84; http://www.ncbi .nlm.nih.gov/pubmed/19712031.

Chapter 13. Applying Discipline 2: Act on the Lead Measures

17 Jim Collins, "Turning Goals into Results: The Power of Catalytic Mechanisms," *Harvard Business Review*, July–August 1999, 73.

Chapter 15. Applying Discipline 4: Create a Cadence of Accountability

18 John Case, "Keeping Score," *Inc.*, June 1, 1998. http://www.inc.com /magazine/19980601/945.html.

19 Eric Matson, "The Discipline of High-Tech Leaders," *Fast Company*, April–May 1997.

Acknowledgments

This book is the product of contributions from literally dozens upon dozens of people from the FranklinCovey organization. Our names are on this book, but we recognize that there are many others who are just as deserving. This truly was a companywide effort and embodies everything we teach about synergy, where the whole is greater than the sum of its parts. So many contributed in so many different ways. Some were instrumental in the design and development of the *4 Disciplines* content. Others refined the methodology through continual application in the field with clients. Still others added an idea or an insight or a new way of viewing an old problem. It seemed that every time we were missing a piece of the execution puzzle, someone showed up who had the answer. The baton was passed again and again as different people led different efforts to commercialize and scale this execution business around the globe. Our heartfelt gratitude goes to everyone who has contributed to this success and particularly to the following individuals:

Jim Stuart, for your extraordinary contribution to FranklinCovey over a period of many years as a senior consultant and for sharing the principles of execution with the rest of us. Without you, there would be no 4 Disciplines. Thank you for your great one-liners and for coining the terms "wildly important," "land one at a time," and "compelling scoreboard," among others. We are forever indebted.

Bob Whitman, our CEO, who recognized years ago that execution was a big idea and then steered us in that direction. Your fingerprints, language, ideas, and influence are all throughout this book. We so appreciate your visionary leadership and support.

ACKNOWLEDGMENTS

The original design and development team (consisting of *Andy Cindrich, Don Tanner, Jim Stuart,* and *Scott Larson*), who conceived and developed the original *4 Disciplines* content from scratch. We also wish to thank the subsequent development teams that followed, who included *Todd Davis, Breck England, Catherine Nelson, Blaine Lee,* and *Lynne Snead.*

Mark Josie, for building the initial execution practice, helping to crack the code on implementation, and creating the vision and strategy behind my4dx.com software. We acknowledge your heavy influence on the content and appreciate your pioneering efforts in getting this solution off the ground.

Breck England, our chief writing officer, for contributing greatly to the development of the *4 Disciplines* content and for your remarkable talents in helping the authors to write and edit this book. Your contributions raised this book to a whole different level.

Andy Cindrich, a key member of the original design and development team, for your contributions to the content, and for the truly excellent work you have done and continue to do with your clients in execution.

Doug Puzey, for helping us crack the code on implementation and building our first 4DX Practice.

Jeff Wadsworth, for thought leadership and content creation.

Michael Simpson, for your contribution on applying 4DX to project management and manufacturing.

Michele Condon, for your constant management support, passionate encouragement, and keeping everyone sane.

Catherine Nelson, for leading the charge on early versions of 4DX, including the development of Manager Certification.

Todd Davis, for leading the version 2.0 development team and for pointing out that people "play differently when they're keeping score."

Sam Bracken, our former general manager over books and media at FranklinCovey, for reestablishing our relationship with Simon & Schuster and negotiating the rights for the first edition of this book, and for your continual support throughout the life cycle of the book.

Our publishing team at Simon & Schuster, including *Stephanie*

Frerich, Emily Simonson, and *Nancy Inglis,* for your enthusiasm and belief in this work and for your ongoing efforts to market it to everyone under the sun.

Our FranklinCovey Publishing Team, *Annie Oswald, Meg Hackett,* and *Zach Kristensen,* for all of their guidance and support in helping us reach the finish line.

Jody Karr, Cassidy Back, and the *CLab* team at FranklinCovey, for helping with the numerous graphics in the book.

Don Tanner, a member of the original design team and one of our best consultants, for your early contributions to the content.

Richard Garrison, for your work on 4DX coaching and for enhancing the implementation process, as well as the excellence you bring to your consulting and to our clients.

Rebecca Hession, for your client leadership and extraordinary innovations.

David Covey, for your exceptional support and commitment to our team over many years.

Shawn Moon, for your leadership and your guidance of the Execution Practice.

Scott Larson, for doing a great job as the project leader of the original development team.

Bill Bennett, our former division President, for challenging us at the beginning to "go out and build the world's best solution on the topic of execution. I don't care if you buy it or build it, just do it."

Doug Faber, for your help in expanding the practice and for your many innovative contributions.

Tom Watson, Jeff Downs, Rick Wooden, and *Lance Hilton,* for your leadership in the Execution Practice.

Paul Walker, Marianne Phillips, and *Elise Roma,* for your organizational support over many years.

To *Stephen M. R. Covey,* for helping, in the early days, identify that *execution* was the issue of our time, and to *Greg Link,* who offered much wise counsel in helping to launch and market the book.

To *Scott Miller* and *Curtis Morley,* for your guidance and support in helping to develop and execute a superb launch plan for this book.

ACKNOWLEDGMENTS

To *Debra Lund,* for your encouragement and friendship, and for the unbelievable way in which you, once again, rounded up so many great endorsements from all over.

Les Kaschner, James Western, Chris Parker, Harvey Young, DeVerl Austin, Coral Rice, Wayne Harrison, Kelly Smith, Craig Wennerholm, Garry Jewkes, Rick Spencer, Bryan Ritchie, and *Pepe Miralles,* for your innovation and dedication to client results.

Index

Page numbers in italics refer to charts and illustrations.

About the Authors

Chris McChesney

Chris McChesney is the Global Practice Leader of Execution for FranklinCovey and one of the primary developers of *The 4 Disciplines of Execution*. For more than a decade, he has led FranklinCovey's ongoing design and development of these principles, as well as the consulting organization that has achieved extraordinary growth in many countries around the globe and impacted hundreds of organizations. Chris has personally led many of the most noted implementations of 4DX, including the State of Georgia, Marriott International, Shaw Industries, Ritz-Carlton, Kroger, Coca-Cola, Comcast, Frito-Lay, Lockheed Martin, and Gaylord Entertainment. This practical experience has enabled him to test and refine the principles contained in *The 4 Disciplines of Execution* from the boardrooms to the front line of these and many other organizations.

Chris's career with FranklinCovey began by working directly with Stephen R. Covey, and has continued over two decades to include roles as a Consultant, Managing Director, and General Manager within the organization. Chris launched the first 4 Disciplines of Execution Practice in the Southeast Region of FranklinCovey and today has seen it expand around the globe. Throughout this period of significant growth and expansion, Chris has maintained a single focus: to help organizations get results through improved execution.

Known for his high energy and engaging presence, Chris has become a highly sought-after speaker, consultant, and adviser on strategy execution, regularly delivering keynote speeches and executive presentations to leaders in audiences ranging from the hundreds to several thousand.

Chris and his wife, Constance, are the proud parents of five daughters and two sons. His love of family is combined with his passion for boating, water sports, coaching, and trying to keep up with his children.

For more information on Chris, visit www.chrismcchesney4DX.com.

Sean Covey

Sean Covey is a business executive, author, speaker, and innovator. He is President of FranklinCovey Education and is devoted to transforming education through FranklinCovey's whole school improvement process, called *Leader in Me*, which is now in more than 5,000 K-12 schools and fifty countries throughout the world. As the former head of Innovations for FranklinCovey, Sean was one of the original architects of *The 4 Disciplines of Execution* methodology and has been an avid practitioner and promoter of the methodology ever since.

Sean is a *New York Times* bestselling author and has authored or coauthored several books, including the *Wall Street Journal* #1 Business Bestseller, *The 4 Disciplines of Execution*, *The 6 Most Important Decisions You'll Ever Make*, *The 7 Habits of Happy Kids*, *The Leader in Me*, and *The 7 Habits of Highly Effective Teens*, which has been translated into thirty languages and sold more than 8 million copies worldwide. He is a versatile keynoter who regularly speaks at education and business events and has appeared on numerous radio and TV shows and print media.

Sean graduated with honors from Brigham Young University with a bachelor degree in English and later earned his MBA from Harvard Business School. As the starting quarterback for BYU, he led his team to two bowl games and was twice selected as the ESPN's Most Valuable Player of the Game. Sean and his family founded and run a global, nonprofit charity called Bridle Up Hope, whose mission is to inspire hope, confidence, and resilience in struggling young women through equestrian training. Visit BridleUpHope.org for more information.

Born in Belfast Ireland, Sean's favorite activities include going to movies, working out, hanging out with his kids, riding his motorcycle, coaching youth football, producing short films, and writing books. Sean and his wife, Rebecca, live with their children in the shadows of the Rocky Mountains.

Jim Huling

Jim Huling is the Global Managing Consultant for FranklinCovey's *4 Disciplines of Execution*. In this role, Jim is responsible for the *4 Disciplines* methodology, teaching methods, and the quality of delivery worldwide. Jim also regularly leads large-scale engagements, including the 4DX implementation for Marriott Hotels, Kroger, Ritz-Carlton, and a number of large hospitals. He is a sought-after keynote speaker for events ranging from senior-executive sessions to audiences in the thousands.

Jim's career spans over four decades of corporate leadership, from Fortune 500 organizations to privately held companies, including serving as CEO of a company recognized four times as one of the 25 Best Companies to Work for in America.

Jim's teams have won national awards for customer-service excellence, business ethics, and an outstanding culture, as well as numerous local and regional awards as a workplace of choice. Jim's personal awards also include being selected for the Turknett Leadership Group Character Award, which recognizes CEOs who demonstrate the highest standards of ethics and integrity.

Jim holds degrees from the University of Alabama and Birmingham-Southern College, and serves on the boards of several organizations, as well as the Siegel Institute for Leadership, Ethics, and Character.

Jim is most proud of his wonderful marriage of over forty years to his sweetheart, Donna, being dad to two phenomenal adults, Scott and Sarah; and "Papa" to his three grandkids. He holds a third-degree black belt in Taekwondo and is an avid runner, backpacker, whitewater rafter, and CrossFit athlete.

For more information on Jim, visit www.jimhuling.com.

Scott Thele

Scott Thele originally joined the Covey Leadership Center in 1993 with the charter to build the public program seminar business. He then began working directly with clients as a client partner, and soon was leading teams. In 1999 he was asked to build a new regional team as a managing director and shortly after spent time focused on delivery and consulting. This led Scott to an external senior leader role that gave him additional experience and perspective. Scott rejoined FranklinCovey in 2009 to work with Chris McChesney in building the Execution Practice. During his tenure he has worked with hundreds of organizations in diverse industries including Dell, Eli Lilly, General Mills, Verizon, Procter & Gamble, and Halliburton.

Scott's broad experience allows him to quickly connect and convey meaningful messages that inspire people to perform at higher levels. He is equally at home with sophisticated global organizations, burgeoning national companies as well as start-up ventures.

He has also served on the boards of small and midsized organizations, providing an outlet for his consulting and coaching passion. Scott has a master's degree in organizational design and effectiveness, adding another dimension to his process of life-long learning.

In his spare time Scott enjoys spending time with his wife, Tracy, and their children on the beach in the South Florida sun. He is a recovering adrenaline junkie and has traded road racing motorcycles for tamer activities like snorkeling and leisurely paragliding flights in the Swiss Alps.

Beverly (BJ) Walker

BJ Walker has managed a broad portfolio of human services programs in the administrations of Governors in Georgia and Illinois and the Mayor of the City of Chicago. As Commissioner in Georgia from 2004 to 2011, she was responsible for child welfare, public health, behavioral health, developmental disabilities, TANF, childcare, food stamps, Medicaid eligibility, aging, and child support. In Illinois, she managed a statewide human services reform effort, resulting in the historical consolidation of many of Illinois's human and social services under one umbrella agency. In that agency, she became the state's welfare reform leader, managing the staff and offices responsible for delivering TANF, Food Stamps, and Medicaid eligibility. In the City of Chicago, BJ served as Deputy Chief of Staff for Mayor Richard M. Daley, leading several major mayoral initiatives in human services and education. Most recently, she served as Acting Director for the Illinois Department of Children and Family Services, following her 2017 retirement from Deloitte Consulting LLP, where she served for five years as a Managing Director in their national public sector practice. Previously, she worked with FranklinCovey in their 4 Disciplines of Execution practice and served as a Senior Fellow with the Annie E. Casey Foundation. She now manages a consulting practice, In the Public Way, Inc., which serves as a platform (inthepublicway.com) for supporting state and nonprofit leaders engaged in transformational change management efforts. In 1993, BJ Walker was awarded a prestigious yearlong resident Fellowship with the Annie E. Casey Foundation. BJ has an MA degree from Northwestern University and a BA from Mount Holyoke College. She serves as a board member with the Algebra Project, Inc, and the Stewards of Change Institute. She is married to Thomas and they have two adult children, four grandchildren, and one great-grandson.

About FranklinCovey

Franklin Covey Co. (NYSE: FC) is a global, public company, specializing in organizational performance improvement. We help organizations achieve results that require lasting changes in human behavior. Our world-class solutions enable greatness in individuals, teams, and organizations and are accessible through the FranklinCovey All Access Pass®. They are available across multiple modalities and in 20-plus languages. Clients have included the Fortune 100, Fortune 500, thousands of small- and mid-sized businesses, numerous government entities, and educational institutions. FranklinCovey has more than 100 direct and partner offices providing professional services in more than 160 countries and territories.

FranklinCovey
ALL ACCESS PASS

The FranklinCovey All Access Pass provides unlimited access to our best-in-class content and solutions, allowing you to expand your reach, achieve your business objectives, and sustainably impact performance across your organization.

AS A PASSHOLDER, YOU CAN:

- Access FranklinCovey's world-class content, whenever and wherever you need it, including *The 7 Habits of Highly Effective People®: Signature Edition 4.0*, Leading at the *Speed of Trust®*, *Helping Clients Succeed®*, and *The 4 Disciplines of Execution®*.

- Certify your internal facilitators to teach our content, deploy FranklinCovey consultants, or use digital content to reach your learners with the behavior-changing content you require.

- Have access to a certified implementation specialist who will help design Impact Journeys for behavior change.

- Organize FranklinCovey content around your specific business-related needs.

- Build a common learning experience throughout your entire global organization with our core-content areas localized into 19 languages.

Join thousands of organizations using the All Access Pass® to implement strategy, close operational gaps, increase sales, drive customer loyalty, and improve employee engagement.

To learn more, visit
FRANKLINCOVEY.COM or call **1-888-868-1776**.

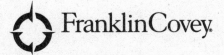

Implement *4DX*® in Your Organization

To learn more about how FranklinCovey's *The 4 Disciplines of Execution*® (*4DX*) can support your team and organization visit **franklincovey.com/the-4-disciplines**.

FranklinCovey's execution system revolves around these four key interdependent parts:

- **Methodology:** *4DX* is the #1 bestselling execution content in the world. The book has sold more than 500,000 copies, in 16 languages, and we've worked with more than 60,000 teams worldwide.

- **Implementation Process:** FranklinCovey has worked with over 3,000 client implementations and has a proven track record of case worthy results in every industry.

- **Technology Tools:** FranklinCovey uses a proprietary software, 4DX OS, to work with all clients who implement *4DX* to ensure success. To date, more than 50 million commitments have been made with over 12 million weekly accountability sessions.

- **XPS:** A single metric that measures the amount of energy and engagement your putting against your strategic targets by unit, team, and individual. XPS allows you to systematically expose your execution reality and act on it.

Join the thousands of companies that have used *The 4 Disciplines of Execution* to consistently deliver year-over-year breakthrough results.

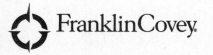

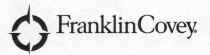

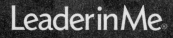

FRANKLINCOVEY
ON LEADERSHIP

WITH
SCOTT MILLER

Join *On Leadership* host Scott Miller for weekly interviews with thought leaders, bestselling authors, and world-renowned experts on the topics of organizational culture, leadership development, execution, and personal productivity.

FEATURED INTERVIEWS INCLUDE:

CHRIS McCHESNEY
THE 4 DISCIPLINES OF EXECUTION

SUSAN DAVID
EMOTIONAL AGILITY

KIM SCOTT
RADICAL CANDOR

DANIEL PINK
WHEN

SETH GODIN
THE DIP, LINCHPIN, PURPLE COW

NELY GALÁN
SELF MADE

LIZ WISEMAN
MULTIPLIERS

GUY KAWASAKI
WISE GUY

STEPHEN M. R. COVEY
THE SPEED OF TRUST

RACHEL HOLLIS
GIRL, WASH YOUR FACE

NANCY DUARTE
DATA STORY, SLIDE:OLOGY

STEPHANIE McMAHON
CHIEF BRAND OFFICER, WWE

STEDMAN GRAHAM
IDENTITY LEADERSHIP

ANNE CHOW
CEO, AT&T BUSINES

GENERAL STANLEY McCHRYSTAL
LEADERS: MYTH AND REALITY

MATTHEW McCONAUGHEY
GREENLIGHTS

Subscribe to FranklinCovey's *On Leadership* to receive weekly videos, tools, articles, and podcasts at

FRANKLINCOVEY.COM/ONLEADERSHIP.